AF323751

FLUX
The Complexity of Changing Minds

STUDIES OF NONLINEAR PHENOMENA IN LIFE SCIENCE*

ISSN: 1793-1428

Editor-in-Charge: Bruce J. West

Vol. 18   *Flux: The Complexity of Changing Minds*
by F Orsucci

Vol. 17   *Crucial Events: Why are Catastrophes Never Expected?*
by B J West & P Grigolini

Vol. 16   *Fractal Physiology and Chaos in Medicine (2nd Edition)*
by B J West

Vol. 15   *Decision Making: A Psychophysics Application of Network Science*
edited by P Grigolini & B J West

Vol. 14   *Fractal Time: Why a Watched Kettle Never Boils*
by S Vrobel

Vol. 13   *Disrupted Networks: From Physics to Climate Change*
by B J West & N Scafetta

Vol. 12   *Mind Force: On Human Attractions*
by F Orsucci

Vol. 11   *Where Medicine Went Wrong: Rediscovering the Path to Complexity*
by B J West

Vol. 10   *The Dynamical Systems Approach to Cognition: Concepts and Empirical Paradigms based on Self-Organization, Embodiment, and Coordination Dynamics*
edited by W Tschacher & J-P Dauwalder

Vol. 9   *Changing Mind: Transitions in Natural and Artificial Environments*
by F F Orsucci

Vol. 8   *Dynamics, Synergetics, Autonomous Agents: Nonlinear Systems Approaches to Cognitive Psychology and Cognitive Science*
edited by W Tschacher & J-P Dauwalder

Vol. 7   *Physiology, Promiscuity, and Prophecy at the Millennium: A Tale of Tails*
by B J West

Vol. 6   *The Complex Matters of the Mind*
edited by F Orsucci

*For the complete list of titles in this series, please go to

http://www.worldscientific.com/series/snpls

Studies of Nonlinear Phenomena in Life Science – Vol. 18

FLUX
The Complexity of Changing Minds

Franco Orsucci

University of Amsterdam, the Netherlands &
Norfolk and Suffolk NHS Foundation Trust, UK

World Scientific

NEW JERSEY • LONDON • SINGAPORE • BEIJING • SHANGHAI • TAIPEI • CHENNAI

To the Muses

Published by

World Scientific Publishing Co. Pte. Ltd.
5 Toh Tuck Link, Singapore 596224
USA office: 27 Warren Street, Suite 401-402, Hackensack, NJ 07601
UK office: 57 Shelton Street, Covent Garden, London WC2H 9HE

Library of Congress Cataloging-in-Publication Data
Names: Orsucci, Franco, author.
Title: Flux : the complexity of changing minds / Franco Orsucci,
    University of Amsterdam, The Netherlands & Norfolk and Suffolk NHS Foundation Trust, UK.
Description: New Jersey : World Scientific, [2025] | Includes bibliographical references and index.
Identifiers: LCCN 2024042827 | ISBN 9789811287367 (hardcover) |
    ISBN 9789811287374 (ebook) | ISBN 9789811287381 (ebook other)
Subjects: LCSH: Thought and thinking. | Change (Psychology) | Biocomplexity.
Classification: LCC BF441 .O77 2025 | DDC 153.4/2--dc23/eng/20241107
LC record available at https://lccn.loc.gov/2024042827

British Library Cataloguing-in-Publication Data
A catalogue record for this book is available from the British Library.

For any available supplementary material, please visit
https://www.worldscientific.com/worldscibooks/10.1142/13705#t=suppl

Desk Editor: Shaun Tan Yi Jie

Typeset by Stallion Press
Email: enquiries@stallionpress.com

About the Author

Prof. Dr. Franco Orsucci is Co-Founder of the Centre for Excellence in Mental Health Sciences at the University of Amsterdam, Netherlands, and leading R&D at Norfolk & Suffolk NHS Foundation Trust. He had been a Visiting Professor at University College London, UK, and a Professor at the University of Siena, University of Chieti-Pescara, and Gemelli University Hospital of Rome, Italy. He is also a Fellow of the European Academy of Science and Arts, a Fellow of the Royal Society of Medicine, and President of the Mind Force Society. He was Editor-in-Chief of *Chaos & Complexity Letters*, now a book series. His empirical and theoretical research is on the complexity science of human dynamics. His multidisciplinary works dealt with psychology, psychiatry, neuroscience, psychotherapy, human interfaces, smart cities, biophysics, language, synchronization, social networks, and co-evolution. He has published over 200 articles and written/co-edited seven books.

Preface

These are not just introductory notes but the opening of an intense journey. The Universe, a grand tapestry, is woven with magnificent, interconnected structures. From the vast galaxies to the intricate cells, from the delicate ecosystems to the complex human beings, all manage to assemble and function. At all levels of magnitude, these organizations are based on interactions, disruptions, order, and disorder in symphonies of rhythms, melodies, accord, resonance, and dissonance. Intervals, gaps, and silence are integral to these cosmic harmonies, just as disorder is integral to any form of order in space and time.

I have been fascinated by complexity and self-organization since my youth. In high school, at some point, I was involved in year-long group projects on the scientific revolution. I was deeply intrigued by the life and discoveries of Leonardo, Galilei, Bacon, and Newton. I discovered non-Euclidian geometry and understood that we could see the world differently. Later, as a university student cycling to lessons, I noticed that the notorious traffic jams in Rome often managed to sort themselves out without an external controller. Instead, in the worst ones, I could usually find someone trying to direct the traffic toward a particular direction, not just helping the traffic flow. These were the early preludes of further insights into Complexity Science. Ancient wisdom in the West and East always advised that we help organisms maintain their vital balance and self-organization for prevention, self-healing, and longevity.

Living systems are so complex that usually, the best way to help them stay systemically healthy is to help them flow within their boundary conditions. This is also called facilitating the spontaneous order of self-organization. The boundaries of living systems are usually porous and open.

Therefore, any interaction should consider their fragility, including possible indeterminacy and equifinality. Nature uses all possible modalities to orchestrate our bodies' symphonies. All these involve enormous numbers of players linked in complex webs. In every case, astonishing patterns emerge spontaneously. The richness of the world around us is due, in large part, to the miracle of self-organization.

This book relies on the vast knowledge scientists, clinicians, philosophers, and artists created. It attempts to synthesize diverse experiences and knowledge accumulated through years of research and clinical practice. I have tried to avoid equations to illustrate the key ideas and make them readable to the broader public. (Relevant mathematical formalisms are included in a concluding Appendix.) I have strived to reveal the underlying unity of these different sources of knowledge, macro and micro universes, using metaphors and images from everyday life and the humanities. The result is a tapestry of knowledge that I hope will inspire and enlighten, fostering a sense of connection and unity among its readers. This might elicit further interest in the relevant papers and books reporting empirical evidence and formal models listed in the references.

I have also tried to make the disciplinary boundaries between clinical and general studies of human dynamics more fluid. The dynamics are the same, and sometimes, using technical jargon for professional pretense might complicate our understanding. This is one of the main goals of this book, and I hope it might have helped make it more open. At the same time, I attempted to continue developing one of my research strategies of fluidifying the boundaries between the so-called hard and soft sciences, including unique insights from the arts. The main caveat in this epistemological approach is to avoid confusion in multidisciplinary practice and always declare where scientific evidence is and where there might be more nuanced perspectives or metaphoric inspirations. I enjoyed the journey, and I hope the readers will feel the pleasure of this voyage through the marvelous and complex landscapes of human nature.

Acknowledgments

I am deeply grateful for the opportunity to have worked with and met so many brilliant and creative minds throughout my career. The research described in this book was a joint effort resulting from fertile collaborations. I want to acknowledge with gratitude for various fruitful interactions related to this book, including the invaluable support and insights of:

Fred Abraham, Mauro Annunziato, Tito Arecchi, Harald Atmanspacher, Joanna Baines, Kevin Beardsworth, Francesco Corrao, Giulio De Felice, Eutizio Egiziano, Peter Fonagy, Walter J Freeman, Mario Fulcheri, Liane Gabora, Omar Gelo, Alessandro Giuliani, Jeffrey Goldstein, Steve Guastello, Stine Steen Høgenhaug, Hozumi Gensho Roshi, Jürgen Kurths, Klaus Mainzer, Norbert Marwan, Ezio Menoni, Chiara Mocenni, Giorgio Parisi, Lou Pecora, Luciano Pietronero, David Pincus, Mario Reda, Sergio Rinaldi, Nicoletta Sala, Sergio Salvatore, Andrea Seganti, Günter Schiepek, Thomas Schreiber, Alan Stein, Graeme Taylor, Wolfgang Tschacher, Pier Christian Verde, Chuck Webber, Joe Zbilut, Giovanna Zimatore.

A special thank you to Bruce J. West for inspiring some of the research lines I followed over the years and hosting this book in his Studies of Nonlinear Phenomena in Life Sciences series at World Scientific.

I am grateful for Shaun Tan Yi Jie's editorial patience, attention, and receptive support throughout the development of this project. I also dedicate my gratitude to Lakshmi Narayan, with whom I started years of rewarding collaborations at World Scientific.

I praise my wife, Bea, daughters Sophia and Jo, and sister Paola, for their musical inspiration and creative support. They are my familiar Muses.

Contents

About the Author   vii
Preface   ix
Acknowledgments   xi

Chapter 1   Flux   **1**

    1.1 Streams   1
    1.2 Emergence   3
    1.3 The Observer   6
    1.4 The Wonder of Complex Systems   7
    1.5 Organized Complexity   9
    1.6 Self-Organization   11
    1.7 An Interdisciplinary Science   13
    1.8 Models & Metaphors   17
    1.9 Personal Patterns   19
    1.10 Fluxes of Change   22

Chapter 2   Embodiments   **23**

    2.1 Beyond Solipsism   23
    2.2 Creating Language   26
    2.3 A World of Experience   28
    2.4 Looking for the Source   31
    2.5 Biosemiotics   34
    2.6 4Es, 5Es, 7Es   38
    2.7 The Necessary Fifth E   40
    2.8 The Nature of Emotions   42
    2.9 Expressing Emotions   47

2.10 The Source of Emotions | 51
2.11 Afflictive or Nourishing Emotions | 54
2.12 Clouds, Rain, and Blue Skies | 58

Chapter 3   Patterns | **60**

3.1 The Self Universe | 60
3.2 The Primary Self | 62
3.3 Dynamical Systems of the Self | 65
3.4 Power of Selves | 67
3.5 The Dynamical Self | 69
3.6 Dynamical Patterns | 72
3.7 Morphogenesis of the Self | 74
3.8 The Self Multiverse | 78

Chapter 4   Landscapes | **80**

4.1 Sceneries | 80
4.2 Personality, Character, Temperament | 81
4.3 Pattern Disorders | 83
4.4 Complexity Maps | 87
4.5 Dynamic Maps | 89
4.6 Formulation Tools | 91
4.7 Ancient Fitness Landscapes | 92

Chapter 5   Dynamics | **94**

5.1 Personal Dynamics | 94
5.2 Pattern Analysis | 97
5.3 Hybrid Couplings | 99
5.4 Chimera States in Human Interactions | 101
5.5 From Determinism to Statistical Dynamics | 103
5.6 Chimeras and Consciousness | 106

Chapter 6   Change | **107**

6.1 Rupture and Repair | 107
6.2 Interpersonal Physiology | 110

6.3 Couplings   112
6.4 Transformations   114
6.5 Factors of Change   119
6.6 Harmonious Couplings   121
6.7 Errors and Enchantments   126

Chapter 7 Play   **128**

7.1 Homo Ludens   128
7.2 Language Plays   129
7.3 Contained Self-Organization   132
7.4 Maladaptive Self-organization   135
7.5 Repairing Biosemiotic Coordination   138
7.6 A Musical Interlude   140
7.7 Biosemiotic Orchestration   145
7.8 The Mozart Orchestrations   148

Chapter 8 Nostos   **150**

8.1 Nostos   150
8.2 Core   151
8.3 Accord   153
8.4 Orience   155
8.5 Descartes Redux   156
8.6 Pattern Dynamics   159
8.7 Beyond Rationalism   161
8.8 Probabilities   162

Appendix   165

References   173

Index   215

Chapter 1

Flux

Συλλάψιες· ὅλα καὶ οὐχ ὅλα, συμφερόμενον διαφερόμενον, συνᾷδον διᾷδον.

Implications: whole and partial, united and dispersed, harmonious and discordant.

Heraclitus

1.1 Streams

Heraclitus was a groundbreaking thinker and a superb writer who received tributes from Plato and Aristotle. Diels defines him as "the most subjective and, in a sense, the most modern prose author in antiquity" (Diels, 1912). Beyond any style consideration, Heraclitus is perhaps the first natural philosopher to make capital statements about dynamical systems. Diogenes Laertius summarizes Heraclitus's philosophy, stating, "All things come into being by conflict of opposites, and the sum of things τὰ ὅλα (the whole) flows like a stream." Furthermore, "one cannot step twice in the same river, nor can anyone grasp any mortal substance in stable condition, but it scatters, and again it gathers; it forms and dissolves, and approaches and departs" (Kahn, 1981). The river is the same and not the same simultaneously, but the streams are similar and different, just as we are similar and different. This strikingly recalls what centuries after would be called self-similarity in the structure of chaotic attractors. "The ray of lightning guides the All. This world order, which is the same for all, was created neither by one of the gods nor by one of the humans, but it was always and will be, eternally living fire, glimmering and extinguishing according to measures" (Kahn, 1981).

As Heisenberg (1952) aptly observed, "Heraclitus' pronouncements can be considered extraordinarily modern: We must substitute the word "fire" with "energy," and the result is modern physics." For Heraclitus, our microcosm is part of the macrocosm, and the opposites are held in unity by a profound concept he called *harmony*, the cosmic law he called *logos*. This harmony, as a cosmic, personal, and social law, is the unifying foundation grounding communities in the order of nature and the ruling principles of the universe. It is a universe where we search for more profound knowledge in ourselves, just as he wrote: "I went in search of myself." (Kahn, 1981). Therefore, he criticized "most men who live as if their thinking were their private possession" as "though the language is common, many live as if they had a wisdom of their own." (Kahn, 1981). Heraclitus's intellectual journey is fascinating as he transitions from Milesian cosmology to the Ionian conception of the world as a cosmos. He incorporates human subjectivity into an overarching dynamical system. Diels correctly identified Heraclitus's central insight into the identity of structure between the PsycheSoma, personal world, and the Universe's natural order. Once he encountered the laws of the microcosm within himself, "he discovered it a second time in the external world."

"The lord whose oracle is in Delphi neither declares nor conceals but gives a sign." (Kahn, 1981). The ignorance of men lies in their failure to comprehend how *logos* as discourse, culture, community, thinking, and emotions flow according to the laws of the *Logos* as the laws regulating the Universe. In his reflections on Heraclitus, Martin Heidegger (Heidegger & Fink, 1993) articulated this perspective as emergence dynamics, "the essential connectedness of emerging and submerging." We formulated the dynamical relations between merging and emergence as follows:

$$M \Leftrightarrow E$$

An object's simplicity, complexity, and consistency depend on the perspective and resolution of the subject (Orsucci, 2002). *Emergence* becomes of increasing importance as an explanatory construct when the following features characterize the system:

- when the emergent patterns are not predictable or directly reducible to those components.
- the organization of the system, its global order, appears to be prominent and different than the sum of single components.
- when single components can be replaced without an accompanying decommissioning of the whole system.
- when the new global patterns or properties are radically novel concerning the pre-existing components.

1.2 Emergence

Living in a world of stability and change, we face known and unknown situations, old and new phenomena, and shifting perceptual patterns and interactions. Emergence is a universal phenomenon that can be defined mathematically in a very general way (Orsucci, 2002). This is useful for studying scientifically legitimate explanations of complex systems, also defined as hyper-structures. Emergence is related to how we consider a given system's structure. In the so-called sciences of complexity, complex phenomena, such as the appearance of life on Earth, the evolution of new species, or the integration of body, language, and thinking, are often considered instances of some emergent higher-order structure. That may explain how the lower-level dynamics generate the collective behavior as an emergent system property. The sciences of complexity offer new important insights, theories, and methodologies for dealing with complex, higher-order phenomena. Scientific explanations should be seen in a more dynamic and context-dependent setting. *Explanations are emergent structures.* The new general framework for describing higher-order structures, *hyper-structures,* includes the processes of observation and eventually allows for self-generation in such systems of new observational frames and observers (Baas, 1994). Understanding a system means creating some generalized resonance as there is a link between understanding and change for both parties, the system and the subject.

Traditional deductive notions of scientific explanation have frequently been criticized for being too crude and reductive to account for complex phenomena. The pure dilemma of reductionism and holism is an illusion:

combining different perspectives, we can gain knowledge and retain the richness of a world of emergent structures.

We must consider a new general framework for describing higher-order structures and hyper-structures. We will return to this later, especially about the higher-order dynamics in complex networks (Orsucci, 2009). Here, we would highlight the mechanisms of observation, which eventually allow for self-generation in such systems of new observational frames (Orsucci, 2002). In recent years, emergence has been studied extensively, but often without precise definition. Here, we will use emergence in the general sense defined by Baas (1994). The crucial point in this definition is the notion of *an observer* in a very general sense. When studying complex systems, one often sees that a collection of interacting systems shows collective emergent behavior. This is intuitively what we understand by emergence.

The observational mechanism may be internal or external. Examples:

- Coupling of dynamical systems.
- Large collections of objects generate new behavior.
- Consciousness resulting from multiscale dynamics.

New observers may also emerge in the system (Baas, 1994). It is always impossible to deduce the properties of the whole from its constituents and the observational mechanisms. With the interactive help from coupling, each may perform tasks that none could do separately; hence, we get a *second-order agent*. It makes a structure related to lower-level interactions and higher-level thoughts and represents a new observational mechanism of the entire system. General causes of emergence would be multiscale interactions, open-ended evolution in heterogeneous environments, and context-dependence of properties in complex systems.

On a personal level, it is a common experience to have sudden "flashes of insight." They involve the emergence in consciousness of a possible solution to a problem that has long occupied the working mind (its conscious and subconscious parts). The sudden "flash" is experienced as the appearance of the solution as a new structure that can be observed at once but must be worked out deductively in detail and tested formally before it can be trusted. Poincare (1929) vividly described this experience. The appearance of a new idea or orderly structure may often be like detecting a pattern, a metaphor, an image, or a particular short description, rule, or algorithm, which may encompass the complicated situation that was the starting point. A ubiquitous feature of consciousness, in general, seems to be the property of "overflow" (Searle, 1992) in which situations experienced in personal life suddenly are seen in a new light, as if a higher-order observational mechanism has accessed the properties of new structures, as generated through the interactions of previous experiences. We propose that the characteristic phenomenon that conscious states refer beyond their immediate content (as seen in the overflow phenomenon, in the so-called "Aha! Experience", and in the well-known *Gestalt* shifts) is deeply related to the hyper-structured constitution of consciousness. Following neural plasticity, we can say that the brain emerges from the mind because mental events keep changing the mind and brain both ways. As in the Möbius band, container and content in the mind-brain relationship can be reversed in their reciprocal function depending on the observer's perspective. Increasing knowledge of the *PsycheSoma* about how specific effects are obtained may reveal that certain products are integrated into the contributed impact by subcomponents of that system.

This process has generated different diagrams in different fields, from the Stacey Matrix in social dynamics (Stacey, 1996) to the Feynman diagrams in quantum physics (Feynman, 1949) and the Calabi-Yau manifolds in topology (Calabi, 1954; Yau & Nadis, 2010).

In the general framework, we must distinguish between different kinds of emergence:

A. *Deducible emergence. This is structural or ontic emergence.*
B. *Observational emergence. This is a phenomenal emergence.*

We must consider the whole as analyzable, its parts as synthetical, and a possible observer function. The observer can also be observed by the emerging entirety or mirrored.

1.3 The Observer

The role of observing self-reference is placed at the core of consciousness studies. Bateson (1987) proposed the seminal metaphor of the possible interactions between a cartographer, the map, and the landscape. Hoffmeyer (1997) evoked the possibility that cartographers could be so involved in their experience that they are swept into the landscape. Mastering his literary elegance, Borges has provided compelling examples of both opposite extremes of mapping models.

"…In that Empire, the Art of Cartography attained such Perfection that the map of a single Province occupied the entirety of a City, and the map of the Empire, the entirety of a Province. In time, those Unconscionable Maps were no longer satisfied, and the Cartographers' Guilds struck a Map of the Empire whose size was that of the Empire and which coincided point for point with it. The following Generations, who were not so fond of the Study of Cartography as their Forebears had been, saw that that vast Map was Useless, and not without some Pitilessness was it, that they delivered it up to the Inclemency of Sun and Winters. In the Deserts of the West, still today, there are Tattered Ruins of that Map, inhabited by Animals and Beggars; in all the Land there is no other Relic of the Disciplines of Geography." — Suarez Miranda, Viajes de varones prudentes, Libro IV, Cap. XLV, Lerida, 1658 (Borges, 1968).

Conversely, meticulous cartographers could follow the example proposed in the *Celestial Emporium of Benevolent Knowledge* (Borges, 1937). The list divides all animals into 14 categories:

1. Those that belong to the emperor.
2. Embalmed ones.
3. Those who are trained.
4. Suckling pigs.
5. Mermaids (or Sirens).
6. Fabulous ones.
7. Stray dogs.
8. Those that are included in this classification.
9. Those who tremble as if they were mad.
10. Innumerable ones.

11. Those drawn with an excellent camel hairbrush.
12. Et cetera.
13. Those who have just broken the flower vase.
14. Those that, at a distance, resemble flies.

This elegantly ironic list has stirred considerable philosophical and literary commentary. For example, Michel Foucault (1971–2002) began the preface to his book *The Order of Things*: "This book first arose out of a passage in Borges, out of the laughter that shattered, as I read the passage, all the familiar landmarks of thought, our thought, the thought that bears the stamp of our age and our geography, breaking up all the ordered surfaces and all the planes with which we are accustomed to tame the wild profusion of existing things and continuing long afterward to disturb and threaten with collapse our age-old definitions between the Same and the Other." A deeper understanding of emergence processes is strictly connected to understanding the role of the Same and the Other in our consciousness processes and their observation.

1.4 The Wonder of Complex Systems

In his recent book, Giorgio Parisi (2023a) recalls his studies on the self-organization of vast flocks of starlings. In the remarkable phenomenon of murmuration, many birds seem to move in formation and make almost simultaneous decisions about sudden changes in direction. How do the birds coordinate so quickly and effectively? They proved that no boss bird drives the rest of the flock without top-down instruction. More practically, each bird keeps track of just a few neighbors and follows simple rules. This simplicity of iterating simple rules and generating complexity had been simulated on computers in the *Boids Algorithm* (Reynolds, 1987). "Generally speaking, we could say that a complex system can stay in many different equilibrium states, while a simple system may stay only in one or a few equilibrium states." (Parisi, 2023b). Therefore, a complex system is dynamically flexible and resilient. The example of the starlings is particularly effective as they follow bottom-up local rules to form a murmuration flock while keeping their flocking maneuver at a regular distance from their neighbors to avoid bumping into each other. However, starlings are also known for their remarkable navigational abilities, allowing them to orienteer and migrate long distances. These birds have a keen sense of direction and can use various environmental cues to navigate, such as the sun during the day, stars at night, and the Earth's magnetic field. Starlings are also known for their adaptability to different habitats. They thrive in urban and rural environments. They can be found across Europe, the Middle East, Central Asia, and North Africa and have been introduced to North America, Australia, and other regions (Hildenbrandt et al., 2010).

If you are interested in observing starlings, look for their iridescent plumage and listen for their diverse vocalizations, including mimicking other birds and even mechanical sounds. With their avian navigation and social behavior, starlings testify to systems' effectiveness, flexibility, and beauty. They also clarify how complex systems organizations integrate local, middle, and large-scale dynamical principles (Bingman & Able, 2002; Ritchison, 2023).

Elsasser (1987) proposed the main principles of complex systems:

1. A complex system includes many components linked to each other through dynamic relationships, enabling its representation in a correlation network.
2. Such a network (independently of the chosen correlation metrics) exhibits a multiscale structure with substantial dynamics at different spatial and temporal scales.
3. The spatial and temporal relationships among the elements are subdued to non-linear dynamics, giving rise to both memories (hysteresis) and multi-stability (different equilibrium states) effects.

As highlighted in these paragraphs, two streams of definitions of complexity can be found (Arecchi et al., 1997). Complexity can be an inherent property of some objects regarding their numbers and relations. This could be called *ontic complexity.* Complexity can also be considered a property of the relations between a system and its observer, including their cognitive attitude. This is also called *epistemic complexity.*

Complex systems are neither entirely disorganized (like a gas) nor steadily ordered (like a crystal). In complex systems, order values change over time, showing dramatic fluctuation at points where the system undergoes critical transitions. This leads to the emergence of new configurations ("phenotypes" in biological parlance) in which order values (i.e., negentropy) are frequently uncoupled from Kolmogorov-based complexity parameters.

1.5 Organized Complexity

Warren Weaver was a very active and exciting man of science for an extended period of the 20th century. For example, in the late 1940s, he not only published the well-known introductory and popularizing paper, *The Mathematics of Communication* (Shannon & Weaver, 1949), and the very influential memorandum *Translation* (Weaver, 1952) on the possible use of early computers to translate natural languages. Nevertheless, Weaver also wrote the groundbreaking article *Science and Complexity* (Weaver, 1991), where he identified a class of scientific problems "which science has as yet little explored or conquered". To revisit Weaver's reasoning, he distinguished between "problems of simplicity" that "physical science before 1900 was largely concerned with" and another type of problems common in "life sciences, in which these problems of simplicity are not so often significant." The life sciences "had not yet become highly quantitative or analytical in character," he wrote. Then, he enlarged on the newly developed approach of probability and statistics in exact sciences at around 1900: "Rather than study problems which involved two variables or at most three or four, some imaginative minds went to the other extreme and said: "Let us develop analytical methods dealing with two billion variables." That is to say, the physical scientists, with the mathematicians often in the vanguard, developed powerful techniques of probability theory and statistical mechanics to deal with what may be considered as problems of disorganized complexity." A problem of *disorganized complexity* "is a problem in which the number of variables is vast, and one in which each of the many variables has individually erratic behavior, or perhaps totally unknown. However, despite this helter-skelter, or unknown, the behavior of all the individual variables, the system possesses certain orderly and analyzable average properties." Weaver emphasized that probability theory and statistical techniques "are not restricted to situations where the scientific theory of the individual events is very well known." However, he also attached importance to the fact that they can also "be applied to situations […] where the individual event is as shrouded in mystery". The entire structure of modern physics, our present concept of the nature of the physical universe, and the accessible experimental facts concerning it rest on these statistical concepts. Indeed, the whole question of evidence and how knowledge can be inferred from it are now recognized to depend on these same statistical ideas, so that probability notions are essential to any theory of knowledge itself (Weaver, 1991).

In addition to, and in between, "problems of simplicity" and "problems of disorganized complexity," Weaver identified a third kind of problem. "One is tempted to oversimplify and say that scientific methodology went from one extreme to the other — from two variables to an astronomical number — and left a great middle region untouched. Moreover, the importance of this middle region does not depend primarily on the fact that the number of variables involved is moderate, large compared to two, but small compared to the number of atoms in a pinch of salt. The problems in this middle region will often involve many variables. The significant characteristic problems of this *middle region*, which science has explored or conquered a little, lie in the fact that these problems, as contrasted with the disorganized situations to which statistics can cope, show the essential feature of the organization. One can refer to this group of problems as those of organized complexity." They are "problems which involve dealing simultaneously with a sizable number of factors which are interrelated into an organic whole."

Here Weaver identified the problems of *organized complexity* "which science has as yet little explored or conquered" to be problems that can neither be reduced to a simple formula nor can they be solved with methods of probability theory: "These problems — and a wide range of similar problems in the biological, medical, psychological, economic, and political sciences — are just too complicated to yield to the old nineteenth-century techniques" and "these new problems, moreover, cannot be handled with the statistical techniques so effective in describing average behavior in problems of disorganized complexity." (Weaver, 1991).

1.6 Self-Organization

Some great minds laid the basis for the science of self-organization, such as Adam Smith, Immanuel Kant, and Charles Darwin. Self-organization is a critical concept in complexity science that refers to the emergence of stable patterns through autonomous and self-reinforcing dynamics. It describes the growth or evolution of more complex forms through simple rules (Haken, 1983; Mainzer, 1994). Emergence must operate through interactions at local or microscales, that is, bottom-up rather than top-down rules (Nicolis & Prigogine, 1977). Self-organization describes characteristic relationships in emergent systems created by feedback mechanisms that either amplify an effect (positive feedback) or dampen an effect (negative feedback). This has also been called autopoiesis (Maturana & Varela, 1980). The theory of self-organized criticality (Bak, 1996) suggests that as systems evolve to ever more complex states, they exhibit variability independent of scale. Change in evolved systems will show a relationship of magnitude and frequency described by a mathematical power law, with very few significant events and many small events. For example, earthquake zones exhibit this behavior, where a magnitude seven will occur, but we cannot tell when! Self-organized criticality also argues that systems evolve to reach critical states where they become sensitive to disproportionately small impacts before they crash or evolve into new configurations.

Co-emergence of systems, parts, and properties can be the conceptual framework to understand the functional integration of organisms, their multilevel patterns, and the way scientific practice approaches such complexity (Bizzarri et al., 2020; Bertolaso et al., 2015). Complex systems (paradigmatically those entailed by living beings) show emergent properties, likely arising from the non-linear dynamics of the relationships established among the entities (molecular components) that comprise the system. This statement implies some non-trivial consequences, both epistemological and ontological. First, as envisioned by Whitehead, biological phenomena consist of processes rather than material objects that exist and function independently of one another (Whitehead, 1978). As "all things flow" (Whitehead, 1985), in a philosophical stance that can be traced back to Heraclitus and which has been adopted recently in the contemporary philosophy of science (Dupré & Nicholson, 2018), it is mandatory to shift our focus from "molecules" to "relationships."

A phenomenon can, in principle, be studied at different levels (sub-atomic, atomic, molecular, cell, organisms, families, groups, communities). However, we are primarily interested in "effective" relationships, i.e., those relations triggering "emerging functional properties" of the system. Effective complex relations thrive at the *mesoscopic level*; we can find effective order and organization (Elowitz et al., 2002). At the microscopic level, objects and their relationships are affected by fluctuations due to both environmental and intrinsic stochasticity. At the mesoscopic level, stochastic fluctuations turn into ordered behavior, thus allowing order to emerge. The co-emergence of systems, parts, and properties is a natural (and hypothesis-free) consequence that can be adopted as a conceptual framework to understand the functional integration of organisms, including their hierarchical or multilevel patterns, and including the way scientific practice proceeds in approaching such complexity (Bizzarri et al., 2020).

Self-organization is the spontaneous, often seemingly purposeful, formation of spatial, temporal, and spatiotemporal structures or functions in systems composed of few or many components. In physics, chemistry, and biology, self-organization occurs in open systems driven away from thermal equilibrium. The process of self-organization can be found in many other fields, such as economy, sociology, medicine, and technology (Haken, 1985; Kelso, 1995; Maturana & Varela, 1980; Nicolis & Prigogine, 1977; Mainzer, 1994). Different authors converged in defining general principles of self-organization, referred to as reducing the degrees of freedom. In this case, for example, the electric current serves as a control parameter in lasers. Above a critical value, the emergent laser light is called an order parameter, as the joint action of its subsystems (atoms, molecules) can establish a new order.

1.7 An Interdisciplinary Science

One of the founding pillars of Complexity Science is that it is interdisciplinary, as similar schemes, patterns, and mathematical descriptions of complex systems can be found in different disciplines. This led to the definition of translational science, a practice that comes with perils and rewards. "*Traduttore, traditore*" is a traditional Italian expression. All translations compromise, and every translation implies some treason of the original meaning. This is already implied in any listening or reading, as the original meaning is always co-produced by the reader and the listener (Eco, 1989). If the translation is too literal, the translator will try to be faithful to the original but might betray the reader by being unintelligent. If the translator tries to please the reader, they might betray the author's original intentions. This essentially ambiguous part of the human experience with language could be paradoxically avoided if we would communicate, as in Gulliver's travels, by producing the natural objects of our reference. However, this might be difficult for many objects, from whales to galaxies, and impossible for others, from sirens to concepts, such as beauty. The magic of language poised Umberto Eco to define that "Semiotics is in principle the discipline studying everything which can be used to lie. If something cannot be used to tell a lie, it cannot be used to tell the truth. It cannot be used to tell at all." (Eco, 1976). Eco's interest in the connection between detective fiction and semiotics can also be seen in his participation with Thomas Sebeok in editing the volume *The Sign of Three: Dupin, Holmes, Peirce* (1988), which deals with this intrinsic connection both historically (Charles Peirce was an aficionado of both Poe and Conan Doyle) and theoretically. Fiction is a lie in what the philosopher Karl Popper (1963) called falsification: "Every genuine test of a theory is an attempt to falsify it or to refute it. Testability is falsifiability, but there are degrees of testability: some theories are more testable, more exposed to refutation than others; they take, as it were, greater risks." (Danesi, 2017).

Throughout history, scientists and philosophers have defined disciplines in different ways. An influential tradition is taking the view that disciplines are tools for dealing with real-world problems and scientists are not "students of some subject matter, but students of problems" (Popper, 1979). Some disciplines, such as mathematics, can be flexible and more adaptable to the nature of problems. Aristotle argued that physics, biology, and psychology could also be considered flexible concerning the nature and properties of matter.

However, the last century has seen an explosion of scientific specializations, sometimes as micro-tools for local problems and sometimes as micro-academic domains for university administration (Menken & Keestra, 2016). The last decades have seen interdisciplinarity's emergence as a counterforce of problem-focused collaborations. This process has seen highly dynamic landscapes of interdisciplinary collaborations, varying degrees from interaction to fusion between disciplines. A possible definition might be: "[Interdisciplinary studies is] a process of answering a question, solving a problem, or addressing a topic that is too broad or complex to be dealt with adequately by a single discipline or profession … and draws on disciplinary perspectives and integrates their insights through the construction of a more comprehensive perspective" (Klein, 1997).

A definition of interdisciplinarity also defines our epistemology in science and everyday life. Boundaries between disciplines change depending on the tools and focus we use to observe and define reality. Historically, they have changed many times, and they will keep changing. The idea of interdisciplinarity is educative because it is innately ambiguous and easily adapted to different times and cultures. In the inherently infinite nature of this approach, a new cohesion has begun to emerge. The prospect of a theory of interdisciplinarity has coalesced around the concepts of integration and complexity (Orsucci, 1998, 2002). After a while, each discipline exists by its technical language or jargon. The boundary work of interdisciplinarity is directed into the integration activity, which is negotiated, situational, and contingent. Therefore, it includes semantic maps and translations between disciplinary jargon. This will imply transcending local ways of thinking and the risk of misunderstandings, which is standard in every translational procedure.

Interdisciplinarity entails the interpenetration of disciplinary boundaries and a meta-cognitive rethinking of how we structure knowledge (Newell, 2001). However, as Klein (1996) suggests, the interdisciplinary approach to epistemology is not reductionist, nor does it seek a grand unification of transdisciplinary truth claims. Instead, interdisciplinarity shifts epistemology "from absolute answers and solutions to tentativeness and reflexivity. In all interdisciplinary activities, time should be devoted to examining the philosophical underpinnings of the challenge they pose to disciplinary approaches. Good interdisciplinary work requires a substantial degree of epistemological reflexivity." Mansilla (2006) identifies three approaches to integration utilized in interdisciplinary research, all of which involve decoding comparative disciplinary epistemologies: conceptual bridging, comprehensiveness, and pragmatism.

Science develops theories and laws, expressed in verbal, logical, or mathematical forms, through cycles of inductive and deductive processes. These will include data collection and observation, operationalization, and investigation. Throughout history, scientists and philosophers have defined disciplines in different ways. The nature of matter, living or nonliving, human or non-human, might contribute to defining the boundaries of disciplines. How we sense and perceive, in qualitative and quantitative ways, also contributes to defining these boundaries. Measures, devices that extend our sensory/perceptive capacity, algorithms, metaphors, and models might further contribute to changing ways we can "cut" reality along different realms. What the ultimately real *Das Ding an-Sich* might be beyond our conventions can be a matter of metaphysics and spirituality. Academia and research funding, with its social and financial constraints, will also contribute to shaping and reshaping disciplines. Then, disciplines might be defined as soft or hard depending on the amount of mathematics and statistics involved in studies and practice. A study of the vital role of metaphor in science and knowledge might also allow a better understanding of the interdisciplinary method (Orsucci, 1998, 2002, 2008). More recently, metaphors describing knowledge have shifted from linear or hierarchical structures to networks, webs, and textures in dynamic interaction. Welch (2009) links interdisciplinarity to a paradigm shift in considering knowledge. Once described as a foundation or linear structure, knowledge today is depicted as a rhizome, a network, or a web with multiple nodes of connection and a dynamical system. The metaphor of unity, with its accompanying values of universality and certainty, has been replaced by plurality and relationality metaphors in a complex world. Images of boundary crossing and cross-fertilization supersede images of disciplinary depth and compartmentalization. Isolated modes of work are being supplanted by teamwork and alliances. Older values of competence and expertise are being reformulated as partnership and negotiation (Klein, 2008). All the interdisciplinary procedures and translations require specific epistemological care and re-testing. As Parisi (2023) highlighted, "Monsters are sometimes created in this translation." Instead of a generative and creative cross-fertilization, we might find monsters and golems.

There might be different gradations of interbreeding or integration between disciplines. For example, Menken & Keestra (2016) propose three grades:

a. *Multidisciplinary*, some complementarity without integration and separate results.
b. *Interdisciplinarity*, with deeper integration and expected results.
c. *Transdisciplinary*, including non-academic knowledge, with integrated results.

The design of an interdisciplinary study includes the implicit or explicit design of a new framework of patterns and algorithms shared throughout different disciplines. Potentially, a new hybrid structure might emerge from old, separated ones. "Seen as a whole, that larger set of variables and relationships can be fruitfully thought of as a [new] complex system" (Newell et al., 2001). He proposed that "we can better understand and carry out interdisciplinary integration if we recognize we are attempting to identify and make sense out of the self-organizing pattern of a phenomenon modeled by a particularly complex system." Newell's formulation of the theoretical framework for interdisciplinary studies is potentially fruitful. However, he does not take all the logical conclusions from its premises. A complex systems approach should imply new patterns, structures, and algorithms that every interdisciplinary study can unveil. The degree of determinism or indeterminacy might vary, depending on the field's complexity and the scholars' or scientists' attitudes. In any case, there might be a new emergence in waiting.

1.8 Models & Metaphors

The scientific extraction, abstraction, or simple clarification of an organizing dynamic pattern is frequently called a model. Apart from models as mathematical objects, the term 'model' is used in many other ways (Verhulst, 1998). A teacher may use the word model for constructions of geometrical shapes, a human skeleton or an organ. A biologist or a medical researcher may use a relatively simple, experimental laboratory set-up as a model for a complicated real-life phenomenon. An entrepreneur could define a business model as a plan to structure production and commercial transactions. The fashion industry might define models in other ways. The orthodox way to define models indicates a schematic representation of reality, connecting the main quantities by laws that form mathematical equations. The model is an extraction of a schematic representation of the order of reality. Empirical measures and applications can keep connecting models to various forms of experience. Sometimes, models can benefit from their translation into metaphors. That is like using different glasses to look at the world, as in Thomas Kuhn's formulation (Parisi, 2023a). One of the most famous scientific metaphors is that of the atom as a mini solar system. It does not respect the atomic world's reality based on quantum indeterminacy, waves, non-locality, and resonances. However, it was a way to create an image that could introduce an otherwise mysterious world in popular culture. Sometimes, metaphors can lead to discoveries and have a heuristic value in science. Henry Poincare (Poincare & Halsted, 1929) clarified how this might have been possible in his understanding of the three-body problem. More generally, metaphors are schematic ways to structure our everyday lives in how we perceive, think, and act (Lakoff & Johnson, 1980). Metaphors can also allow embodied imagery from sensory-motor experience to organize our experience and everyday life (Lakoff & Johnson, 1999).

What is a metaphor, and why do we find them helpful? Using a metaphor, as Aristotle & Telford (1985) said, "consists in giving the thing a name that belongs to something else." Describing and theorizing about new things is impossible without referring to well-known things (Verhulst, 1998). We can only understand or place something if it is or seems like something we already know. Even physicists who use all the abstract characteristics of an electron still find it helpful to think of it as a small particle with a charge. It turns out that metaphors are unavoidable in scientific concept formation and discussion. As we have seen, a scientific model is not reality itself; it is a description of reality and, in fact, a metaphor. A model, however, is a metaphor with something added; it has qualitative and quantitative aspects, which adds to the precision of the description. We use the expression 'approximation of reality, which is as accurate as possible.' This implies the validation of the model. Modeling and validation can take many different forms. Although famous for its way with numbers — the quantitative side — mathematics is about structures and the deeper relations between mathematical objects, the qualitative side. The solvability of an equation and its relations with other equations is often more attractive to the mathematician than the solution itself. In mathematics, moreover, images are created that are new and that are an inspiration for metaphoric thinking, in particular modeling.

Mathematical language is the tool of modern science; its consistent use, together with the unsparing rule of experimental verification, started modern science. However, it is an open question why mathematics, studying the laws of imaginary abstract objects in an imaginary abstract world, is so efficient in modeling reality. This must have something to do with how we perceive the world and the corresponding pattern formation, schemes, and orders, which play a part in wiring the human brain.

1.9 Personal Patterns

Idiographic and nomothetic are slightly unusual terms in everyday language. The term 'idiographic' comes from the Greek word '*idios*,' which means 'own' or 'private.' Psychologists who take an idiographic approach focus on the individual and emphasize the unique personal experience of human nature. They favor qualitative research methods, such as case studies, unstructured interviews, and thematic analysis, allowing in-depth insight into individual behavior. The idiographic approach does not seek to formulate laws or generalize results to others. In the late 19th century, the German philosopher Wilhelm Windelband coined the words 'idiographic' and 'nomothetic' to refer to different forms of evidence-based knowledge (Windelband, 1998). These two words entered American psychology thanks to the philosopher/psychologist James Hayden Tufts, who was well-versed in Windbelband's philosophy. Hugo Munsterberg, the seventh president of the American Psychological Society (APA), referred to the idiographic/nomothetic distinction in an address to the APA, warning psychologists against implying that individuals and theory are in some sense opposed (Franck, 1986). He suggested that individual particulars and general theory are complementary sides of all science. For example, history concerns specific events and explanatory theory, and natural scientists aim to develop theory and study highly particularized phenomena. For 30 years after Munsterberg's paper, the individual case was typical in psychology journals, as findings were frequently presented as a series of cases. Both the early experimental quantitative psychologists, such as Ebbinghaus, Pavlov, Cattell, Titchener, and Watson, and early qualitative, observational clinical research by Kraepelin, Freud, James, and Piaget, all of them employed a 'case-by-case' research approach that both drove and tested theory. This approach is called the *Wundtian methodological model* (Jovanović, 2018). In this approach, individuals are studied and analyzed one at a time. Then, generalizations and their distribution can eventually be verified in large cohorts.

In the 1930s, Gordon Allport popularized the adoption of the idiographic/nomothetic distinction in psychology by equating each term with a particular research method (qualitative/quantitative) in the study of personality. However, he changed their meaning (Allport, 1998). He pinned the label nomothetic to the group-based methodology devised in Galton's intelligence testing and heredity research, which was gaining popularity across psychology at the time. This Galtonian methodology combined cases into aggregated group samples for statistical analysis purposes and presented data at the level of the group (Popple & Levi, 2000). In the Galtonian approach, which we now recognize as the standard quantitative model of contemporary psychology, data is collected for a group of cases or into multiple groups (e.g., experimental/control). Then, each group is analyzed using cross-case statistics such as frequencies, means, standard deviations, variance, and correlation coefficients. Group parameters, rather than individual cases, are the fundamental units of analysis in this form of research. Significance testing will pertain to effects observed at the group level to explore relationships between variables or in an experiment to infer cause-and-effect by viewing group-level differences between the experimental group and control group. This method was given additional support in the 1930s by the development of inferential group-based statistics developed by the agricultural statistician R. A. Fisher, which then developed into the General Linear Model, upon which are based many critical statistical treatments for grouped psychological data (Nelder & Wedderburn, 1972).

Allport thought that this group-based research in personality psychology was what Windelband had in mind when he referred to nomothetic science. In Allport's formulation of idiographic/nomothetic, the Galtonian group-based approach received the label of a nomothetic science, while the Wundtian case-by-case approach faded away. At about this same time, the Wundtian model disappeared from much of psychology. For decades, it became confined to experimentalists working in the operant tradition, following Skinner (1998), who had publicly disavowed the group-based Galtonian heterodoxy.

So, there are two distinct forms of nomothetic work available to psychology — one to establish what is common to all individuals in a sample or category (the Wundtian model) and the other to establish what is expected of a sample or group of persons as an aggregated whole (the Galtonian model). The Wundtian approach employs individual cases in theory development and theory testing, as to make a 'common to all' claim; a researcher must look at all cases in a sample, one at a time, to establish the same pattern within each. The theory that results from this painstaking process can be tested on any individual within the class to which the theory is said to apply, for the theory predicts what is common to all. If one individual does not conform, this is a challenge to the theory. If predictions about single cases are repeatedly not borne out, then the theory may be falsified (Popper, 1963).

This methodology differs from predictions made within the Galtonian model, which are made about a group as an aggregated whole and must be tested at that group level. Despite Allport's intentions, the polarity became antagonistic rather than complementary, and idiographic research was considered the antiscientific adversary of nomothetic progress. Still, in the 1970s and 1980s, writers denounced idiographic methods as unscientific and opposed to nomothetic science. In the last few years, the notion of idiographic methods has enjoyed a revival. However, the use of the term in journal articles across the last decade shows a plurality of different meanings, many of which bear little relation to Windbelband's or Allport's meaning. The concept seems untethered from its philosophical moorings and can mean almost anything that can be contrasted with the standard (i.e., Galtonian) quantitative method. The fundamental problem is that idiographic research is not premised on a specific method. Idiographic is the objective of describing or explaining an individual thing. The loss of the Wundtian paradigm has meant that Psychology has had a widely accepted empirical basis for developing or testing fundamental, non-probabilistic theory for many decades. However, this has not deterred mavericks. Newell and Simon's research on problem-solving is a rare and superb modern example (Newell & Simon, 1972). In the Wundtian paradigm, every case matters. As you will see, we adopted this paradigm in a deep exploration of single cases and then generalized it with care of individual and personal differences.

1.10 Fluxes of Change

Moving to the next steps in our explorations of Flux in the Complexity of Changing Minds, we would resort again to one of the prominent inspiring masters, Leonardo da Vinci. Karl Jaspers proposed considering Leonardo a scientist and a philosopher who conveyed his research in his visible productions (Jaspers, 1953). Leonardo, in his pluriverse, is a progenitor incarnating the early uncertain steps of complexity science. Knowledge, for him, comes from eyes and hands. His paintings are universal topologies and microcosms where reality is sublimated and modeled. In his paintings and drawings, he recognized embedded mathematical patterns as he wrote in archaic Italian: *"Nissuna umana investigazione si puo' dimandare vera scienza, s'essa non passa per le matematiche dimostrazioni"* ("No human investigation can be considered true science, if it does not pass through mathematical demonstrations.") (Richter, 1970). In Leonardo, the world is *Vita Universa*, the wholeness of a universe of life. Earth is flesh, stones are bones, water is blood. Sea waves and tides are breathing. Lava, sulfur, and volcanoes express its fire of life. That is its immense force and fragility, as even the weight of a little bird can change its position (Richter, 1970). This might recall the *clinamen* of Epicure and Democritus and later the Butterfly Effect (Lorenz, 1993). As in hurricanes, force in Leonardo can easily become violent. He described and fascinatingly pictured natural catastrophes, deluges, cosmic destructions, and violent phase transitions. Water and fire can bring life as harmonious change and devastation as brutal transformation. Leonardo always admired the universe, in harmony or devastation, as in the following passage from his *Notebooks* (Richter, 1970): "Here forms, here colors, here the character of every part of the universe are concentrated to appoint; and that point is so marvelous a thing…Oh! Marvelous, O stupendous Necessity, by thy laws thou dost compel every effect to be the direct result of its cause by the shortest path. These are miracles…In so small a space, it can be reproduced and rearranged in its whole expanse."

Chapter 2

Embodiments

What I try to translate for you is more mysterious,
it is entangled at the roots of being,
at the impalpable source of sensations.

Paul Cézanne

2.1 Beyond Solipsism

Paul Cezanne (1839–1906) is one of the most highly regarded and enigmatic artists of the late 19th century. By approaching painting as a process and investigation, Cezanne linked the formal process of artmaking, which he called *realization*, to his personal experiences or *sensations*. For Cézanne, landscape painting touches the primordial trans-modal, synesthetic experience of encountering and being part of a scenery. He translates to us the way it vibrates with him. It has been reported that before painting, he was motionless, his eyes dilated and immersed in a sensory field that he called a *motif*. Then, he converted the *motif* into the canvas, translating its forces for our vibrations (Merleau-Ponty, 1966; Petitmengin, 2007). This was his way of producing a masterpiece, from a personal experience to an interactive art artifact. Within this process, the artistic object acts as an interpreter, translating an intimate perceptual and emotional experience from presentation to representation into a social object, projecting and potentially inducing analog experiences. This transition from the unique individual, private, *umwelt* to shared culture and knowledge was explored in a seminal case study on Cezanne by Maurice Merleau-Ponty (1966).

Ludwig Wittgenstein investigated these liminal areas of human experience from a different perspective. He proposed a thinking experiment on the border between personal and social boundaries in his famous *private language argument* (Kripke, 1982; Orsucci, 2015). In some well-known paragraphs of the *Philosophical Investigations* (1967), Wittgenstein posed this problem: "The words of this language relate to what can be known only to the speaker, to his immediate and private sensations. So, no one else can understand this language." He later described: "The words of this language refer to what only the speaker can know, to his immediate private sensations. So, another person cannot understand the language." (Wittgenstein, 1967). Wittgenstein did not consider encryption and secret coding; he thought a language intelligible only to its single originator and inaccessible to others.

As an example of a possible private language, we might consider the *Voynich Manuscript*, an illustrated codex handwritten in an unknown, eventually meaningless, writing system. Wilfrid Voynich, a Polish book dealer, purchased the manuscript in 1912. The material has been carbon-dated to the early 15th century (1404–1438), possibly composed in Italy during the Renaissance as an elegant hoax. Many professional and amateur codebreakers have studied the Voynich manuscript but never deciphered it. As a result, no one has independently verified the many hypotheses proposed over the last hundred years. Nevertheless, it is fascinating that the manuscript became a *cause célèbre* in cryptology and, at some point, even a subject for novels. In 1969, Hans P. Kraus donated the manuscript to Yale University's Beinecke Rare Book and Manuscript Library, where it remains. Additional resources about it are available on the library website (http://www.voynich.nu). The Voynich Manuscript, though written in unusual signs, presents an apparent natural language structure in sequences and recurrences (Barlow, 1986; Brumbaugh, 1975, 1978; Landini, 2001). We find an imaginary linguistic universe with unusual signs, grammar, syntax, and a dictionary.

Would it then be possible to conceive a peculiar language that is not understandable to anyone except its creator, who might use it just for private writing, thoughts, and solitary conversations? After introducing the idea, Wittgenstein clarifies that, from his point of view, there can be no private language because all language is essentially the result of personal and social interactions. The importance of drawing philosophers' attention to an unusual idea and then arguing that it is impossible lies in the fact that implicit confidence in the possibility of a private language has been essential to idealistic epistemology and metaphysics. Most representational theories of mind imply some privacy of mental contents. This position is significant in philosophy, linguistics, psychology, and epistemology (Baker, 1998; Kripke, 1982). Wittgenstein's paradox is relevant because the possibility of a private language is a vague assumption of standard theories of knowledge and philosophy of mind from Plato to Descartes and most of the cognitive science of the late 20th century.

Wittgenstein dedicated part of his investigations to "healing grammar diseases" and "infections" from conceptual confusion. Similarly, early Freud's attention went to all the anomalies that jut out of speech as puns, slips of the tongue, and narrative of dreams, regarded as rebuses or cryptic texts needing deciphering. For Wittgenstein, language is not intrinsically misleading or deviant. On the contrary, Wittgenstein seems to find the cause of "linguistic disorders" in a metaphysical desire to "[run] its head up against the limits of language" (Wittgenstein, 1967). So, in principle, he confirms that grey regions of uncertain language privacy might be possible. However, from his point of view, they might be potential sources of linguistic disorder. From that point of view, thinking and language disorders have developed over the centuries, spreading like epidemics. In these dynamics of linguistic epidemiology, the *meme* conceptual framework is a source for further reflection and research (Blackmore, 2000; Dawkins, 2006). As Merleau-Ponty explored in Cezanne, the private language paradox could find its roots in the ambiguous phase transitions between sensations and perceptions, presentations and representations. Human language has the remarkable property of admitting usage for both interpersonal communication and thinking, often in inner monologues or virtual dialogues. Not surprisingly, a line of linguistic research has suggested the notion of *idiolect* as a unique individual semiotic identity pattern (George, 1990; Kraljic et al., 2008). The idiolect manifests itself in lexicon forms, idioms, grammar, and pronunciation unique to each of us (Higginbotham, 2006). As Prieto (Martinet, 1989; Simeonidou-Christidou, 1998) proposed, linguistic understanding could be considered a transitional area between private idiolects in a shared system of meanings that he called shared *noetic fields*. In Prieto, the double articulation between the noetic and the semantic fields in a language renders communication possible.

2.2 Creating Language

As Wittgenstein wrote, "To imagine a language is to imagine a form of life." What forms of life could we find in artificial languages? We might consider the mysterious Muslim *bailabalan*, the Dogon *sigi* secret language society, or the *ignota lingua* of Hildegard von Bingen. Moreover, why not consider that mathematical languages are artificially produced and not regularly spoken? Alessandro Bausani (1974) explored the field of invented languages in depth. Claude Hagege (1993) applied an ecological approach to the studies of language evolution. Similarly, in his *Rise and Fall of Languages* (1997), Dixon applies a dynamical systems model of punctuated equilibria to linguistic evolution. Particularly relevant was the example of Ben Jehudah, the 19th-century visionary in Paris, who imagined bringing the Jewish language back to life, though it had not been an everyday language for more than 2,500 years. His successful enterprise established a seminal component of the cultural foundations of Israel. Similarly, we might mention the successful *linguistic nest* projects established to protect the Māori language from near-extinction. When we speak about languages, we also speak about cultures, *weltanschauung*, and values.

However, states of mind can alter personal semantic fields and produce individual changes in syntax and grammar (Merleau-Ponty, 1960; Lorenzer, 1977; Lacan, 1978; Orsucci, 1981a; 1981b). Mental states and conditions are associated with changes in thinking and social communication. Therefore, every social and therapeutic communication occurs in the grey areas between private dialogue and public conversation. Communication is constantly developing in the transitional-transactional areas of understanding and misunderstanding. The psychopathology of language highlights how neologisms and neo-languages can be related to mental health conditions (Andreasen & Grove, 1986; Condray et al., 2002; Crow, 2000; DeLisi, 2001).

Language develops in a coordinated flow of interactions, not in single gestures, sounds, words, or attitudes extracted from the communication streams. Inner and outer streams constantly merge or diverge. Language is a manner of living together in a flow of consensual behaviors (Maturana & Varela, 1980). Language evolves as a structural coupling in which living systems interact, engage, and affect each other. The concept of coupling between systems is present both in physics and biology. Coupling can facilitate the entrainment in synchronization (Pikovsky et al., 2001) and coevolution (Durham, 1992; Lumsden et al., 1981). In this perspective, following the pathways traced by Wittgenstein (1967), language can be considered a tool for cognition and social interaction. Language can produce the weaving of presentations between agents in distributed cognitive systems and social networks. Language is "a skillful, joint activity through which interlocutors attune to each other and the task at hand co-constructing a shared cognitive niche" (Fusaroli et al., 2014; Fusaroli & Tylén, 2016). Language is a joint action through multiple attunement-and-coupling dynamics of cognitive and motor processes (Tschacher & Bergomi, 2015). Communication involves body movements (kinesics, kinesthetics), posture, gesture, facial expression, voice inflection, sequence, rhythm, and pitch of the spoken words, including the words themselves, culture artifacts, and media. Communication in modern societies can be synchronous and asynchronous, in presence or at a distance, direct or indirect, and even mediated by artifacts and objects. About the meaning of objects, for example, we could refer to the seminal essay by Marcel Mauss on the social dynamics of gift donation and related anthropology (Adloff, 2016; Mauss, 2000).

Some current approaches to social cognition rarely emphasize the intersubjective dimension, and even when they mention interaction, they frame the problem in terms of two minds communicating across a gap (Gallagher, 2001, 2013). In the Theory of Mind (ToM), the inference about what is going on in others' minds bridges the grey gap between minds. The ToM bridging inference is a simulation that will permit a form of mind-reading, also called mentalizing. However, we rarely take a detached observational stance in everyday social life. As agents and partners in situations, we directly interact with our own verbal, motor, and emotional systems. Developmental studies provide evidence of these active processes that the developmental psychologist Colwyn Trevarthen called *primary intersubjectivity.*

Dynamical system theory can be an excellent toolbox for understanding the synergy between symbolic and dynamical aspects of language (Elman, 1996; McWhinney, 1999; Orsucci, 2002; Rączaszek-Leonardi & Kelso, 2008). Human language evolved — through a series of intermediate stages of mimetic culture — due to pressure for increasingly sophisticated means of socio-cultural coordination and cooperation (Orsucci, 2008). The main features deriving from the dynamical system nature of language are: 1) higher balance of dynamical synchronization between interlocutors, 2) increased stability and complexity of collective evolved symbolic patterns, 3) better coordination, 4) higher synergy performance in everyday tasks, and 5) emerging symbolic patterns of trans-subjective cultural repositories of collective knowledge. Semiotic patterns come to constitute communal cognitive niches structuring and coevolving with coordinative dynamics. Semiotics can be considered a tool for social and ecological harmonization. Synchronization on complex heterogeneous networks spanning and weaving in subjective and intersubjective dynamics produces the emergence of semantic patterns from indexes, icons, and symbols (Orsucci et al., 2013; Orsucci, 2015; Orsucci et al., 2016). This intersubjective perspective replaces the monologue-based monadic rationalism of the cognitivist approaches to language, such as Generative Grammar.

2.3 A World of Experience

A musical approach to semiotic interactions can help to grasp the dynamic nature of language and communications. In present circumstances, gestures seen, felt, or heard reveal the motivating force and coherence of central neural plans for immanent action. They tell stories by mimesis and may allude to imaginary adventures over time scales, in rhythmic units from present moments to lifetimes. In this way, music is a natural resonance of the human body (Trevarthen et al., 2011). However, every piece of music, even the smallest melody, is made with a social purpose. All communicative gestures of animals, such as the head bobbing and hand waving of lizards, singing of whales or nightingales, cries of migrating geese, squeaking of mice, and grunts of baboons, are both self-regulatory (felt within the body or guided by interested subjective attention to objects and events in the world) and adapted for social communication (Darwin, 1977; Panksepp & Trevarthen, 2009). Gestures represent embodied intentional actions that signal moving experiences in several domains of consciousness. They can sense, show, and regulate the state of the body of the person who makes them; they can manifest and direct interests to the objective world of physical 'things'; and they can convey the purposes of communication with other persons or any combination of these three. In social life, the distinction between a movement or posture made in communication and, therefore, a gesture, as opposed to one not intended for communication but entirely for individual purposes, is unclear. It would appear to depend on the abilities of one individual to 'feel with' the motives that cause and direct any action of the other. The process will gain direction and subtlety by learning in real-life communication. However, this learning would appear to require adaptations for an innate intersubjective awareness that is active from the start of life with others (Trevarthen 1998; Beebe et al., 2015).

Music seems to be a privileged way of encountering the human semiotic dynamics dimension of our experience. A piece of music, or a song, awakens and causes us to vibrate, a zone of us that is difficult to situate, intimate, and diffuse without precise limits (Petitmengin, 2007). As many psychotherapists have pointed out, it is at this level that we play any therapy. A patient can understand their problem conceptually and be capable of explaining it without addressing it simultaneously. The liberation comes during an experiential process, generally far longer, and consists of becoming aware of the felt meaning. The felt dimension of the difficulty will gradually become relaxed, expanded, and diluted. It is a process of embodied understanding and transformation, an inner distillation rather than an intellectual arrangement of concepts. We find this dimension also in the process of the emergence of an idea, for example, in scientific research: very often, a new idea, before taking a precise and communicable form, first shows on the surface of consciousness as a blurred and fuzzy sensation, a presentiment, or a direction of thought, an interior line of force which silently guides research, as Einstein once observed to the psychologist Max Wertheimer who questioned him in great detail about concrete events in his thoughts that led to the theory of relativity: "For all these years, there was a feeling of direction, of heading straight for something concrete. It is, of course, challenging to express this feeling in words. Nevertheless, I had it in a sort of overview and in a certain way, visually." (Holton, 2000). William James drew our attention to the instant at which, before appearing and developing, a thought is preparing, still unarticulated, with no determined sensorial form, in what he called the 'fringe' of consciousness (James & McDermott, 1967). "One may admit that a good third of our psychic life consists of these rapid premonitory perspective views of schemes of thought not yet articulate. (...) In short, the reinstatement of the vague to its proper place in our mental life which I am so anxious to press on the attention." Francisco Varela (Varela et al., 1991) and Antonio Damasio (1998) studied this dimension. The latter calls these fleeting feelings (which he considers as the root of self-consciousness) 'background feelings' because although sometimes intense, they are not usually present in the mind's foreground. This dimension of our mental life is panoramic, peripheral, floating, holistic, and lateral, though it is fine and sensitive to subtle discontinuities. It is also described as receptive, through free associations, in a stream of consciousness that can be blurred and fuzzy. This kind of felt meaning can call, simultaneously, on several sensory forms: the visual (shape, shadow, fuzzy), the kinetic, the tactile (vibration, pulsation, pressure, density, weight, texture, temperature), the auditory (echo, resonance, rhythm), and even the olfactory or the gustative. Very well-known descriptions of felt meanings confirm these multisensorial experiences. Some authors call this dimension *synesthetic*, while others prefer the definition of *trans-modal* (Petitmengin, 2007). Plato & Conford (1957) and Aristotle & Irwin (1999) had already identified these characteristics, which they called *common sensible*. Along these lines,

Daniel Stern (1977) concludes that the world the child experiences is not a world of images, sounds, and tactile sensations but a world of shapes, forms, movements, intensities, and rhythms. In other words, a world of trans-modal qualities, which can transfer from one mode to another, and he calls vitality affects (distinct from categorial or discrete) such as happiness, sadness, fear, anger, disgust, surprise, and shame). "This global subjective world of the emerging organization is and remains the fundamental domain of human subjectivity. It operates out of awareness as the experiential matrix from which thoughts, perceived forms, identifiable acts, and verbalized feelings will arise later. It also acts as the source for ongoing affective appraisals of events. Finally, the ultimate reservoir can be dipped into for all creative experience." (Stern, 1985). He refers to a first matrix of affective attunement, a stratum of experience that remains active throughout life, although generally below the threshold of awareness. The roots of this affective subliminal dimension are in the pre-reflective way mother and child attune their internal rhythms. For example, a mother will reply to the babbling of her baby with a caress of the same intensity and rhythm. This rhythmic synchronization, which enables the resonance or tuning of two interior universes, is the basis of affective intersubjectivity.

2.4 Looking for the Source

The source of vital dynamics develops through multiple systems of the highest complexity. Freud wrote in his unpublished *Project* (1966), "The intention is to furnish a psychology that shall be a natural science: that is, to represent psychical processes as quantitatively determinate states of specifiable material particles, thus making those processes perspicuous and free from contradiction…The neurons are to be taken as material particles." Let us dive into the background of the Source. The brain is a polyfunctional generator of information. A population of neurons can use many different combinations of signals in response to internal or external stimulation. Neural pathways form, dissolve, and reform in streams of conduction and physical connections. The brain contains about 10^{15} (one quadrillion) specialized junctions or synapses (Black, 1994). Many other levels of the nervous system have communication pathways. Synapses modulate in such a way that the brain can change itself (Doidge, 2007). The mix of electrical and biochemical information is augmented in degrees of freedom by multiple modulating factors: density and strength, pulse rhythms, recruitment and synchronization, dynamically changing pathways, ions, neuromodulators, and hormones. The combinatorial informational power of this system is beyond finite determination as transmission can develop along continuous spectra of concentrations. The boundaries between hardware and software are blurred, while structure and function constantly change. For instance, many transmitters can mediate electrical communication, elicit synaptic changes, and modulate circuit functions, survival, and growth of neurons. Some ions, for example, Ca^{2+}, can activate enzymes modulating synapses, facilitating or inhibiting inter- and intracellular connections.

Neurons appear using multiple co-localized modulated signals, providing immense potential for combinations even at the synaptic or neuron level.

These combinations are mixed and electrochemical, with various degrees of freedom in the resulting codes. Environmental stimuli and internal body dynamics can be encoded, communicated, and stored flexibly. The resulting systems are complex and diverse to be resilient and fault-tolerant. There is an overall modularity of partially self-contained subsystems, as the dynamics can be local, specialized, or global. The trophic function of the nerve growth factor and brain-derived neurotrophic factor (BDNF) might be an example, as they can regulate physical circuits and increase the biosynthetic enzymes of catecholamines.

The brain is a complex system consisting of different types of networks, such as structural, functional, and dynamic (Park & Friston, 2013). These networks can be studied using various methods and models, revealing essential aspects of the brain's organization, function, and development.

Structural networks are the physical connections between brain regions, such as axons, synapses, and white matter tracts. They can be measured by techniques such as diffusion tensor imaging, which can map the direction and strength of water diffusion along the brain's fiber pathways. Structural networks can be represented by graphs, where nodes are brain regions, and edges are connections between them. Graph theory can be used to analyze the properties of structural networks, such as their topology, modularity, efficiency, and resilience.

Functional networks are the statistical dependencies between brain regions, such as correlations, synchrony, or causality. They can be measured by functional magnetic resonance imaging techniques, which detect changes in blood oxygenation level-dependent (BOLD) signals reflecting neural activity. Functional networks can also be represented by graphs, where nodes are brain regions, and edges are measures of functional connectivity between them. Functional connectivity can vary depending on the brain's task, state, or condition (Yao et al., 2015).

Dynamic networks are the changes in structural or functional networks over time, such as adaptation, learning, or development. They can be measured by techniques that capture the temporal evolution of network properties, such as dynamic causal modeling, which can infer the causal effects of one region on another based on their BOLD signals. Dynamic networks can also be represented by graphs, where nodes are brain regions, and edges are measures of effective connectivity between them. Effective connectivity can reflect the underlying mechanisms of information processing and integration in the brain (Uddin et al., 2011).

Structural, functional, and dynamic networks are interrelated and influence each other. For example, structural networks constrain functional networks by providing the anatomical substrate for communication. Functional networks modulate structural networks by inducing synaptic plasticity and neural growth. Dynamic networks reflect the interaction between structural and functional networks by showing how they reconfigure in response to different stimuli or demands.

The study of brain networks can provide insights into the brain's complexity and diversity. Using different methods and models, researchers can explore how the brain's structure supports its function, adapts to its environment, and develops its cognition (Park & Friston, 2013). The Source is a dynamical process, not a place.

2.5 Biosemiotics

At the beginning of the 1970s, Umberto Eco opposed transpositions of the linguistic model on other phenomena, which he assigned to the lower threshold of semiotics (Eco, 1976). At least since the Hellenistic period, we mean by semiotics the study of the phenomenon of emitting and interpreting signs. According to an ancient definition, a sign is something that stands in the place of something else. Something is present, and in some ways, either due to convention or some relation of homology or analogy, it brings the thought of something else to us. If this is the definition, verbal language undoubtedly is only one of the forms of semiosis. Semiosis also involves domains in which an interpreter still decides to interpret an unintentional interaction event as a sign. The activity of the physician who scrutinizes the patient's symptoms is a semiotic activity, as is one of the hunters who interpret tracks in the wood. In the mid-1950s, catalyzing a series of suggestions across the entire history of human thought, from philosophy to linguistics, from psychology to anthropology, the vogue of semiotics exploded, and scholars of diverse disciplines threw themselves into discovering communication processes and underlying signification processes in all domains, from architecture to nonverbal expressions and body postures. With such enthusiasm for discovery, it was natural that somebody would seek to identify semiotic processes among animals (zoo-semiotics), plants (phyto-semiotics), and at the cellular level. The discovery of the genetic code at the beginning of the 1950s proved that communication processes were also at the heart of the biological domains. Some seminal papers on information theory came around that time (Shannon & Weaver, 1949).

To understand the forms of semiosis, we could consider the conditioned reflex. One could think that the Pavlovian dog "interprets" the bell as a sign of food and "decides" to salivate, but only if it were possible, as it happens in a Russian joke, to imagine a clever dog who goes daily to the Pavlov Institute and salivates to induce a conditioned scientist to ring the bell and bring food. We may go back to Charles Sanders Peirce, one of the founding fathers of modern semiotics. He wrote, "Every relationship with the world comes in three phases that may never be complete: first, second, and thirdness. Suppose that I place my hand on a stove and burn myself. Firstness is the moment at which I perceive pain. Secondness is the moment at which, although still confused, I identify the stove as the cause of my pain. Thirdness is the moment I pass to the order of the symbolic and say (and think): "Stove! It is the stove that burned me." From this point, I have entered the order of language and thought, and I will also be able to make inferences about what will happen if I bring my hand closer to something that is not stove but may be under the same category. I entered the order of language because I passed from the particular to the universal. The space separating secondness and thirdness is the space of semiosis and interpretation."

It is possible to speak of animal or cellular semiosis only if such a virtual space and time exists. When a lymphocyte T recognizes an antigen, it calls other lymphocytes — suppressors, effectors, and inductors — to collaborate to target it adequately with the antibody. The question posed by semioticians was whether there was a choice, a space, or only key-lock processes, and the lymphocyte had no choice. Since the cultural universe is not born in a vacuum, because it appears if not as the final, then as the most recent result of the evolution of the species, let us go back to where nature is not yet culture, but from where culture, as the terminus of evolution, originates. "The elementary sign condition is a physical state whereby a structure bears significance with another structure since it selectively interferes with it. A substrate is a sign for an enzyme because it is complementary to one of its parts and therefore appears as meaningful [...]". (Hoffmeyer, 1997).

One main concern of biosemiotics is thus to see the phenomena of significance, meaning, and interpretation in the human sphere as rooted in and, to some extent, continuous with the kind of phenomena in the non-human sphere (Emmeche, 2003). We can take the words of Short (1983) to symbolize this non-reductionist perspective of biosemiotics: "The distinctive power of human speech is not a supernatural gift but is a remarkable development of basic principles found elsewhere in nature." Biosemiotics is an attempt to study life not only by chemical approaches, seeing cells and organisms as assemblies of molecules, but from the perspective of semiotics, seeing those same molecules and interactions as vehicles for information and signification processes. Scientific fields like molecular biology, ethology, cognitive science, robotics, and neurobiology deal with information processes at various levels and thus — in that minimal sense of semiosis as informational processes in living organisms — spontaneously contribute to knowledge about biosemiotics and living sign action. From a biosemiotic perspective, human and non-human cognitive systems are non-dual, as there is no evident separation between hardware and software, *res extensa* and *res cogitans*, and body and mind. Sign processes are active all through the physiology of living and artificial systems. Molecular biology, cognitive science, robotics, and virtual environments are all considered within a biosemiotic unified framework. Information is a process in which something stands as a sign (simple or composite representamen) that makes a difference (interpretant) to some system (interpreter) (Peirce, 1953). Biosemiotics add value to the dynamic aspects of semiotics (Sebeok, 1992; Peirce & Fisch, 1982) as signification generates in interactions, either in physical, biological, or cultural forms, and their integrations. In this way, it almost inadvertently helps to resolve remnants of Cartesian dualism and metaphysical ghosts. Embodiment is the way to overcome the dualistic nature of old cognitivism. Biosemiotics might even go further as signification processes are so pervasive that mind and body blend seamlessly. Organisms live in their ecological niches defined by porous boundaries. Humans are techno-cultural beings integrating meaningful hybrid interactions. The definitions of cyborg (cybernetic and biological) point in that direction, though they still almost fail to address flawless integration and fusion. Hoffmeyer (1997; 2008) sees the body as swarms of cells organized into a super swarm through semiotic communication between the nervous, hormonal, and immune systems. In this cybernetic, systemic, and semiotic view (Brier, 2015), intelligence is not understood as coming from a central controller. Intelligence is an emergent self-organization phenomenon arising out of these swarms of cells. Hofstadter (1985) also claims that the autopoietic thinking system is not organized from above in a classical logical way but from below through subconscious and non-conscious activity.

"The brain itself does not manipulate symbols; the brain is the medium in which the symbols are floating and trigger each other. There is no central manipulator, no central program. There is simply a vast collection of *teams* — patterns of neural firings that trigger other neural firings like teams of ants. The symbols are not *down there* at the level of the individual firings; they are *up here* where we do our verbalization. We feel those symbols churning within ourselves in somewhat the same way we feel our stomach churning. We do not do symbol manipulation by some act of will, let alone some logical deduction rules. We cannot decide what we will think next or how our thoughts will progress. Not only are we not symbol manipulators, but quite to the contrary, we are manipulated by our symbols!" (Hofstadter, 1983; 1985).

The more researchers studied how people think, as opposed to how philosophers, logicians, and computer scientists said they ought to consider, the clearer it became that our bodies impose the conditions of our experience, thinking, and communicating with others (Newen et al., 2018). This new perspective has come to be known as the cognitive science of the embodied mind or, more simply, embodied cognitive science (Lakoff & Johnson, 1999; Feldman, 2006). The origin of meaning and thought is the activity of a bounded, embodied organism as it engages its various environments in ways that allow it to maintain the primary conditions for life and growth. The more complex the organism is, the more ways it has by which it can meaningfully interact with the energy structures that make up its environment. Situations will provide for the organism what James Gibson (1979) called affordances, patterns for meaningful perception and action relative to the nature of the organism, its needs, and its purposive activity in the world it inhabits. Meaning, in this way, is taking a phenomenological perspective, more expansive than in linguistics or analytic philosophy. Conceiving meaning in this embodied, experiential manner enables us to go beyond the narrow confines of language-based meaning to embrace the full range of human meaning-making in such practices. Exploration of the implicit assumptions of the affordance concept will reveal the underlying intentional character of the ecological approach to perception (Heft, 1989). Affordances shape conversations' virtual space of speech (Worgan & Moore, 2010). There are essential structural similarities in how higher animals and humans engage in unreflective activities, including unreflective social interactions. It is a form of unreflective embodied intelligence that is 'motivated' by the situation (Merleau-Ponty, 1945; Rietveld, 2012). The living space's intentional shaping depends on psychophysical shaping created by our perception, motor structures, and skills. This perspective extends what the philosopher Thomas Nagel proposed with his famous paper "What is it like to be a bat" (Nagel, 1974, 2007). In recent years, this general orientation toward the grounding of mind in organism-environment interactions has come to be known as "4E cognition", that is, cognition as embodied, embedded, enactive, and extended.

2.6 4Es, 5Es, 7Es

We can find the origin of this debate in Plato's *Phaedo,* where Socrates discusses the position that he attributes to Anaxagoras as a purely physical explanation of bodily mechanisms (Plato et al., 1988). Afterward, Aristotle reassessed that position, accepting that the body has a role in human rationality (Aristotle & Bostock, 1994). This position later established value in Neoplatonists, Aquinas, and others, including more recent thinkers such as Spinoza, de La Mettrie, and Condillac. Pragmatists and phenomenologists continued the debate, discussing behaviorism, cognitivism, and psychodynamics. More recently, in the 90s, *The Embodied Mind* by Varela, Thompson, and Rosch (1991), drawing on phenomenological and neurobiological resources, proposed an enactive account of cognition that emphasized the role of the *dynamical coupling* of the brain-body-environment. Around the same time, a paper by Hutchins (2020) introduced *distributed cognition* as a "new branch of cognitive science" for which the unit of analysis includes external structures, collectives, and artifacts organized as performing systems. Hutchins's (1995) *Cognition in the Wild* influenced Clark and Chalmers's (1998) now-classic philosophical essay, *The Extended Mind.* Throughout this time, additional work inspired by Gibson's ecological approach to psychology contributed to a growing realization that cognition was not limited to "processes in the head" but was embodied, embedded, extended, and enactive. The concept of 4E cognition brings these different approaches together under one heading and conceives them as coherently opposed to the internalist, brain-centered views of cognitivism. The issues that continue to be debated concern the very nature of embodiment — how brain, body, and environment are coupled or integrated into cognition, and how much we can generalize from observing embodiment in one type of cognitive performance to others. Furthermore, there are questions about the role of representation and what it means to say that bodily and environmental processes constitute cognition.

The functionality of the motor system carves out a pragmatic *Umwelt*, dynamically surrounding our body (Gallese, 2018). The profile of peri-personal space is not arbitrary: it maps and delimits a perceptual space expressing and constructing the motor potentialities of the body. All objects are the potential target of intentional action, mapped as such by the cortical motor system. An essential component of the perceptual experience of handling objects is determined, constrained, and constituted by the limits posed by what the body can do with it (Rizzolatti et al., 1996). Based on his research in mirror neuron functions, Vittorio Gallese proposed a theory of Embodied Simulation (ES) that might be based on active embodiment, not on mind reading or propositional representation. Empirical research demonstrated that the very same nervous structures involved in the subjective experience of emotions and sensations are also active when such emotions and sensations are recognized in others. Therefore, ES extends beyond Mind Reading and Simulation Theory as a general mechanism, including action, perception, imagination, and language. The other relevant feature of ES is that it is primarily intrapersonal since it pertains to the mental states or processes that an individual undergoes when planning action or experiencing emotions and sensations and when observing someone else's actions, feelings, and sensations. ES theory can also be applied to distinctive forms of human social cognition, like mental imagery and the experience of symbolic fictional worlds, like when beholding artificial images, hence in the absence of real-world motor action (Gallese & Lakoff, 2005). ES is also entirely interpersonal, as the shared intersubjective space in which we live from birth constitutes a substantial part of our semiotic space. Self and others relate to each other because they are opposite extensions of the same correlative and reversible, we-centric space (Gallese, 2005). The observer and the observed are part of a dynamic system governed by reversible rules. Using intentional attunement, *the other* is much more than a different representational system; it becomes a bodily self, like us. From a semiotic perspective, the mechanism of ES can produce *iconic signs* (Cuccio & Gallese, 2018). This is because simulations are natural signs whose denotative relation depends on their similarity with the objects or events they refer to. Thus, as in the Peircean perspective, icons are signs that signify an object neither for a conventional relation to it, as symbols do (words are the best example of symbolic relations), nor for their spatiotemporal contiguity with the object, as indexes do (a classic example is the relation that holds between smoke and fire: the former is always an index of the latter), but only in virtue of their qualities, of their structure. The mechanism of ES provides us with categorical schematization of objects, actions, emotions, and perceptual experiences. The icons produced in ES are the first and primary sources of categorization at our disposal (Cuccio & Gallese, 2018).

2.7 The Necessary Fifth E

We were surprised that there was no mention of the emotions between the 4E forms of embodiment proposed by Shaun Gallagher and others (Newen et al., 2018), as emotions represent a most relevant "5th E". This absence perhaps indicates that a hidden cognitivist bias might still influence the 4 Es project. Emotions and their expression are a constant and crucial component of embodiment, as affects constantly permeate the *PsycheSoma* or Mind-Body as just one integrated domain. Emotions, affect, and moods present an exciting interdisciplinary exploration field for studies involving developmental psychology, personality psychology, neurobiology, psychoanalysis, biological psychiatry, psychophysiology, psychosomatic medicine, cognitive science, cognitive and behavioral psychology, and communication sciences (Taylor et al., 1999).

Historically, emotions receive different statuses depending on the dominant cultural *milieu*. For example, they might provide inspiration, transcendence, and intuitive illuminations. In this context, ecstasy and enthusiasm refer to enjoyment, lively interest, transcendence of individuality, and inspiration. Conversely, emotions might perturb the purity and clarity of reason. For example, one of the speakers in Plato's *Symposium* (Plato et al., 2001), Eryximachus, a pythagorizing Athenian physician, sets two contrasting conceptions of Eros as the representative of all emotions. He favors an orderly Eros of union and harmony in opposition to the Eros of excess. The orderly Eros regulates the joyous blending of hot, cold, dry, and wet. They bring health to men, animals, and plants when mixed in gentle harmony. When, instead, excessive Eros prevails, there is injustice, destruction, and disease. The physician believes medical art aims to establish an orderly and harmonious Eros balancing opposites in the body (Orsucci, 2002). Significantly, Plato involved an Athenian physician in discussing the role of emotions. Asclepiades had attributed mental disorders to emotional disturbances; Galen classified passions between the reasons of non-natural disease. He also proposed the four temperaments theory, a proto-psychological theory that suggests four fundamental personality types based on emotion prevalence and physiological embodiment: sanguine, choleric, melancholic, and phlegmatic. Plato promoted *eudaimonia* as a positive balance of emotions (Orsucci, 2001). It might be worth mentioning that Socrates affirms in multiple dialogues that he kept joyous communion with his daemon as a spirit of nature representing his emotional identity. In this, we might find residual links to the shamanistic roots of early philosophy (Cornford, 1957; Orsucci, 2002).

The publication of seminal studies about a century ago opened a new phase in the scientific status of emotions. In 1872, Charles Darwin published his monumental work *The Expression of Emotions in Man and*

Animals (Darwin, 1972). He reported observational findings that facial and bodily expressions of emotions were similar between human infants and adults across diverse cultures. He also noted similarities with other primates. So, in his perspective, the expression of emotions was universal and related to general evolutionary processes. He thought emotions might be innate, though he had not acknowledged genetic inheritance, and Mendel's papers found in his library were unopened, with uncut pages. The evidence provided in his book is anecdotal and not based on structured studies. However, he proposed that the expressions might involve face, voice, and movement. He suggested that innate and discrete emotions manifest in specific expressions. Darwin recognized that emotional expressions promote bonding between mothers and infants and relations in social groups. Emotions are relevant components of human evolution, as they organize behavior and increase the chances of survival. He proposed that body movement and gestures might be influenced by culture, while facial and vocal expressions of emotions might be more independent from cultural constraints. This proposition opened a relevant *nature vs. nurture* debate as the anthropologists Margaret Mead and Gregory Bateson advocated a cultural influence on all emotional expressions, including facial ones (Ekman, 2006, 2009).

2.8 The Nature of Emotions

A few years after Darwin's book, William James published his famous essay, "What is an Emotion" (1884, now in James & McDermott, 1967). He brought neuroscience into the scientific framework by proposing that emotions result from the afferent feedback to the brain of different patterns of peripheral autonomic nervous activity and bodily states. In his perspective, emotions were forms of awareness of physiological changes. The Danish physician Carl Lange independently developed similar ideas (Lange, 1894). James and Lange defined emotions as feelings of physiological changes, but they focused on different aspects of the emotions. James was more focused on the conscious experience of emotions, for example, a person crying because they might be sad. Lange's theory was more biomedical, operational, and testable. However, both agreed that removing physiological sensations could remove emotional experience. From their perspective, physiological arousal causes emotion. Other pragmatists extended the naturalization of the human mind. Peirce (1968) fondly reminded his readers that humans' capacity for reason reflects the mind's affinity with nature and its continuity with the instincts of so-called lower animals.

However, Walter Cannon (1987) soon criticized the James-Lange theory, arguing that emotions arise from subcortical regions of the brain and that the autonomic physiological responses are an output of brain processes. Walter Cannon's article on the James-Lange theory of emotions attacked the fundamental notions of emotion held by most psychologists since its postulation by William James and C. G. Lange. In this classic study, Cannon analyzes the assumption and premises of the James-Lange theory and offers the best criticism of that position. Cannon held that the viscera and the innervation of muscles were not the sources of the qualities of emotion. Instead, emotions derive from subcortical centers. Cannon's theory, which developed from these beginnings, replaced the James-Lange theory in most textbooks.

A complexity science-integrated perspective will help to consider that multiple feedback loops are in place in emotional arousal, expression, and recognition. As Tschacher noted (Tschacher et al., 2012, 2023), the Autonomic Nervous System activation is an example of the circular relationship between mind and body addressed by the embodiment perspective: mental arousal or relaxation has the consequence of bodily arousal or relaxation, whereas the reverse is also true, as the mind becomes alerted by sympathetic physiological activation or relaxed by parasympathetic activation. In analogy to the reciprocal relationship of physiological and mental activation, there is also an interchange between body movement and so-called body language. An example is gait, where increased vertical movement while walking predicts increased positive mood and distinguishes the gait of depressed patients from that of control subjects (Adolph et al., 2021). In another study on gait, the reverse sequence was explored experimentally. Non-depressed participants found that depressed gait favored depressed cognitive styles (Michalak et al., 2015). Such findings point to an interchange between cognition, movement qualities, expression, and reaction in an integrated embodied perspective.

There is a general agreement that emotional responses involve at least three systems: a) neurophysiological autonomic and endocrine systems, b) motor and expressive behavioral systems, and c) cognitive and experiential systems. Affects are composite states encompassing all three domains: mental presentations, representations, and memories of personal meaning. Most authors use emotion and affect as synonyms; some include feelings in the same semantic areas. We will try to draw a preliminary map of the definitions of emotional states, the basic emotions, and their relevant combinations. Emotion, mood, feeling, passion, sentiment, and atmosphere are all related to human experiences, but they have different meanings and implications. Here are the main semantic differences between their definitions:

1. *Emotion* is a complex psychological state involving physiological and cognitive responses to a specific stimulus or event. It is often intense, short-lived, and has a clear trigger or cause.
2. *Mood* refers to a more generalized and longer-lasting emotional state. Moods can be positive or negative and influence how we perceive and interpret the world.
3. *Feeling* is a conscious experience of an emotional state. It is the subjective experience of an emotion or mood specific to an individual. Individual experiences, cultural backgrounds, and beliefs can influence feelings.
4. *Passion* refers to intense emotions and feelings towards something or someone. It is often associated with a strong desire, enthusiasm, or drive to pursue a particular activity or goal.
5. *Sentiment* refers to a general attitude or feeling towards something or someone. It can be positive or negative and influences behavior, decision-making, and communication.

6. *Atmosphere* refers to the overall mood or feeling related to a place or environment. It combines physical and social factors, such as lighting, sound, and social interactions.

7. *Instinct* refers to a fixed, patterned, innate, and genetically determined behavior. Emotion and instinct are two different concepts that relate in some ways. Emotion is a subjective state of mind typically accompanied by physiological changes and expressed through behavior. The main difference between emotion and instinct is that emotions are acquired responses to stimuli, while instincts are innate responses to stimuli. In addition, experiences, culture, and environment shape our emotions, which can vary between individuals and cultures. In contrast, instincts are universal and shared by all species members. Emotions can also be complex and involve various components, such as cognitive processes, physiological changes, and behavioral responses. On the other hand, instincts are usually straightforward and involve a specific, predetermined behavior. Despite these differences, emotions and instincts can interact with each other. For example, a robust emotional response like fear can trigger an automatic fight-or-flight response. Similarly, instincts can sometimes influence our emotions, such as when we feel a sense of satisfaction or pleasure after fulfilling a basic instinctive need, like eating or mating. The instinctual component is primarily related to our body's physiological responses to certain stimuli. It is a natural and automatic response based on our genes and not subject to direct conscious control. For example, when we feel hungry, our body automatically produces certain hormones that trigger the instinctual behavior of seeking food. Similarly, when we sense danger, our body's instinctual response triggers physiological changes that prepare us for fight or flight. These physiological responses are not conscious and are controlled by our autonomic nervous system, which operates independently of our conscious control.

Primary emotions are a set of universal and biologically based emotions experienced by all humans regardless of culture, language, or socialization (Ekman, 1999). Therefore, primary emotions link or mix with instincts. Emotional expression and recognition can involve automatic and reflective processes, depending on the context and individual's experience. Let us explore each of these aspects:

1. *Reflexive.* Reflexive emotional expression refers to spontaneous and automatic reactions to emotional stimuli. It involves immediate and automatic responses, often driven by the amygdala and other subcortical regions of the brain. These reflexive expressions can include facial expressions, vocalizations, body language, and physiological responses like tears or increased heart rate. Similarly, automatic emotional recognition refers to the quick and automatic identification and interpretation of emotions in others based on their expressions or behaviors.

2. *Reflective.* Reflective emotional expression involves a more deliberate and conscious process of choosing how to express emotions. It may include introspection, self-awareness, and the consideration of social norms and appropriateness. Reflective emotional recognition consists of the cognitive appraisal and interpretation of emotions, often requiring conscious thought and reflection. It involves analyzing cues from others' behavior, context, and verbal expressions to understand their emotional state.

Automatic and reflective processes are not mutually exclusive but frequently mix on a continuum. Emotional expression and recognition can involve a combination of both. Reflective processes may follow initial reflexive responses as individuals become aware of their emotions, consider their implications, and choose how to respond or interpret them. Similarly, reflective processes can inform and shape future reflexive responses through learning and socialization. Cultural, individual, and contextual factors can influence the balance between automatic and reflective emotional processes. For example, cultural norms and upbringing can impact how individuals express or suppress their emotions reflexively or engage in more reflective emotional regulation. Similarly, individuals with high emotional intelligence or those who have undergone emotional self-reflection may rely more on reflective processes for emotional expression and recognition. In summary, emotional expression and recognition can involve both reflexive and reflective processes, with reflexive responses being more automatic and spontaneous and reflective processes involving conscious thought, introspection, and interpretation. The interplay between these processes varies based on individual characteristics and contextual factors. Paul Ekman (2009) suggested the essential criteria summarized in the following table that should distinguish basic emotions from one another and other affective phenomena:

1.	Distinctive universal signals
2.	Distinctive physiology
3.	Automatic appraisal
4.	Distinctive universals in antecedent events
5.	Distinctive appearance during development
6.	Presence in other primates
7.	Quick onset
8.	Brief duration
9.	Unbidden occurrence
10.	Distinctive thoughts, memories, images
11.	Distinctive subjective experience

2.9 Expressing Emotions

Panksepp and Watt confirmed that a scientific study of emotions is possible only if we consider their foundations "in the nested hierarchies in BrainMind organization" (Panksepp & Watt, 2011). They believe that a better appreciation of such a level of organization can diminish confusion and disputes among investigators working at various levels of *MindBrain* control. They explain their preference of conflating the terms mind and brain into one word, equally used in the reversed version of *BrainMind*, to reflect the monistic ontology, emphasizing that "these are two sides of a coin." We might follow their interesting suggestion in terminology or use an elegant equivalent such as the *PsycheSoma*. As Damasio suggested, in rejecting any dualism, emotions constitute rationality (Damasio, 2006).

The brain is the only body organ where it is empirically evident, anatomically, histologically, and functionally, that the pressures of evolution left clear historical imprints on its organization. This history is apparent in the layered stratifications where more ancient systems are situated in the middle and back and the more recent systems lateral and frontal. We can better understand the organization of emotions in these nested hierarchies, where the basic levels can combine to produce emergent and more complex levels. Hierarchical controls are also evident in the brain regulation of emotionality. As a heuristic simplification, they prefer the following levels of analysis and a vocabulary with an early Freudian reference: (a) primary-process core affects arise from ancient subcortical processes (Panksepp, 1998b), (b) secondary-process elaborations, including emotional learning, arise from Pavlovian/classical conditioning and instrumental/operant learning principles, and (c) tertiary process emotions, as complex cognitive-affective amalgams, emerge via neocortical interactions with paralimbic and limbic structures. In the higher mind, these nested hierarchies interact with working memory to plan alternative courses of action to cope with ongoing affective opportunities and challenges. Various top-down and bottom-up controls exist within the *PsycheSoma*. Ludwig Wittgenstein wrote in his *Remarks on the Philosophy of Psychology*: "We see emotion. — As opposed to what? We do not see facial contortions and infer that he feels joy, grief, or boredom. We immediately describe a face as sad, radiant, or bored, even when we cannot give any other description of the features. One would like to say that grief is personified in the face." (Wittgenstein et al., 1980).

Emotional expression can present an emotion that enables sensation and perception in ourselves and others. We can also highlight a third level, as an emotion can induce a similar state in others. If we see sadness, we can feel sad, as it can happen in implicit, non-conscious, explicit, or conscious ways. Expressions can make emotions perceptible.

We might differentiate natural and spontaneous reflex *expression episodes*. Examples include facial expressions (smiles, pouts, scowls), gestures (waving one's hands, covering one's face, clenching one's fists), postures (puffed chest, slumped shoulders, hunched back), vocalizations (hoots, sobs, snarls), and tones of voice (high-pitched, brittle, stentorian) (Glazer, 2017). LeDoux (1996) has drawn attention to the importance of the amygdala in what he calls a "quick and dirty" automatic emotional response (Fonagy, 2002). The second type of emotional expression, *speaker or action expression,* occurs when someone intentionally performs one of the above behaviors to communicate an emotion. LeDoux clarified that this involves the neocortex, though he repeatedly emphasizes that there is no single place in the brain where emotions reside, as most of the brain can be involved (LeDoux, 1996; Fonagy, 2002). Unlike natural expressions, speaker expressions can be insincere, and there can be "lies" in these emotional expressions. Therefore, following Eco's criteria (Eco, 1976), we could consider this part of a higher-level semiotic communication process. Finally, a third type of emotional expression, *cultural expression,* includes artifacts that convey emotions to observers. These can be artworks, music, or theatre that explicitly depict emotions (such as Auguste Rodin's *Shame* or Edvard Munch's *The Scream*) or implicitly elicit emotions (such as Beethoven's *Fifth Symphony* or Van Gogh's *Starry Night*). An entire corpus of literature in aesthetics focuses on determining how artworks convey emotions to their audiences. Notoriously, for example, the Greek tragedy was supposed to provoke cathartic emotions. Modern art is less straightforward, though indeed implicitly working as an open framework to provoke readings, meanings, and emotions in spectators (Merleau-Ponty, 1973; Eco, 1989).

Within the *PsycheSoma,* nested systems of layered evolutionary stratifications interact. The most ancient systems are situated medially and rostrally, with the higher and newer systems distributed (Panksepp & Watt, 2011). There is evidence for hemispheric asymmetry in some emotional life elements but not others. Indeed, the cortex itself is essential only for some aspects of the broad phenomenon of emotion, for example, how emotions are perceived and expressed, which often show effects of hemispheric asymmetry, especially on some emotional regulation and neuropsychological skills.

On the other hand, the role of deep subcortical structures in generating emotions is clear for powerful feelings, moods, and emotions (Turnbull & Salas, 2021). A recent data-driven meta-analysis revealed that the perception, experience, and expression of emotion are each subserved by distinct large-scale networks (Morawetz et al., 2020). For example, Morawetz et al. (2020) identified four large-scale brain networks. The first two were related to regulation and functionally characterized by a stronger focus on response inhibition or executive control versus appraisal or language processing. In contrast, the second two networks are related to emotion generation, appraisal, and physiological processes. Thus, it has been proposed to move from hypotheses supporting an overall hemispheric specialization for emotion processing toward dynamic models incorporating multiple interrelated networks that do not necessarily share the same lateralization patterns (Palomero-Gallagher & Amunts, 2022). There might be interactions between the following systems:

- The *amygdala-centered network* constitutes the neurobiological substrate for integrating sensory input and emotional arousal to decode the stimulus's significance for the organism. It includes the amygdala, areas of the olfactory, orbitofrontal, insular, anterior, and midcingulate cortex, and the *ventral striatal-pallidum.*
- The *hippocampus-centered network* mediates the integration of information processed by multiple large-scale brain networks involved in the different memory types to incorporate cognition into emotion processing. It includes the hippocampal complex, entorhinal and retro-splenial cortex, areas of the anterior (discussed above) and posterior cingulate cortex, and the thalamus.

Regarding the secondary involvement of cortical areas, the *right-hemispheric dominance hypothesis* proposes that the right half of the brain is dominant for processing all emotions, independent of their valence or emotional feeling. A valence lateralization hypothesis gradually replaces this *hypothesis.* According to the valence lateralization hypothesis, both hemispheres process emotions and feelings. However, depending on the emotional valence, there is a preference for the left hemisphere for positive emotions and the right for negative ones. This pattern of findings led to hemispheric accounts of emotion, of which Davidson and colleagues are best known (Davidson, 2001), with the suggestion of a right frontal system involved in negative (withdrawal-related) emotional states, with left frontal regions associated with positive (approach-related) emotion. In a variant of this hypothesis, *motivational valence* would drive lateralization, with the left hemisphere being dominant for approach motivational tendencies and the right for withdrawal ones (Palomero-Gallagher & Amunts, 2022). A meta-analysis addressing the neuroanatomical structures underpinning emotional experiences demonstrated that happiness, sadness, fear, anger, and disgust are associated with distinct regional brain activation patterns. There would be a wider distribution and competence of brain areas and lateralization patterns. Since emotion perception is a multi-layered phenomenon, increasing task demands would redistribute activity among the hemispheres as an adaptive mechanism to ensure continued accurate and prompt responses. Since environmental requirements modulate psychological responses, there is evidence that altered conditions, such as acute stress, could result in network redistributions and even reversed lateralization. Thus, a dynamic systems perspective is now becoming predominant in abandoning hypotheses of an overall hemispheric specialization and moving beyond a global lateralization model in emotion processing.

2.10 The Source of Emotions

Survival depends on the maintenance of the body's internal and external integrity. The first requires keeping physiology within an optimal homeostatic range. Body state changes are mapped topographically in the central nervous system (specifically, in the upper brainstem and cerebral cortex). Feelings facilitate learning the conditions responsible for homeostatic imbalances and their respective corrections and anticipation of future adverse or favorable conditions (Damasio & Carvalho, 2013). From both evolutionary and ontogenetic perspectives, the experiential aspect of homeostatic neural mappings rests at the primary level of the mind and consciousness. The available evidence indicates that phylogenetically recent sectors of the nervous system, such as the cerebral cortex, contribute to but are not essential for the emergence of feelings, which are likely to arise instead from older regions, such as the brainstem, suggesting that feelings are not exclusive to humans or even mammals.

Evidence suggests that emotional experience is somehow preserved after cortical lesions but distorted or altered in several ways (Turnbull & Salas, 2021). Explaining this paradox requires identifying a source of emotion generation outside the cortex and identifying the contribution of neuropsychological components that produce the distortion in emotional processes. Emerging evidence suggests that the source of emotion generation lies in a range of deep subcortical structures, the most important of which is in the upper brain stem. In contrast, the cause of the distortion appears to be a range of cortical areas devoted to managing feelings and other higher cognitive processes. The source of emotional experience is deeply subcortical, as cortical lesions do not disrupt the ability to generate emotions. The core of the emotional experience is in systems underpinning consciousness in the dorsal regions of the mid-brain (Panksepp, 1998a, 2004), especially the periaqueductal gray (PAG), as all the primary emotion systems (which include the various subcortical regions named above) terminate in the PAG. In addition, in the PAG, one finds the maximal emotional outcome (pleasurable or aversive) for the most negligible electrical current. Stimulation of the amygdala, striatum, insula, hypothalamus, or anterior cingulate produces fewer substantial effects, and lesions to those brain areas produce changes in global emotional experience. Critically, this expands the debate on the neural basis of emotion beyond the problem of hemispheric asymmetry to the 'vertical' dimension of hierarchy (Turnbull & Salas, 2021). In evolutionary terms, these higher-order cognitive functions have emerged not only to help us successfully deal with demands from the external world but, most notably, to successfully manage internal states of the body (the inner world) in the light of contextual constraints: to manage feelings adaptively, in the light of environmental and social limitations. These tools allow us to use emotions to fuel and direct behavior, to inhibit emotional responses when they are not adequate to our long-term goals, to predict the future based on relevant past experiences, and to read or hide emotional expressions when necessary.

No doubt we can combine the top-down (cognition to affect) with bottom-up (affect to cognition) perspectives in various ways, but we believe the most coherent and defensible evolutionary approach is to have clear bottom-up primary-process views, namely, some neuroscientific basic emotion approach that cannot be clarified just through human research. Animal neuroscience models are essential for envisioning more explicit evolutionary processes. Based on these assumptions, Panksepp and Watt (2011) defined cross-species primary-process (basic) emotions as prototype emotional states based on subcortical networks of the brain. Something about emotionality is neuro-genetically foundational for the BrainMind emergence, and primary-process emotional networks are among such functional specializations. The emotional lives of mature individuals consist primarily of secondary and tertiary processes, while pure primary-process emotions are rare (Panksepp & Watt, 2011). We should be clear again that there is no evidence that the neocortex can independently generate feelings on its own (without accompanying arousals of paralimbic and subcortical emotional effector systems). Neocortex can engender emotions, regulatory processes, and social and cultural emotional expression dynamics but no strong basic emotions. We will expand the examination of these dynamics in the following chapter. While Panksepp and Freeman focused on foundational emotions and their brain roots, other authors, including Ekman, focused on emotional expression with their cognitive/cultural, and cortical dynamics.

The perspective later proposed by Panksepp and Davis (Davis et al., 2003; Davis & Panksepp, 2018) clarifies the neurobiological foundations of the main emotional types and proposes psychometric testing for it. Just as the instruments that preceded the Affective Neuroscience Personality Scales (ANPS) relied upon taxonomies of personality that were generated by blind statistical measures of its superficial features (or worse, culturally and linguistically mediated self-conceptions of those features), so too the classification and measurement of psychiatric disorders are embarrassingly arbitrary — grounded in and confounded by the history and conventions of the discipline, rather than empirically based understanding of how the emotional brain works. They aim to establish neurobiological foundations of basic emotions on the limbic subsystems and their dynamics. The psychometric tool has been more recently criticized as the ANPS has several problems, including an ill-defined factor structure, overly long scales, poorly worded, ambiguous items, and questionable content validity. To address these issues, Barrett, Robins, and Janata constructed an improved short form of the ANPS — the Brief ANPS (BANPS) (Barrett et al., 2013). Three studies demonstrated that the 33-item BANPS has a clear and coherent factor structure, relatively high reliabilities (for short scales), and theoretically meaningful correlations with a wide range of external criteria, supporting its convergent and discriminant validity. Unlike typical short-form scales, the BANPS improves upon the psychometric properties of the long form, and we recommend its use in all research contexts.

2.11 Afflictive or Nourishing Emotions

The immune system provides the basis for embodied and embedded body-mind integration (Goleman, 1997). We can recognize emotional states that can help to stay healthy and emotional states that can facilitate disease. Afflictive emotions can facilitate illness, while wholesome states of mind promote health. The quality of the emotions directly affects the immune and cardiovascular systems. Other body systems are also indirectly affected. Anger and hostility may contribute to developing specific cardiovascular diseases, blood pressure dysregulation, and related mortalities (Gavrilova & Zawadzki, 2023; Harris et al., 2020; Sadeghi et al., 2020). Low mood, sadness, grief, chronic stress, and depression can dysregulate cortisol levels, impacting the immune system (Knezevic et al., 2023; Nandam et al., 2020; Rothe et al., 2020).

Looking at wholesome mental states, equanimity, calm, satisfaction, optimism, confidence, friendliness, joy, happiness, play, and compassion can foster higher levels of dopamine, serotonin, oxytocin, endorphins, and neurotrophins (Alexander et al., 2021; Diener et al., 2020; Li et al., 2020). This would facilitate further positive emotions and neuroplasticity. The experience of positive emotions, feelings, and affect are fundamental building blocks for cultivating resilience, flourishing, vitality, happiness, and life satisfaction (Bryant, 2003; Cohn et al., 2009; Diener et al., 2020), which ultimately contribute to physical and emotional wellbeing.

Gautama Buddha (c.563/480 — c.483/400 BCE), the founder of Buddhism, believed that happiness is concerned with good life and starts from understanding the root cause of suffering. Living a good life involves avoiding extremes, specifically self-indulgence and self-affliction, and following the 'Middle Path' of moderation (Hallisey, 1988, 2022). In Ancient Greece, Aristotle (384 — 322 BCE), following his predecessors Plato and Socrates, asserted that happiness resides in moral or ethical virtues, termed eudaimonia (Aristotle & Irwin, 1999). Such virtues include courage, justice, temperance, benevolence, and prudence. To be happy, one needs an excellent moral character to do the right thing even under challenging circumstances and to achieve virtue excellence. Epicurus (341–270 BCE) also viewed happiness as the ultimate purpose of human existence (Sellars, 2021), implying avoiding extreme passions.

The British utilitarian Jeremy Bentham (1748–1832) held a more extreme hedonistic view, whereby happiness was defined as an experience of pleasure and a lack of pain (Guidi, 2007). Such pleasures included wealth, skill, friendship, a good reputation, power, piety, benevolence, memory, imagination, expectation, association, and relief.

Ikigai is a Japanese concept that combines the terms *iki*, meaning "alive" or "life," and *gai*, meaning "benefit" or "worth." It represents what gives your life worth, meaning, or purpose. Essentially, ikigai is the reason why you get up in the morning. Ikigai is said to have evolved from the essential health and wellness principles of traditional Japanese medicine, which holds that physical well-being is affected by one's mental-emotional health and a sense of purpose in life. Japanese psychologist Michiko Kumano has said that ikigai is a state of well-being that arises from devotion to activities one enjoys, which also brings a sense of fulfillment (Kono & Walker, 2020). The concept of ikigai is often associated with a Venn diagram with four overlapping qualities: what you love, what you are good at, what the world needs, and what you can be paid for. However, one's ikigai may have nothing to do with income. Finding our ikigai brings more meaning and purpose and facilitates enhanced physical health and mental well-being. For instance, ikigai has been shown to influence immune function, increase life expectancy, reduce anxiety, and improve resilience (Fido et al., 2020; Kotera et al., 2021). In summary, ikigai is a comprehensive concept that incorporates values in life, giving a sense of purpose and leading to a more fulfilling life. It focuses on a particular sphere of life or activity that makes life worth living and is essential for our well-being.

Three dominant paradigms of wellbeing presently exist in psychological research (Jayawickreme et al., 2014): 1) *hedonic (subjective wellbeing)*, 2) *eudaimonia (psychological wellbeing)*, and 3) an integrative approach spanning hedonic and eudaimonia. Integrating theoretical perspectives on subjective and psychological well-being, Gatt et al. (2014) developed a composite well-being scale called COMPAS-W (Composure, Own-worth, Mastery, Positivity, Achievement, Satisfaction). The COMPAS-W scale provides an overall measure of total well-being and specific subscales of subjective well-being and psychological well-being along a continuum ranging from flourishing to languishing. For example, "calmness" is considered a positive emotion that represents relatively low levels of arousal compared to "happy," which represents approximately the same level of pleasant valence but higher levels of arousal (Anderson & Adolphs, 2014). Positive affect is associated with flourishing and success across life domains, including social, work, physical, and psychological health (Pressman et al., 2019). From an evolutionary perspective, the functional role of positive emotions has been theorized to build physical, intellectual, and social capacities that promote adaptation and long-term survival (Fredrickson, 1998).

The neurotransmitter dopamine has received the most attention concerning positive emotions, and dopamine has been implicated in reward-related processes. Reward is conceptualized as comprising of (1) objective and subjective 'liking' reactions, which translate to the hedonic experience of pleasure; (2) 'wanting' or incentive salience, which describes the motivation to seek reward; and (3) reward-based learning (Berridge & Kringelbach, 2008, 2013). Oxytocin is a nonapeptide hormone released from the posterior pituitary and multiple organs (uterus, placenta, amnion, corpus luteum, testes, and heart) in response to social bonding, interactions, and the emotional context of social relationships (Shamay-Tsoory & Abu-Akel, 2016; Orsucci et al., 2013). Dopamine and endorphin systems have been theorized to mediate the link between oxytocin and social relationships (Pearce et al., 2017). In summary, positive moods, emotions, and stimuli appear to modulate specific cognitive control processes differentially, and additional neuroscience research across cognitive domains would contribute to developing more unified theories regarding how positive moods, emotions, and stimuli influence cognitive control and vice versa.

Social relationships and connectedness promote thriving. Interdependent solid and healthy relationship bonds are critical for human survival, and positive emotions contribute in complex ways to this equation (Pressman et al., 2019; Sbarra & Coan, 2018; Shiota, 2014; Shiota et al., 2017). Whereas evolutionary theories generally suggest that negative emotions support short-term survival (Stockdale et al., 2020), positive emotions such as joy, contentment, interest, and love have been broadly theorized to increase physical, intellectual, and social capacities, connections, and resources that facilitate survival in the long run (Fredrickson, 1998). Relatedly, the size of social networks increases longevity and enhances the capability to cope with stressors (Pearce et al., 2017). However, specific positive emotions, such as pleasure, may also reinforce behaviors that lead to short-term survival, such as goal-directed consummatory behaviors related to food, procreation, and social connections (Berridge & Kringelbach, 2008, 2015). Momentary happiness often increases when spending time with friends.

Across the human lifespan, positive emotions are generally experienced during play (Winnicott, 1971), which is a critical form of social interaction that builds relational capacities and facilitates general well-being (Nijhof et al., 2018; Russ, 2009; Storli & Hansen Sandseter, 2019). Play occurs across cultures and is observed in mammalian species, certain bird species, and reptiles (Nijhof et al., 2018). Given that play requires a significant time and energy expenditure for humans and animal species alike, play likely serves an essential evolutionary purpose, facilitating survival (Nijhof et al.,

2018). For children, play enables the development of a broad repertoire of social capacities and affective processes, including understanding and regulating emotions and empathy (Nijhof et al., 2018; Russ et al., 2009). Play also scaffolds cognitive development in the domains of problem-solving and creativity (Nijhof et al., 2018). In humans, the play experiences represent a wide range of activities, including attunement/mimic play, body play, movement, object play, social play, imaginative and pretend play, storytelling-narrative play, and creative play. Environmental factors are critical to cultivating positive emotions and well-being beyond contextual factors such as strong social relationships and healthy social interactions. Play is related to enriched environments and learning gamification. Since the discovery that enrichment leads to positive effects on brain development and behavior (Rosenzweig et al., 1962), enrichment has been widely used to study the effects of the environment on brain development and particularly on neuroplasticity and neurogenesis (Van Praag et al., 2000). Environment enrichment and physical exercise attenuate illness and promote positive emotions and learning through enhanced levels of BDNF and neuroplasticity (Sadegzadeh et al., 2020; Santoso et al., 2020; Xu et al., 2021). There has been growing interest in human research regarding the link between mental well-being and physical health, as indicated by the immune response (Pressman et al., 2019). Environmental enrichment in mice attenuated the effects of a flu infection (Jurgens & Johnson, 2012) and lipopolysaccharides (Ji et al., 2017), and enriched housing of pigs reduced the impact of a co-infection with two common respiratory viruses (van Dixhoorn et al., 2016) and affected levels of autoantibodies (Luo et al., 2017). In humans, there is some evidence of a relationship between positive emotions and lower levels of inflammatory cytokines (Stellar et al., 2015). Meditation, mindfulness, contemplative practice, and flow experiences are linked to positive emotions and their neural correlates (Kabat-Zinn, 2003a, 2003b).

2.12 Clouds, Rain, and Blue Skies

We started this exploration on sensations, feelings, and the inner and outer worlds, and Cezanne was a unique case study for Maurice Merleau-Ponty.

Leonardo had a different experience of landscapes when he wrote, "The air was darkened by the heavy rain whose oblique descent, driven by the rush of the winds, flew in drifts through the air… However, it was tinged with the color of the fire kindled by the thunderbolts by which the clouds were rent and shattered, and whose flashes revealed the broad waters of the inundated valleys…" (Richter, 1970). His drawing of a mighty deluge is one of eleven in the Royal Collection. It was probably executed during his last years in France and is among the Renaissance's most enigmatic and visionary works.

To the painter John Constable, the sky was full of emotion (Smith, 2015). In a letter written in 1812, he called it the keynote and chief organ of sentiment in painting. He dedicated much of his time to collecting and classifying cloud shapes and colors. At the time, he lived in Hampstead, a village near London, and he would walk to the nearby countryside, collecting sketches of clouds that he would later organize at home. He wanted to master the language of the sky, looking for taxonomies, though the clouds kept folding, merging, and drifting away.

It is a well-known experience, that of pareidolia on non-structured shapes. On that basis, Swiss psychologist Hermann Rorschach developed the Rorschach Inkblot Test in 1921 (Vecchio et al., 2023). His interest in inkblots began in childhood with a game called *Klecksography*, which involved creating inkblots and making up stories or poems about them. Piet Mondrian reduced his work to simple geometric elements and primary colors in a simplified reality (Jones, 2020). In his action painting, Jackson Pollock almost returned to Leonardo's deluges, and to avoid any possible pareidolia added further complexity to his shapes (Parkinson et al., 2020). Mark Rothko produced field paintings characterized by expanding dimensions and an increasingly simplified use of form, brilliant hues, and broad, thin washes of color (Guan & Liu, 2023). In his large, floating rectangles of color, which seem to engulf the spectator, he explored the expressive potential of color contrasts and modulations with a rare mastery of nuance. The mysterious source of sensations evoked by Cezanne is entangled at the roots of being, the impalpable source of sensations, translated into the expression of emotions. Like colors, emotions flow, merge, and weave complex configurations in the streams of life.

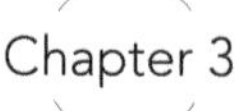

Chapter 3

Patterns

Most of an organism most of the time is developing from one pattern to another, not from homogeneity to a pattern.

Alan Turing

3.1 The Self Universe

Fernando Pessoa was a prolific writer, not only under his name, for he created approximately 75 other fictional authors, each with their personality. Three stand out: Alberto Caeiro, Álvaro de Campos, and Ricardo Reis (Jennings & Pessoa, 2019; Pessoa, 2002). These imaginary figures sometimes held unpopular or extreme views. He provided them with biographies, individualized psychologies, religious and political points of view, and distinctive literary styles. Too radically different from him and from each other to be considered simple pseudonyms, Pessoa called them *heteronyms*. In a *Bibliographical Summary* of his works published in 1928, he explained the conceptual distinction: "Pseudonymous works are by the author in his person, except in the name he signs; heteronymous works are by the author outside his person. They proceed from a full-fledged individual he created, like the lines spoken by a character in a drama he might write." (Zenith, 1993, 2021). The main three heteronyms boasted a large and exquisite body of work stylistically unlike the poetry of his fellow heteronyms or Pessoa himself, and one could say that Portugal's four greatest poets from the 20th century were Fernando Pessoa. Pessoa's last name is the Portuguese word for "person,"; there seems to be a universe of personae and poems within the person. A panorama of the human self to display and magnify some of the features of its nature. The history of literature contains some pale parallels to his performance of multiple authorship.

The explorations of identity and diversity of selves within their transformations are far from new. For example, Diotima in Plato's *Symposium* articulated: "For even during the time in which each living being is said to be alive and to be the same — for example, someone is said to be the same person from when he is a child until he comes to be an old man, and yet, if he is called the same, that is even though he is never made up of the same things, but always comes to be new and loses what he had before, hair, flesh, bones, blood and the whole body." (Plato et al., 2001). Not much later, Plutarch (Perrin, 1926) formulated the *Ship of Theseus* thought experiment after the Athenians preserved the ship that supposedly Theseus used by replacing part by part as they decayed. In its original formulation, the Ship of Theseus paradox concerns a debate over whether a ship with all its components gradually replaced one by one would remain the same ship.

Many centuries after, William James asked: "Each of us, when he awakens, says, here is the same old Me again, just as he says, here is the same old bed, the same old room, the same old world." (James, 1985). We have an emotional sense of intimacy and warm feelings embracing our body, clothing, family, and familiar spaces. This is "how the I appropriate the Me" in James's formulation. In the first moments of the awakening, it is clear how thoughts, feelings, and sensations mix and blur into what we might call a sensed and thought Self. There is a "sameness in the Self as known" every morning and a self-similarity and continuity in the difference in the rest of the days. An emotional sense of personal identity provides a safe enough foundation for the active cognition of everyday life. James (1895) defined this nucleus of our Self-identity as "the very sanctuary of our life." He attributed this core to the spiritual Me, belonging to the empirical Self. The Empirical Self, the *Me*, is emerging from integrating sensations, activities, family and friends, work and reputation, clothes, house and cars, and personal histories. Our bodies form the innermost, implicit, and concrete parts of the *Material Me* and our *Social Me*. Further extensions might include the intricacies of collaborations, friendships, and cultures. "Properly speaking, a man has as many social selves as there are individuals who recognize him and carry an image of him in their mind." At the same time, we show our Selves in many ways, depending on the context and interactions, sometimes creating synergies or conflicts between our different identities. In parallel, our biological selves keep transforming as cells are replaced, while the immune system guarantees that our biological identity keeps persisting while changing over time.

3.2 The Primary Self

Darwin, James, Lange, and Freud started exploring analogous landscapes in the same years. In his first relevant writing, the unpublished *Project for a Scientific Psychology* (Freud, 1895–1966), Freud intentionally distanced himself from verifiable brain matters. His contemporary biophysics influenced his initial stance, though he was not particularly open to accommodating verifications, perhaps because of the limited neuroscience knowledge of his days. However, a famous passage from that early seminal writing was: "Mind is extended but knows nothing about it." Since his earliest studies, emotions have seldom had an implicit but relevant role in defining human identity and its circumstances. Freud borrowed the term *Affekt* from the earlier German psychophysiology and psychology. Generally, in his terminology, it encompasses any affective state representing the qualitative component of instinctual representations. In Freud's successive works, we could find a clinical discussion of the role of emotions since the early *Studies on Hysteria* (Breuer & Freud, 1956), where the causes of illness were traced back to emotionally traumatic events. They hypothesized that the emotion remained dissociated from representations, repressed, and accumulated in emotional congestion. Therefore, treatments initially focused on the therapeutic value of releasing congested emotions in cathartic abreactions. Early psychoanalysis considered that a recollection of traumatic memories would have been therapeutic only if accompanied by the expression of corresponding repressed and congested emotions. In his later years, Freud returned to examining the role of emotions in his meta-psychological writings on *Repression* and the *Unconscious* (Freud et al., 1959). With another biophysical metaphor, he intended emotions as the subjective experience and expression of quantities of instinctual energy. A significant disparity persisted between the marginal role accorded to affects in psychoanalytic theory and their enormous importance in the clinical realm and everyday life (Fonagy, 2002). In *The Ego and the Id*, Freud's concluding remark that "The ego is first and foremost a bodily ego" is well known. However, how Freud reached this conclusion has seldom been examined, given the growing interest in embodiment in psychoanalysis (Sletvold, 2011, 2013). Kernberg (1993) highlighted that Freud conflated the German *Ich-ego* as a mental structure and psychic agency with the personal, subjective, and experiential self. In other words, in his use of the term *das Ich,* Freud never separated the theoretical *system* ego from the empirical *experience* self. He built his argument from the assumption that the origin of the ego is to be found in primordial feelings and internal perceptions of the body's emotional states. In his view, the Ego is formed by an interaction of external and internal perceptions. The combined experience of the external world and the state of our own body somehow lays the foundation for 'the feeling of our self, of our ego.' The internal perception of the emotional body states creates the 'feeling of our self' unique quality.

This view of the double nature of the body and the ego echoes in Maurice Merleau-Ponty (1945). On the one hand, Merleau-Ponty suggests that the body is seen as an object, a site to touch, the *me.* On the other hand, the body is the experiencing subject, the self-sensing/feeling of the touch, the *I.* Years later, in *The Self and the Object World* (1964), Edith Jacobson referred to children's first expressions of communication as an *affective organ language.* In her opinion, the *affective organ language* survives in adult age in different forms. Her definition might be a forerunner of what later would be defined as human biosemiotics (Hoffmeyer, 2008; Sebeok, 1992). This perspective contributes to the foundations of the *Primary Self* by establishing individual boundaries, interchanges, and negotiations with human, non-human, and physical environments. The Primary Self has the capacity of permanence and invariance through change. Jakobson was the first psychoanalyst to confront that emotions were not fully considered in their relevance for developing the Self and its psychopathology.

Later, Jaak Panksepp (1999) proposed probing Freudian theories on emotions with neuroscientific approaches by (1) seeking essential brain processes that synchronize the visceral and somatic motor expressions of emotions, (2) defining the crucial ingredients in the cognitive and memory aspects of emotions, and (3) combining these experimental findings with a study of the subjective reports of humans. In his perspective, emotional behavior might be a low-level background stream of *moods* affecting whole clusters of experiences, patterns of thinking, and behavior. Jacobson suggested defining this foundation of subjectivity as a *Proto-Self*. We prefer calling it the *Primary Self* as a lifelong foundation of human identity and personality. Panksepp identified this substrate of affective brain functions as "emotional evolutionary qualia" that constitute an affective core of human experience. In another paper, Panksepp (1998b) proposed, "Primitive emotional feelings appear to lie at the core of our beings, and the neural mechanisms that generate such states may constitute an essential foundation process for the evolution of higher, more rational forms of consciousness." Evidence indicates that certain affective states arise from the neuro-dynamics of a Primary Self. They are based on emotional and motivational systems situated in subcortical regions of the brain. These deep emotional streams represent a biological system of existential values, our Ship of Theseus. At this level, they are integrated with the immune system, maintaining a biological identity that is continuously transforming (Tauber, 1994, 2008).

The proto-self might be in a critical brain area: "within the center-medial-diencephalic midbrain areas such as the Periventricular and Peri-Aqueductal Gray (PAG) and nearby tectal and tegmental zones" (Panksepp, 1998). Walter J. Freeman's approach to this crucial matter is concordant, including other brain areas and widening the implications (Freeman, 2001). He located the emotional Primary Self in a more comprehensive network of brain areas, the Limbic System. The Limbic System, also known as the paleomammalian cortex, is a set of brain structures located on both sides of the thalamus, immediately beneath the medial temporal lobe. It works with emotion, intentional behavior, long-term memory, and olfaction. It is a system integrating sub-units with different functions, all relevant to the Primary Self. Its systemic structure entails neuro-psychological dynamics between areas and functions. These dynamics are contained within the system but involve other cortical regions. Most authors would include the cingulate gyrus, amygdala, mammillary bodies, hippocampus, entorhinal cortex, and the PAG in the limbic system.

The Primary Self would resonate with primitive sensory and emotional values and subjective experiences of pleasure, lust, anger, hunger, desire, fear, loneliness, loss, and sadness. The Primary Self can establish a balanced mental presence, providing emotional unity and continuity (Strawson, 1997). Moods constitute a springboard for intentions and the atmosphere for the ecological niche of the embodied mind. The Primary Self is a source of the brain's higher affective and cognitive states. This primal intentionality stream can structure temperaments. The cognitive components and the narrative fiction of the personal and social Self (Dennett, 1991) emerge from other higher areas of the brain.

3.3 Dynamical Systems of the Self

The sensed Self develops into perceived and remembered selves. Ulric Neisser (1988, 1993) provided a template for a realistic synthesis of the dynamic organization of the Self as a system. The Self is physical and mental, private and public, sensed, perceived, imagined, thought and social, all the same time. Its dynamical system organization can be flexible, stretched or compressed, stressed and resilient to all sorts of activities and events of a lifetime. The overarching Self-system will include the core Primary Self and other Selves of differing origins, developmental histories, phenomenology, and variants, including possible pathologies. Neisser encapsulated the subsets in a list that we found interesting (Neisser, 1988, 1993), and we decided to integrate:

- The *biophysical Self* includes molecular biology, physiology, and immunology. This Self equates with self-identification, preserving identity and integrity with physical survival (Tauber, 2008).
- The *ecological Self* is the Self in the physical environment: "I am the person here in this place, engaged in this particular activity."
- The *interpersonal Self* engages in rapport and communication: "I am the person who is engaged, here, in this particular human interchange."

- The *extended Self* is made of memories, associations, and anticipations: "I am the person who had certain specific experiences, who regularly engages in certain specific and familiar routines."
- The *private Self* appears when children first notice that others do not share some of their experiences: "I am, in principle, the only person who can feel this unique and particular desire, pleasure or pain."
- The *conceptual Self* thrives in narrative assumptions and cultures, social roles and socially significant personality dimensions (intelligence, attractiveness, wealth, etc.) (Holstein & Gubrium, 2012).

The Self can be understood as embedded in brain systems, including explicit and implicit knowledge. These systems work in various contexts, private and social. We must consider the trilogy of thinking, emotion, and motivation to understand their actions and interactions. Different systems interact and integrate, intermingled in biosemiotic dynamics (LeDoux, 2002). Therefore, as James envisioned, the Self is plural (James & McDermott, 1967). Mind, for James, does not exist apart from the operations of the brain, the body, and the senses. Consciousness is not an entity but an unceasing flow, stream, or field of impressions. James assumed that no mental state "once gone can recur and be identical with what was before ... There is no proof that an incoming current ever gives us just the same bodily sensation twice." (Richardson, 2007). We might say that, as in chaotic attractors, recurring events can be similar but not identical.

Damasio (1998) highlighted that language might not be the source of the Self, but it certainly is the source of the I. He ascribed the primary sense of self to the nervous system's continuous mapping of the body as the primary source of embodiment: "The moral of this story is that some parts of the brain are free to roam the world and map whatever sound, shape, taste, smell, or texture the organism's design enables them to map. However, other brain parts representing the organism's structure and internal state are not free to roam; they can map nothing but the body and are the body's captive audience. It is reasonable to hypothesize that this is the source of the sense of continuous being that anchors the mental self." (Damasio, 2003). There is a remarkable variety in people's beliefs about themselves, whether false or true. Nevertheless, the plurality of selves intermingles in the fabric of individual experience. They establish personal values and social identities in distinctive forms of coherence.

The foundation of the dynamical system of the Self is rooted in the embodiment of the Primary Self. The psychobiological perspective established by James Bowlby and later by Myron Hofer's empirical studies can foster an integrative perspective on how the Self subsystems interact and integrate into a functioning complex system (Orsucci, 2002).

3.4 Power of Selves

W. J. Freeman considered "the neural populations that compose the limbic system as the key to understanding the biology of intentionality […] the principal agent of action in space-time." (Freeman, 2001). Intentions create the ecological niche of the Self-personal meaning, its *Umwelt*. The etymology of intention highlights action and direction. Franz Brentano, in his *Psychology from an Empirical Standpoint,* launched *intentionality* in two famous paragraphs: "Every mental phenomenon is characterized by what the Scholastics of the Middle Ages called the intentional (or mental) in-existence of an object, and what we might call reference to content, direction toward an object (which is not to be understood here as meaning a thing), or immanent objectivity. In the presentation, something is presented; in judgment, something is affirmed or denied; in love, loved, hated, hated, desired, desired, and so on. This intentional in-existence is characteristic exclusively of mental phenomena. No physical phenomenon exhibits anything like it. Therefore, we can define mental phenomena by saying that they contain an object intentionally within themselves." (Brentano, 2012).

Some of the leading ideas of the phenomenological tradition originate from this conceptual area. Edmund Husserl (1980) defined phenomenological analysis as reaching the essence of intentionality as *noema* as the internal structure of mental acts. The practice of *Epoché,* a phenomenological reduction by suspension of presuppositions, can help to find *noemata,* the essence of cognitive acts. Scholastics and Jean Piaget called *assimilation* the process of integrating intentionality (Piaget & Cook, 1952) as an active co-adaptation between the Self and the world. In this process, the active creation of meaning creates an *Umwelt*. This personal niche, a semi-private ecosystem, becomes a reality *simulacrum* of the world. Scholastics included emotionally charged imagination in this process. Merleau-Ponty called this creation of unique landscapes *the intentional arc* (Merleau-Ponty, 1960). W. J. Freeman expanded these perspectives within the nonlinear dynamics of neural populations (Freeman, 2001).

The concept that *the Self is a complex dynamical system* has gained attention in various fields, including psychology, cognitive science, and philosophy. It suggests that the Self can be understood and described using the principles of complex systems theory. Complex dynamical systems refer to systems that exhibit emergent behavior arising from the interactions between their components. Nonlinearity, feedback loops, sensitivity to initial conditions, and self-organization characterize these systems. They often demonstrate adaptability, resilience, and the capacity to transition phase-changing while maintaining system cohesion. When applied to the Self, considering it a complex dynamical system implies that the self emerges from the interactions between its various components, such as thoughts, emotions, memories, beliefs, social influences, actions, and biological foundations. These components interact with each other in nonlinear and dynamic ways, with a high degree of freedom, leading to the emergence of self-organization and self-regulation.

Considering the self as a complex dynamical system offers a framework for understanding the intricate interplay between internal and external factors, the constant change and adaptation, and the emergent properties that arise from the system's interactions. Therefore, the Self has dynamical flexibility and meta-stability within certain possible states. Vittorio Guidano (1987, 1991) and Mario Reda (1988) sustained this position from a constructivist perspective: ongoing dimensions of selfhood dynamics "in the praxis of living." In their view, synchronization and mutual coordination in action build the learning experiences, constructing the self as a complex system. From a developmental perspective, the increasing ability of synchronic attunement with others creates self-organizing states and structures in physiology and cognition. This comes with the ability to enter enactive socializing towards experiencing the *I* and the *Me* dimensions. The interdependency and rhythmic reciprocity facilitate the self-organization of the Self subsystems and the *Umwelt*. It is an intermodal coordination organized around prototypical emotional schemata. These processes gradually build, from the interactions with the prominent attachment figures, in a rhythmic and self-regulating modulation of intermodal patterns of sensory-motor-affective modules into a unified configuration, resulting in a sense of self and the world (Reda, 1988; Guidano, 1991; Balbi, 1996).

3.5 The Dynamical Self

Terry Marks-Tarlow (1999) extended a comprehensive perspective of the Self as a dynamical system. In her opinion, a dynamical systems perspective is ideal for addressing individual differences in how the Self works without needing to speculate about or confound function with origins. A dynamical systems perspective contributes to conceptualizations of the self by being process-oriented and content-free. This non-reductionistic perspective easily integrates bottom-up factors, like physiological underpinnings, with top-down ones, such as theories of cultural or political driving forces with bi-directional influences. One can attend to how the body is enculturated and how historical eras are affected by changing family relationships. To take this approach necessarily involves crossing disciplinary boundaries. The Self is ever in *flux*, with fluid boundaries. Within complex dynamical systems theory, we can understand how the Self is a *process* that is continually reconstructed by local interactions occurring at multiple levels between neurons in the brain, between an infant and its mother, between individuals, their partners, and culture at large. It can adopt any number of discrete states from moment to moment based on a complex interplay between events, their cognitive interpretation, and the emotions they engender. From a dynamical systems perspective, the Self is an open system, a *dissipative hyper-structure* characterized by metastability requiring a continuous flow of energy, matter, and information. Thus, even when viewed as a succession of stable states, the self is still characterized by dynamical flux. Marks-Tarlow (1999) emphasized the dynamic nature of the Self, its potential for emergent self-organization, its high degree of freedom, and its continual reconstruction while open to the environment. The dynamical notion of process structure provides a new dialectic that bridges structuralist, constructivist, and functionalist positions, helping to shed new light on the age-old controversy. As the Self is an open self-organizing system, its emergence and development neither occur in an experiential nor a social vacuum.

Evidence for entrainment and coupling in physiological and semiotic domains holds at the emotional level. Infant research (Beebe et al., 2015) suggests that not only are the mother's or other primary caretaker's emotions and responses critical in shaping the developing baby's sense of self, but the reverse holds as well. There is a bidirectional influence, sometimes called mutual or co-regulation, between infant and caretaker, through which the selves of mother and child are integrally linked. Following Bowlby's observations (1978, 1982) on attachment behavior, psychobiologists studied the mother-infant bond as a strong coupling organization mainly regulated by inner emotional signals in its early stages of development. In a series of studies on rodents and primates, Myron Hofer and other developmental biologists demonstrated many hidden regulatory mechanisms (Hofer, 1994b). These hidden factors act on different sensorial channels: nutritional, olfactory, tactile, thermal, visual, and vestibular. The body temperature of infant rats, mainly determined by the mother's body temperature, has been shown to regulate levels of brain peptides, nucleic acids, and neuro-amines. All of them are reduced if the young rats are prematurely separated from their mother. Olfactory stimuli are also involved in regulating crucial aspects. For example, infant rats are unable to locate their mother's nipple in the absence of a pheromone secreted from the mother's areolar glands.

Most regulatory mechanisms remain hidden from a passive third observer outside the "nursing couple" and can only be discovered in experimental contexts. Similar hidden regulatory mechanisms in humans continue in adulthood, but their functioning combines with other emotional, cognitive, and social factors. The works by Margaret Mahler (Mahler, 1968; Mahler et al., 1975) on early symbiotic coupling stages of development and the evolution of decoupling towards individual identity can be considered relevant in a general framework for these findings. The interactions between the self and its self-objects (as transitional objects or sensation objects) regulate the psychosomatic balance (Orsucci, 2002). How children come to view themselves depends critically upon the mother's emotional responsiveness; how the mother views herself depends critically on the baby's emotional responsiveness. The reciprocal influence between mother and infant is modeled well by nonlinear dynamical theory (Schore, 2001). Non-reductionist concepts allow for highly complex feedback systems and multilayered, multidirectional conceptualizations of causality. Co-regulation occurs between the selves of parent and child, which are coupled with one another. This is akin to the eventual lockstep of two relatively same-sized people walking or the synchronous ticking of two cuckoo clocks hung on the same wall. Extensive work on the neurophysiology of development highlights the physiological substrates of emotional entrainment between mother and child. (Stern, 1977; Trevarthen, 1993; Schore, 2001). A multiplicity of multilayered coupling occurs when the child's self is coupled to specific caretakers and the phenomenon of culture at large. Postmodern social constructivism supports the coupling of individual selves to the culture at large, where an increasing body of literature (Kitayama & Markus, 1994; Markus & Kitayama, 1994) provides evidence of a reciprocally interactive relationship between culture and emotion.

Emotions are formed through active adaptation to culture, which serves to maintain, regulate, and sometimes challenge the cultural environment to which they are tuned. Along with the cultural regulation of emotion, this view posits the centrality of enculturated emotion to the developing self. For example, in Western cultures, validation of anger functions to uphold individualistic values, whereas, in other cultures, suppression of anger functions to uphold collectivist ones. This tuning of physiology, emotion, cognition, and motivation to cultural landscapes gives rise to fundamental differences in the core organization of the independent self (Greenfield & Cocking, 1994). The conceptions of an independent Self pervade much Western literature and arise from a view of the individual as self-contained and autonomous. This contrasts with the interdependent view held by many Asian, African, and Latin American cultures, where the self is seen as inextricably connected with others, encompassed, and organized by social relationships (Cross & Madson, 1997). Each level of self is formed through interaction and complex feedback loops at various physiological, psychological, and social levels. Each level of self is emergent and embedded in the next; in the same way, Schwalbe (1993, 2009) describes the fully conscious self's neurological, imagistic, and linguistic subsystems. Each level appears to contain similar interaction across open boundaries, feedback loops that move in both bottom-up and top-down directions, self-organization, autogenesis, and emergence.

3.6 Dynamical Patterns

Wiley integrated Peirce and Mead to produce an account of what he calls 'The Semiotic Self' (Wiley, 1994). The process that supports human selfhood is, in its adult form, a cultural-semiotic one (Smolka et al., 1997). However, its origins are biological (Sebeok, 1992). Hoffmeyer sets out this semiotic interpretation of biology and suggests that organic relations are based on meaning (Hoffmeyer, 1997). He combines Peirce and the Umwelt theory of Jacob von Uexküll to show how the interaction, exchange, and development that underlie biological order are fundamentally semiotic processes. When animals perceive patterns in their surroundings and use them to guide their actions, they respond to stimuli and interpret signs. This is what James Gibson called 'affordance' in his theory of direct perception (Gibson, 1979), a term for which he proposed an interesting ontological status: affordance cuts across the dichotomy of subjective-objective and helps us understand its inadequacy. It is both physical and psychical, yet neither. An affordance points both ways, to the environment and the observer. 'Thought is within us, but we are within thought; just as language is engendered by our minds and directly dependent on the mechanisms of the brain, we are within language. Furthermore, unless we were immersed in language, our brain could not engender it (and vice versa: if our brain were incapable of generating language, we would not be immersed in it)' (Lotman, 1990). The assumption is that the self is a biosemiotic process that emerges within a web of relationships. The process has biological origins but, in the human case, is strongly influenced by the world of cultural meaning, and this influence grows as selfhood. Human psyche-soma seems (Stern, 1985) predisposed to achieve selfhood. Primitive feelings appear to lie at the core of our beings, and the neural mechanisms that generate such states may constitute an essential foundation for the evolution of other rational forms of consciousness.

At present, abundant evidence indicates that affective states arise from the intrinsic neurodynamics of primary self-centered emotional and motivational systems situated in subcortical regions of the brain. The roots of the Self go back to specific mesencephalic and diencephalic sensory-motor action circuits within the mammalian brain, which can generate a primitive sort of intentionality (action readiness) and primitive forms of psychic coherence (global affective states of the brain) by interacting with various emotional and attentional circuits that encode fundamental biological values (Panksepp, 1998). For instance, anger may reflect the generation of an energized bodily stance, a sensory-motor dynamic that inundates the Self-schema when rage circuits of the brain are aroused. Fear circuits may generate a qualitatively different, up-tight, trembly type of neural dynamic within the Self.

Scott Kelso's dynamical patterns formulation states that a pattern comprises various factors or processes and their dynamical relations. The pattern theory of emotion claims that emotions are complex patterns of bodily processes, experiences, expressions, behaviors, and actions, and all these factors can make up an emotion pattern. Different patterns of processes constitute different emotions. Newen et al. (2015) provide a catalog of different features that may contribute to specific patterns that constitute emotions. They emerge in a self-organized fashion, without any agent-like entity ordering the elements, telling them when and where to go. There is no self within a Self pattern, and questions arise about stability and self-identity over time. Understanding will be sought regarding essential variables that characterize behavior patterns regardless of the elements involved in producing the patterns or at what level these patterns are studied or observed. Top-down versus bottom-up and macro versus micro can be misleading. After all, what is macro at one level can be micro at another. As addressed by Gestalt psychology, the "genesis of the whole by the composition of the parts is fictitious. It arbitrarily breaks the chain of reciprocal determinations" (Merleau-Ponty, 1962). Reciprocal and circular causal relations between multiple system levels are autopoietic and allow for recovery, repair, and reorganization, a threefold distinction proposed by Francisco Varela: the elementary scale (varying roughly across tens to hundreds of milliseconds), the integrative scale (varying roughly from 0.5 to 3 seconds), and the narrative scale involving memory (above 3 seconds) (Varela, 1999). As already discussed, we focus on the integrative mesoscale scale. Varela characterizes these dynamics as involving self-generating operational closure, which not only does not rule out interaction with the environment but is a necessary condition for such interaction. Varela indicates that the notion of operational closure emphasizes that closure is used in its mathematical sense of being recursive and not in isolation from interactions. Varela's notion of a selfless Self is consistent with Kelso's notion that there is no Self within the pattern, understood as a substantial agent that controls the pattern. A non-substantial self can nevertheless act as if present, like a virtual interface, an illusory self. Our sense of a personal 'I' can be construed as an ongoing interpretative narrative" (Freeman, 2012).

The self-pattern is coherent, changing, invariant, flexible, stable, and unstable. The general parameters of a more significant part of the self-pattern remain intact, even if modified, with friends and strangers. These changes may lead to small changes in some other aspects of the self-pattern, but the overall arrangement and set of relations hold steady. Minor breakdowns in autopoiesis can be repaired in biosemiotic sense-making.

3.7 Morphogenesis of the Self

Three seminal figures in biology, mathematics, and philosophy have significantly contributed to our understanding of patterns and morphogenesis: D'Arcy Wentworth Thompson, Alan Turing, and René Thom. Their transformative work has reshaped our understanding of pattern formation and continues to inspire new research. D'Arcy Wentworth Thompson (1860–1948) argued that physical laws and mathematical equations could explain biological structures. He used concepts like coordinate transformations and scaling to show how different forms relate. For example, he demonstrated how the shapes of shells, fish, and plants could be mathematically derived from simple geometric principles (Thompson, 1963). Alan Turing (1912–1954) contributed critically to the mathematical model for biological pattern formation. Turing's reaction-diffusion model proposes that patterns can emerge from the interaction of two or more chemical substances that diffuse across a space. The model suggests that minor differences in the initial distribution of these substances can lead to large-scale patterns. René Thom (1923–2002) developed the morphogenetic theory of catastrophes to understand abrupt system changes. He also proposed a form of semiophysics. Thom's catastrophe theory uses mathematical topology to describe how systems can undergo sudden, discontinuous transitions (Thom, 1975, 1988). He argued that these transitions could be related to several "elementary catastrophes." Thompson, Turing, and Thom have provided foundational frameworks for understanding the development and evolution of patterns in the PsycheSoma. Their work, which emphasizes the mathematical underpinnings of form, introduces a model for pattern formation based on chemical reactions and diffusion, and develops a theory for understanding sudden system changes, continues to inspire and guide our research in these fields.

As a dynamic duo, pattern formation, and synchronization are crucial in emerging new structures in various PsycheSoma systems. Pattern formation, the process of creating organized structures from initially disorganized systems, often acts as a foundation for further dynamics. On the other hand, synchronization refers to the coordinated behavior of multiple individual components. These two phenomena are closely intertwined, with patterns often providing the framework for synchronization. For instance, the underlying neural network architecture facilitates the rhythmic firing of neurons in the brain. Conversely, synchronization can also be a driver of pattern formation, as synchronized activity can lead to the emergence of new patterns. For example, the coordinated movement of cells during development can contribute to the formation of complex structures, such as the synchronization of neural networks. Neurons can fire synchronously, forming oscillatory patterns underlying cognitive functions like memory and perception. The connectivity patterns within neural networks influence the patterns that can emerge. For example, the heart muscle cells must contract in a coordinated manner to pump blood effectively. The arrangement of heart muscle cells contributes to the overall structure and function of the heart. As we can visualize in flocking birds, they can synchronize their movements to form intricate patterns in flight. The flock's overall pattern emerges from the interactions between individual birds. The flock then can follow specific directions. So, function and structure can synergize. Mechanisms of synchronization can highlight the dynamics in place. Coupling is the degree to which individual components are connected or influenced by each other. Stronger coupling can lead to more synchronized behavior. Random fluctuations can disrupt synchronization. However, in some cases, noise can promote synchronization by providing a shared signal. Positive or negative feedback loops can influence the synchronization of a system. Positive feedback can amplify synchronization, while negative feedback can stabilize it. Understanding pattern formation and destruction in phase transitions is essential in various fields, including materials science, condensed matter physics, chemistry, ecology, biophysics, neuroscience, and biosemiotics. At the same time, patterns in individual subjects involve embodied complex multidimensional networks (Wu, 2007). Patterns in language are involved in scaling synchronization dynamics. A language's sounds are organized into patterns known as phonemes, expressed in morphemes. These patterns can be analyzed in terms of their features, such as voicing, place, and manner of articulation. Morphemes form patterns of informational structures analyzed in information combinatorics (Orsucci et al., 2006). Syntactic patterns of word combinations to form sentences follow specific syntactic rules. These rules can be analyzed in terms of phrase structure, dependency relations, and grammatical categories. Words and sentences' meanings are determined by their semantic relationships, which can be analyzed in terms of semantic features, fields, and networks. The body's physiological processes, such as heart rate, breathing, and hormone levels, exhibit rhythmic or cyclical patterns, coupling and decoupling, sync and desync, alternate in different yet connected streams.

Kelso proposed that unified coordination dynamics could be seen as the partnership of well-known small- and large-scale synchronization models. The former is based on Synergetics and nonlinear dynamics concepts as the extended Haken–Kelso–Bunz or HKB (Kelso, 2021), and the latter on the statistical mechanics in ensembles of many oscillators (Kuramoto, 1984b). Most research supporting the extended HKB model has involved coordinating only two interacting components, whether two joints of a single limb or two persons interacting. In contrast, Kuramoto captured the statistical mechanics features of large-scale coordination among many oscillators. Kuramoto's model, in the hands of mathematical biologists like Steven Strogatz (2004) and Art Winfree (2001), soon became a paradigm for large-scale coordination in complex living systems that ranged from the flashing of fireflies to heart cells and neurons to the concert audiences composed of human beings. This modeling and empirical work suggested that the integrated patterns sustain a dynamical structure of synchronization and coordination, multistability, and metastability. Later, Kuramoto and Battogtokh (2002) observed that their previous model was based on ideal homogeneous forms of synchronization in large ensembles. In empirical research, we can frequently observe the coexistence of coherence and incoherence even in a network of identical, nonlocally coupled, complex Ginzburg–Landau oscillators. Coupled nonidentical oscillators were already known to exhibit mixed complex behavior (frequency locking, phase synchronization, partial synchronization, and incoherence). Identical oscillators were supposed to either synchronize in phase or incoherently drift. They showed that oscillators that were identically coupled with similar natural frequencies could behave differently from one another for specific initial conditions. Some could synchronize, while others remained incoherent in a stable state. Later, Abrams and Strogatz (2004) named this mixed synchronization a *chimera state* from the mythological Greek creature made up of parts of different animals and introduced some theoretical clarifications for such behavior. Chimera states are everywhere as patterns come and go, with gaps in between. Chimera states were later found in limit-cycle oscillators, chaotic oscillators, chaotic maps, and neuronal systems. In the beginning, chimera patterns were observed in nonlocally coupled networks, but afterward, these states were also found in globally and locally (nearest neighbor) coupled networks and in modular networks. The usage of Markov chains for mapping couplings and chimera states was also explored. C. R. Laing studied chimera state in heterogeneous networks, analyzing the influence of heterogeneous coupling strengths. Of further interest for human dynamics is the emergence of chimera states in multiscale networks that result from coupling different networks (Laing, 2009), as usual in biosemiotic dynamics. The dynamical Self patterns hyper-structure results from networks of synchronized oscillators coupled in fields spanning heterogeneous biosemiotic domains (Freeman, 2012; Orsucci, 2009). The ubiquity of chimera mapping of synchronization and its different typologies extended its original definition to areas that might include human non-identical coupling oscillators in hybrid networks and multiscale networking of networks already known to present chimera-like dynamics before this definition started to be used (Orsucci, 2021). The dynamical integration of patterns will include fast and slow synchronization dynamics. For example, there will be fast physiological reactions in emotions, movement, neuromediators, breathing, and heart rate, and slow reactions in neurotrophic factors, hormones, and attachment dynamics. Speech and cognition might be fast, moderate, or slow, ideally placed in a mesoscopic dynamical area (Kahneman, 2011). Topological methods may provide additional insights into system coordination pattern dynamics that are irreducible to the properties of individual parts (Orsucci, 2006).

3.8 The Self Multiverse

Borges & I (1964). "The other one, the one called Borges, is the one things happen to. I walk through the streets of Buenos Aires and stop for a moment, perhaps mechanically now, to look at the arch of an entrance hall and the grillwork on the gate; I know of Borges from the mail and see his name on a list of professors or in a biographical dictionary. I like hourglasses, maps, eighteenth-century typography, the taste of coffee, and Stevenson's prose; he shares these preferences but in a vain way that turns them into the attributes of an actor. It would be an exaggeration to say that ours is a hostile relationship; I live, let myself go on living, so that Borges may contrive his literature, and this literature justifies me. It is no effort for me to confess that he has achieved some valid pages, but those pages cannot save me, perhaps because what is good belongs to no one, not even to him, but rather to the language and to tradition. Besides, I am destined to perish, definitively, and only some instant of myself can survive in him. Little by little, I am giving over everything to him, though I am quite aware of his perverse custom of falsifying and magnifying things. Spinoza knew that all things long to persist in their being; the stone eternally wants to be a stone and the tiger a tiger. I shall remain in Borges, not in myself (if it is true that I am someone), but I recognize myself less in his books than in many others or in the laborious strumming of a guitar. Years ago, I tried to free myself from him and went from the mythologies of the suburbs to the games with time and infinity, but those games belong to Borges now and I shall have to imagine other things. Thus, my life is a flight and I lose everything and everything belongs to oblivion, or to him.

I do not know which of us has written this page." (Borges, 1964).

Landscapes

Consciousness is a process,
what we call objects are really bundles of relations.

William James

4.1 Sceneries

The last novel of the Nobel Laureate Luigi Pirandello was *One, None and a Hundred Thousand* (Pirandello, 2021). He wrote: "This book not only depicts dramatically but simultaneously demonstrates by what might be termed a mathematic method, the impossibility of any human creature being to others what he is to himself." The protagonist discovers by way of a completely irrelevant question that his wife poses to him that everyone he knows, everyone he has ever met, has constructed a different persona of him and that none of these personas corresponds to the image he has constructed and believes himself to be. Critical reviews described this novel as ingeniously stating and restating that everyone has multiple personalities and that if anyone tries to examine their multiplicity, nonentity, and possible unity deeply, they will quickly be called a madman. Others even referred to the book's themes, following Pirandello's comments, to the foundational crisis of mathematics that arose at the end of the 19th century and the beginning of the 20th century with the discovery of several paradoxes or counter-intuitive results. The book almost reads more like an essay in psychopathological metaphysics than a plot-driven narrative.

4.2 Personality, Character, Temperament

Some constructs are frequently associated with the Self. Personality, a unique set of behaviors, traits, and emotions, plays a pivotal role in determining behavior. The relationship between personality and the Self is not a straightforward one, but rather a complex and multifaceted interplay. Personality traits, which are characteristics that relate to our motivational system, determine what we tend to be motivated to do without a strong influence on the situation. This intricate relationship between personality and the Self is a dimension or a continuum from healthy features to maladaptive ones, characterized by a coherent sense of the self and identity, engagements in satisfying relationships, relatively flexible functioning when stressed by external events or internal conflicts, appropriate expression of impulses and emotions, internalized moral values and maladaptive features. In the context of the relationship between personality and the Self as a system, there is a large consensus in considering the constructs of self and relatedness as central criteria to assess personality and its disturbances. However, the relation between the psychological organization of personality, the construct of self, and its neuronal correlates remains unclear, adding a layer of mystery to this complex relationship.

As Cloninger (1994) clarified, there is a long tradition in psychology that distinguishes two significant domains of personality: temperament and character. According to early psychologists, temperament refers to our congenital emotional predisposition, whereas character is what people make of themselves intentionally. It is helpful to operationalize this distinction regarding individual differences in neuroadaptive processes. Temperament can be related to habits and moods. Personality includes voluntary intentions and attitudes. They might be related to a distinction between procedural versus propositional memory and learning. Based on the framework of our dynamical system, they represent different components concurring with the Self. In a non-determinist and pluralist approach, the Self is a network of patterns, a dynamical gestalt, and most relevant is the connectivity and the dynamical relations of the different self-aspects (Daly & Gallagher, 2019; Gallagher & Daly, 2018). Studies of psychiatric or neurological disorders can help us understand the precise nature of the dynamic relations in self-patterns and how they can eventually fail. Dynamical self-patterns are revealed in self-narratives, which track regenerative self-organizing processes and their various disruptions. Such patterns and disruptions are also reflected in dynamic neural processes. The Self, described in terms of such dynamical neural and narrative processes, is not a fixed entity but is instead an ongoing production that brings an actual but contingent coherence to an evolving (or, in some cases, devolving) stream of sensations, thoughts, emotions, desires, memories, and anticipations (Gallagher & Daly, 2018). While the brain is not the sole generator of self-dynamics, mapping self-related brain functions may help demonstrate self-patterns' dynamical and relatively coherent nature. The complex dynamical systems theory of the Self attempts to capture the plurality of factors involved in it and their related dynamical structure. The multi-layered hypernetworks of the Self can be modeled and empirically validated in human change dynamics, narratives, artifacts, clinical settings, and psychopathology (Freeman, 2012; Lindahl & Arhem, 1994; Orsucci, 2009). Mapping the changes across different configurations should reveal a set of underlying dynamics that get disrupted or adjusted as one change impacts the whole pattern. Suppose the pattern is, in fact, a dynamical gestalt. In that case, we expect to find isolated symptoms affecting one aspect alone and readjustments (disruptions or compensatory adjustments) in other aspects (Gallagher & Daly, 2018). Limanowski and Blankenburg (2013) argue that the minimal and pre-reflective experiential elements of the bodily self, including the first-person perspective and the senses of agency and ownership, all of which depend on multisensory integration, including interoception, can be mapped onto a dynamical model and may constitute the basis for higher-level, cognitive forms of self-narrative. Beyond minimal experiential aspects of the self, multisensory integration on the predictive processing model can also explicate connections to affective factors (Seth, 2013) and solve problems of self-recognition, which may involve recognition of the self-as-object, for example, mirror self-recognition (Apps & Tsakiris, 2014). The notion of a dynamical complex system of the Self is, in biophysical terms, parsimonious and accurate. The embodied system predicts and integrates exteroceptive and interoceptive multisensory variations probabilistically as we perceive, move, and experience. This cross-modal, self-correcting interoceptive, proprioceptive, efferent/afferent, and exteroceptive integration generates a self-model (Metzinger, 2004), manifested phenomenologically in a body-centered spatial frame of reference. This suggests a dynamical integration between the embodied and experiential aspects of the self-pattern and the extended and normative aspects (understanding the environment to be social/cultural as well as physical). Some dynamical configurations of the Self have been historically defined in psychopathology. Historically, there has been a slow evolution from deterministic paradigms challenged by the high complexity of this field and non-deterministic paradigms following fluid dynamics, the multiplicity of configurations, and personal differences.

4.3 Pattern Disorders

Classifications, including psychiatric nosology, are not immune to the influences of the scientific and social worlds in which they exist. The methods and application of psychiatric nosology are confined within a specific 'paradigm' or 'episteme,' and the assumptions they rest upon should not be unquestioningly accepted (Berrios, 1999). Foucault (1973) observed that the modern psychiatric classification system originated from Enlightenment notions of rationality and representation. The implicit acceptance of Kantian notions of the classifying activity inherent to the human mind within psychiatric nosology has been much debated. Category-based diagnosis, which strives to align with the third-person, objective measures of science, often falls short in terms of diagnostic accuracy, demarcation problems in the presence of comorbidities, well-documented issues of symptom amplification, and the complexities of stigmatization and looping effects. These limitations call for a critical examination and discussion, urging us to question the status quo and explore alternative approaches.

Psychiatric categories might have been convenient for clinicians in identifying a recognizable constellation of symptoms typical for a particular disorder for communication and eligibility for treatment regimes. However, the reification of these categories has, without doubt, had negative consequences for the patient and the general understanding of psychiatric disorders (Daly & Gallagher, 2019). Classification systems in psychiatry emerged out of the broader effort within medicine to classify diseases. In 1682, Thomas Sydenham asserted that "nature, in the production of disease, is uniform and consistent" and proposed that diseases could be described distinctly and reliably as plant species (Pichot, 1994). Sydenham understood disease as a set of observable and regular symptoms with predictable course. Following Francis Bacon, he emphasized the importance of empirical observations. Sydenham distinguished three types of insanity: 'hysteria,' 'mania,' and 'melancholia,' based on the prominent symptoms. Although he identified a predictable course of illness, it did not play any relevant role in his classification. Soon after, Linnaeus, de Sauvages, and Vogel created symptom-based disease classifications, including various psychiatric conditions. William Cullen published the first widely used system of medical nosology in 1769. He disagreed with symptom-based classifications and argued for the importance of underlying causation in determining disease groups (Pichot, 1994). He later theorized that the nervous system's conditions affected all medical illnesses. The tension between symptom-based (i.e., descriptive) versus causation-based (i.e., etiological) classification systems has been present since the 18th century and has continued until recently. An important landmark in psychiatric nosology occurred in 1801 when the French physician Phillipe Pinel proposed a classification of 'mental alienation' into four species: melancholia, mania, dementia, and idiotism. He did not see these as separate entities but as modes of expression of a single disease of mental alienation. This disease classification reflected only his patient population, i.e., individuals who had been admitted to asylums for the insane and excluded conditions such as 'hysteria' and 'hypochondriasis.' This conceptual bifurcation along asylum vs. clinic fault lines continued in the late 19th and early 20th century, and the study of 'neurosis' seen in the clinic was taken up by neurologists such as Jean-Martin Charcot and Sigmund Freud. This divergence was an early precursor of the later distinction between organic and functional mental illness. Emil Kraepelin's nosology is widely recognized as a watershed moment in psychiatric nosology (Berrios & Hauser, 1988; Hippius & Müller, 2008). At the heart of his work is the distinction between dementia praecox and manic-depressive insanity. The former was marked by a deteriorating course, the latter without deterioration. Kahlbaum and Hecker recognized that psychiatric diagnostic terms like 'melancholia,' 'mania,' and 'dementia' represented heterogeneous symptom complexes, in the same way that 'abdominal pain' or 'headache' was diagnostically non-specific (Aftab & Ryznar, 2021). They believed that reliance on such diagnoses had only furthered diagnostic confusion and had led to the near-complete failure of neuroanatomical and neuropathological research (which dominated 19th-century European psychiatry) to shed light on the etiology of mental illness. They did not think that etiological research would yield results until it was guided by clinical, proto-disease entities that considered symptoms and the whole course of illness. Later, Bleuler emphasized the heterogeneity of the dementia praecox, which he classified as a group of schizophrenias based on inner psychic dissociation. However, as Berrios & Hauser (1988) and Hippius & Müller (2008) accepted the possibility of 'psychogenic' etiology for some disorders and recognized that disorders could pass over "without sharp boundary into the domain of personal predisposition," classifications, psychopathology, and nosology were still a work in progress. A contemporary of Kraepelin, Carl Wernicke, sought to develop a psychiatric classification based on brain localization (Ban, 2013; Ungvari, 1993). He hypothesized that psychic impairments stemmed from disruptions in the interconnections between neural systems, which resulted in hyper-function, hypofunction, or parafunction of the three specific systems: psychomotor, psychosensory, and 'intrapsychic' (the center between the psychomotor and psychosensory pathways). Hallucinations, for instance, were assumed to be due to psycho-sensory hyperfunction, anxiety due to psychosensory parafunction, melancholia due to intrapsychic hypofunction, mania due to intrapsychic hyperfunction, and catatonia due to psychomotor hypofunction (Lanczik & Keil, 1991). Wernicke's theory was dismissed by Karl Jaspers (1997) as "brain mythology psychopathology" as he endeavored to establish a space of critical methodological self-reflection and delineated a scientific methodology specific to psychiatry. Jaspers' approach laid the foundation for the psychopathological phenomenology that would become the hallmark of the Heidelberg School of Psychiatry. His work has profoundly influenced the field, and many modern diagnostic criteria derive from ideas found within it.

The notion that categorical classification is inappropriate for psychiatry has existed since the earliest days. It was one of the main criticisms against Kraepelin's nosology (Engstrom & Kendler, 2015). In 1894, Wilhelm Dilthey introduced the distinction between '*erklaren*' (scientific explanation in terms of general laws) and '*verstehen*' (understanding in terms of individual personality and biography), with the suggestion that psychiatry must be idiographic and not nomothetic (Pichot, 1994). The anti-categorical attitude assumed greater prominence in the 20th century with the rise of Meyerian and psychoanalytic ideas. Adolf Meyer's concept of 'psychobiology' and Freudian psychoanalysis conceptualized mental disorders as reactions of the personality to various life circumstances or products of unconscious mental forces and emphasized the uniqueness of the individual (Pichot, 1994; Stengel, 1959). The Kraepelinian view of diagnosis did not fit well with such an understanding of psychopathology, and this led to an overall neglect of psychiatric classification within clinical psychology. Dimensional and unitary approaches were also influential among psychoanalysts like Karl Menninger who viewed the various types of mental disorders as different only in their quantitative aspects (i.e., in the degree of disintegration of the personality) (Stengel, 1959).

In the mid-19th century, medical statistics experienced burgeoning growth driven by the need to accurately report hospitalizations and causes of death. The most widely used current psychiatric nosology, the Diagnostic and Statistical Manual of Mental Disorders (DSM) and the International Classification of Diseases (ICD), have their roots in this tradition. Unlike earlier taxonomies, these systems were developed by large organizations (thereby necessitating consensus between multiple stakeholders) for pragmatic purposes and incorporated elements of prior taxonomies. The ICD-6 marked a new era of medical statistics in that a combined morbidity and mortality classification was created with the explicit intent of international cooperation and uniform statistical reporting (Moriyama et al., 2011). The DSM-III ushered in a new approach to mental disorders, one in which descriptive and operational diagnosis formed the cornerstone of research and practice (Mayes & Horwitz, 2005). It was the culmination of a long history of proposals for the adoption of 'operational definitions' in psychiatry based on observational criteria and was widely considered revolutionary (Aragona, 2014; Fulford & Sartorius, 2009). However, as it was built on Feighner's criteria (Feighner et al., 1972; Kendler et al., 2010), it brought an underlying Kraepelinian aspiration that reliability would bring validity to a linear medical disease paradigm. On the positive, DSM-3 was multiaxial, assigning developmental and personality disorders, medical conditions, social factors, and a general assessment of functioning independent axes to emphasize their importance in an overall diagnostic assessment. Developers of the DSM-5 publicly expressed hope that the latest revision would deliver a 'paradigm' shift towards etiologically based diagnoses, which was the ultimate hope of the neo-Kraepelinian DSM-3 (Zachar et al., 2019).

4.4 Complexity Maps

The DSM-5 and the ICD-11 embedded a combination of categorical and dimensional structures, emphasizing that diagnostic categories exist in spectra of severity. The complexity of psychiatric disorders does not offer any straightforward solutions to questions of nosology; furthermore, reliability remains problematic for many DSM diagnoses. For example, the DSM-5 field trials reported that several diagnoses, including major depressive disorder and generalized anxiety disorder, had their reliability in a questionable range (Regier et al., 2013). The failure of DSM to move from reliability to validity has led to a loss of confidence in the neo-Kraepelinian assumptions underlying the manual (Aftab & Ryznar, 2021). Therefore, new diagnostic mapping tools emerged as alternatives combining idiographic and nomothetic tools, possibly along the Wundt mesoscopic perspective.

The Psychodynamic Diagnostic Manual (PDM) was developed to compensate for some of the limitations of the DSM. The first edition of the PDM was published in 2006 (Ferrari, 2006), with the collaborative efforts of members from five sponsoring psychoanalytic organizations. Its second edition was published in 2017. It articulates a psychodynamic-oriented diagnosis and a classification system grounded in developmental, cognitive, and neuroscience research. The PDM is strongly influenced by and draws extensively on the Shedler-Westen Assessment Procedure (Lingiardi & McWilliams, 2015). It uses a multiaxial system and encourages assessment along the following axes: level of personality organization and prevalent personality styles or disorders (Axis P); level of overall mental functioning (Axis M); symptoms and syndromes and the patient's subjective experience of them (Axis S) (Lingiardi & McWilliams, 2015). The PDM describes itself as a taxonomy of people rather than diseases. Interestingly, it attempts to merge diagnosis and therapeutic formulation. However, its usage is limited to small pockets of scientists and clinicians.

Mounting evidence that DSM categories do not map onto genetic and neurobiological constructs has raised concern that excessive reliance on DSM categories has prevented the field from advancing the pathophysiological understanding of mental disorders. The US National Institute of Mental Health launched a new transdiagnostic research paradigm in 2009: the Research Domain Criteria (RDoC) (Insel et al., 2010). The RDoC conceptualized mental illnesses as disorders of neural circuits, hoping that data from clinical neuroscience and genetics will yield biosignatures that will inform future nosology (Insel et al., 2010). The RDoC applies its units of analyses (from genes to psychosocial factors) to several predetermined neuropsychological domains (negative valence systems, positive valence systems, cognitive systems, social processes, arousal, regulatory systems, and sensorimotor systems) in the form of a matrix. Each domain is subdivided into constructs; for example, positive valence systems include the constructs of reward responsiveness, reward learning, and reward valuation (Insel, 2014). While the RDoC generated broad interest, especially in the research community, fruits are still to be seen, probably because it underestimated the complexity and integration of neurobiological, developmental, and environmental factors.

Another novel dimensional and transdiagnostic approach to nosology that has been proposed is the Hierarchical Taxonomy of Psychopathology (HiTOP), which uses a quantitative nosology based on factor analysis for psychological/behavioral phenotypes. The nosology rests on six spectra: internalizing, thought disorder, disinhibited externalizing, antagonistic externalizing, detachment, and somatoform, which can be further subdivided into subfactors and symptom components (Kotov et al., 2017). Although HiTOP offers a promising approach for transdiagnostic research, it has yet to see widespread adoption, and concerns exist that it may be too impractical for routine clinical use. Its hierarchical structure is deterministic and still too simplifying.

In an editorial, perhaps ironically entitled "Chaos in Psychiatry" in vol. 31 of *Biological Psychiatry*, Walter Freeman (1992) stated that psychiatrists "are no strangers to complexity, because, during their daily management of mental illness, they must connect data overall levels, from genetics to behavioral and social factors. Few know that new and powerful tools are available to treat complexity." Freeman noted how the amount of data produced in neurosciences is now so vast that the main task might be to get more data and acquire proper scientific tools to integrate the existing information into robust and coherent theories.

4.5 Dynamic Maps

Along these lines, Merlin Olthof and his research group (Olthof et al., 2020, 2023) proposed ADAPT, Adaptive Dynamic Pattern Theory of Psychopathology, based on a theory of psychopathology grounded in the principles of complex adaptive systems. They suggest that psychopathology can be understood as a dynamic pattern that emerges from self-organized interactions between interdependent biopsychosocial processes in a complex adaptive system comprising a person in their environment. Psychopathology is emergent because it refers to the person-environment system and cannot be reduced to specific system parts. Psychopathology as a dynamic pattern is also self-organized, meaning that it arises solely from the interdependencies in the system: the interactions between countless biopsychosocial variables. All possible manifestations of psychopathology will correspond to a wide variety of dynamic patterns. They propose that general principles of pattern formation in complex adaptive systems can describe the development of these patterns over time. They base their tools on the principles that in complex adaptive systems, interdependence implies inseparability: it is impossible to isolate unique contributions of system parts, as any given state of one process is necessarily dependent on the states of all other methods (Van Orden et al., 2011). As a metaphor for inseparability, consider psychopathology as a piece of fabric in which all intertwined threads represent biopsychosocial processes. Separating the threads to study them makes it impossible to recover how they were intertwined in the fabric. Interdependence thus implies that psychopathology cannot be fully understood by separating it into 'smaller pieces' (Van Geert & Van Dijk, 2021; Wallot & Kelty-Stephen, 2018). Whether behavior emerges from interactions between interdependent parts has been addressed in empirical studies that examined variability over (extended) time (for a review, see Wijnants, 2012). Such studies seek to determine the randomness of the values of a variable measured over time (i.e., a time series). A time series that reveals a stable, predictable pattern of values is rigid, whereas a time series that yields unpredictable, widely varied values is random noise (Wallot & Kelty-Stephen, 2017). Notably, systems that behave halfway between rigid and random regimes seem most flexible or healthy (Van Orden et al., 2011). The term used for this type of variability is pink noise, as opposed to random white noise and rigid Brownian motion. Pink noise in a time series is, in fact, a mixture of stable and unstable patterns that allow the system to adapt to a changing environment. Studies on behavioral variability have found numerous examples of pink noise in various measures such as electroencephalography, heart rate, postural sway, reaction, and self-ratings (Wijnants, 2012). Moreover, multiple studies found deviations of pink noise related to pathology. Goldberger and West (2002), for example, showed that a heart rate pattern with pink noise variability characterizes a healthy heart. A heart that beats too regularly or too randomly signifies pathology. Deviations from pink noise patterns also appear to be related to transdiagnostic psychopathology: higher rigidity compared to control participants has been found in reaction time series of individuals diagnosed with attention deficit hyperactivity disorder (Gilden & Hancock, 2007) and dyslexia (Wijnants et al., 2012), and in postural sway data for individuals diagnosed with psychosis (Kent et al., 2012) and bipolar disorder (Bolbecker et al., 2011). Furthermore, decreasing rigidity over time in self-ratings has been found to predict clinical improvement in psychotherapy (Fisher & Newman, 2016). The implications of interdependence for psychopathology research practices are enormous. As Jaspers puts it, "It is difficult to bring diagnostic order … into shifting phenomena which continually keep merging into one another" (1997, p. 32). This might be true unless we understand the need to implement a complex dynamical systems methodology to understand the kind of order and organizations in place.

4.6 Formulation Tools

Complexity science facilitated the evolution of case formulation toward personalized care. The 'bottom-up' case formulation, focusing on individual patient's characteristics, is argued to be the 'royal road' for personalized clinical practice (Krause & Behn, 2022). Case formulation may also function as a bridge between clinical practice and research, for instance, by pointing out person-relevant processes to assess and monitor throughout a therapeutic process (Kramer, 2020). This dynamical systems approach represents an evolution of previous formulation tools. Some precursors to be mentioned are the R-STAR developed by Burns et al. (2008); the Wellness Recovery Action Plan (Canacott et al., 2019); and Cope, Comprehend, and Connect (Descartes & Clarke, 2009) self-mapping tools. These personal mapping tools create individual maps of components and interactions within the Self toward its possible transformation. Complexity science-inspired research has developed tools that allow further measures and models. Idiographic, personalized mapping has evolved using self-monitoring tools and computer graphics (Schiepek, 2003). This has also empowered frequency feedback approaches to human change in psychotherapy, coaching, and other non-clinical areas. Case formulation is at the heart of personalized care in psychotherapy. Scientific research into case formulations can provide new insights into the heterogeneity of psychopathology, which are relevant for advances in personalized psychopathology research and practice. Ideally, person-specific (idiographic) and general (nomothetic) aspects of psychopathology can be integrated into a complex systems approach to psychopathology, which may combine 'the best of both worlds' (Olthof et al., 2023).

A network view of psychiatric disorders, their clusters of symptoms, and their network dynamics can provide powerful visual landscapes (Goekoop & Goekoop, 2014). A large sample of patients with unselected mental disorders were tested on the Comprehensive Psychopathological Rating Scale. Principal component analysis was performed on the bootstrapped correlation matrix of symptom scores to extract the principal component structure. An undirected and weighted network graph was constructed from the same matrix. Network community structure was optimized using a previously published technique. Results clarified network clusters, hubs, bridging, and most frequent associations and evolutions. This research further confirmed that the categorical approach of multiplying the number of syndrome names in the DSM and ICD must be replaced by a dynamical systems approach integrating personalized mapping and therapeutic formulation. This would aid further advancements and new strategies in treatment (Orsucci, 2006).

4.7 Ancient Fitness Landscapes

The *Conference of the Birds*, a 12-century Sufi allegorical poem by the Persian Farid Ud-Din Attar, holds significant relevance in the context of our explorations on self-organization and complexity science as it represents a metaphorical journey through a fitness landscape of personal transformations (Attar et al., 1984). The story is about the quest of their King Simurgh, undertaken by the world's birds. They cross seven valleys, each with a different name and significance. The hoopoe tells the birds that they must cross seven valleys to reach the abode of Simorgh. These valleys are as follows:

1. Valley of the Quest, where the Wayfarer begins by casting aside all dogma, belief, and unbelief.
2. Valley of Love, where reason is abandoned for the sake of love.
3. Valley of Knowledge, where worldly knowledge becomes utterly useless.
4. Valley of Detachment, where all desires and attachments to the world are given up. Here, what is assumed to be "reality" vanishes.
5. Valley of Unity, where the Wayfarer realizes that everything is connected and that the Beloved is beyond everything, including harmony, multiplicity, and eternity.
6. Valley of Wonderment, where, entranced by the beauty of the Beloved, the Wayfarer becomes perplexed and steeped in awe and finds that he has never known or understood anything.
7. Valley of Annihilation, where the self disappears into the universe, and the Wayfarer becomes timeless, existing in both the past and the future. Some birds give up, some die, some decide to return, and many fail. Finally, 30 birds make it, and when they reach the final mountaintop, they find that the King Simurgh they came to look for is a mirror. In Farsi (Persian), *si* means 30, and *murgh* means birds. A discovery in transformations can be a rediscovery.

The poem's allegory is a metaphorical journey through a fitness landscape of personal transformations (Attar et al., 1984). Its representation of travel in a metaphorical fitness landscape of challenges and discovery resonates with similar and different personal explorations, from Homer's *Odyssey* to Dante's *Divina Commedia* and Joyce's *Ulysses*.

Dynamics

Physics is just a set of methods for ordering and surveying human experience.

Niels Bohr

5.1 Personal Dynamics

In the *Elective Affinities*, Goethe produced an extraordinary hybrid (Goethe, 1962). One minute, we read an aristocratic comedy of manners; the next, a philosophical essay; the next, a brooding, proto-symbolist, mythopoetic exploration of the workings of fate as if in physics. Chemistry is, to be sure, hardly the most inventive metaphor for romantic feeling. Nevertheless, as Charlotte (one of the main characters) observes, we often forget how much natural science, which we take to be the inalienable reality of our existence, is informed by the human experience it is meant to illuminate. Elements do not elect to do anything; they rush together blindly, machine-like. Nor are the "laws" of thermodynamics freely legislated — they just are. Everywhere Goethe's characters look, they see portentous signs that give the action a sense of fatefulness, as though it were being propelled by an "invisible, almost magical force of attraction." Eduard discovers that he and Ottilie have the same handwriting; a visiting Englishman reads from a novella that perfectly describes the plot up to that point. All the while, Goethe reminds us, via the supporting cast, how often we misread the world to dress up self-serving behavior for which we are reluctant to take responsibility. What begins as a relatively slight take on the romantic tribulations of the moneyed class gradually unspools, in Goethe's hands, into a meditation on hidden laws that rule us, on the "riddle of life," as the narrator calls it, for which we only ever find the answer in one another.

Our research delves into the interdisciplinary realm of psychology, philosophy, and literature, where each conversation is a complex interplay, an implicit dance or theater of personas searching for an author. In this, the great Stanislavsky meets Pirandello. We also consider the implicit and explicit conversations within us, such as internal verbal dialogues or silent coordination/collaboration between organs. The human body, a longstanding social and political metaphor, further enriches our understanding of the intricate nature of human interactions (Matelli, 2019). Interpersonal communication is a multimodal activity (Paxton & Dale, 2013). Conversation incorporates multiple channels of communication that enrich the interaction, like hand gestures, facial expressions, posture, and speech. Interlocutors cue into each channel simultaneously to effectively communicate with one another, often without realizing the importance placed on each of them. Considerable work has surveyed multimodal interaction qualities (e.g., Norris, 2006; Norris & Maier, 2014). As we might well know from everyday life, sometimes communication channels might not be aligned or even provide discordant messages. However, in general, experimental study of interpersonal communication in cognitive science tends to simplify and target single behavioral channels. This has led to significant advances in our understanding of these specific channels, but there is still much work to investigate their connections and interactions.

We developed an advanced multidimensional methodology to analyze human dynamics, mainly focusing on synchronization within an embodied mind framework (Orsucci et al., 1997; 2016). Synchronization patterns between embodied systems are thought to form the basis of cognition (Bansal et al., 2019). The interplay of synchrony among subsets of brain regions is essential in normal brain function task performance (Shine et al., 2018) and in the continuum between healthy states and disease (Hizanidis et al., 2016). Structural coupling and synchronization occur in human dynamics in many situations, including the coordination between conversation partners. This might be one of the best settings for a study of human dynamics, as synchronization occurs in many modalities: language, movement, emotions, and physiology (Glass, 2001; Orsucci et al., 2006, 2016; Wiltshire et al., 2020; Tschacher & Meier, 2020; Repp & Su, 2013; Ali et al., 2018). Psychotherapy is a unique environment designed for human dynamics (Tschacher et al., 2015; Orsucci, 2016). It is a partially self-contained, controlled setting and practice to observe and facilitate transformation in human conditions and relations. Psychotherapy has been described as one of the most complex bio-psycho-social systems in which patterns of language, cognition, emotion, and behavior are formed and changed through the dynamics of therapist and patient interactions (Gelo & Salvatore, 2016; Schiepek et al., 2016). Studies in psychotherapy are relevant beyond clinical research as they can lead to a general understanding of human dynamics integrating the linguistic, behavioral, and physiological realms. Studies on synchronization and complex systems in psychotherapy are universally relevant for understanding the general dynamics of human change.

We started focusing our studies on verbal language. The study of language is differentiated on its complex levels of structuring: from informational microscopic systems to morphological mesoscopic patterns to semantic and narrative macroscopic frameworks. In verbal interactions, voice tonality, volume, pitch, cadence, rhythm, and turn-taking have additional relevance. At the molecular linguistic level, Claude Shannon (Shannon & Weaver, 1949; Shannon, 1951) laid the foundations of modern studies on the informational structure of texts and speech. However, human linguistic synchronization always develops at multiple levels.

The Pyramid of Life (Oltvai & Barabási, 2002) adequately represents the degrees and scaling of order in living systems. Schreiber (1999) offered a graph mapping scattered areas of different forms of order and knowledge, still interspersed with areas of *unknown*, as in ancient charts. Following this chart mapping, we can find periodic and noisy oscillations, deterministic and stochastic areas of chaos, stochastic resonance, self-organized criticality, nonlinearity, or noise. Then, there are a few other islands where a connection between our models of knowledge and real-world phenomena has yet to be established. This dynamical mapping might be synchronic and diachronic in space distribution and time transitions.

Order and structure in different systems can be known and modified through the emergence of self-organization or by external actions, casual or planned perturbations, including measurements. Measuring and trying to know more about a system can always perturb and change it. Interactions can lead to coupling between systems, and if they are repeated in time, they might produce forms of synchronization. Maturana and Varela (1980) suggested that synchronization is a form of structural coupling that occurs when two systems repeatedly perturb each other. Synchronization is a basic nonlinear phenomenon discovered in interactions between dynamical systems at the beginning of the modern age of science (Strogatz, 2003). In its classical definition, synchronization refers to periodic oscillator adjustment or entrainment in frequencies and phases due to weak interactions. This leads to the development of structural fit between systems. There is a relationship between this process and the emergence of adaptive behavior in the interplay between interacting systems. Furthermore, Pecora & Carroll (1990), Ott, Grebogi, & Yorke (1990), and Pyragas (1996) discovered how synchronization can be reliably used to modify the dynamic behavior of complex systems.

5.2 Pattern Analysis

Our primary aim was to develop a statistical tool for reliable measures of a symbol flow's degree of organization (in the basic sense of recurrence of motifs). Our empirical method has been based on Recurrence Quantification Analysis — RQA (Eckmann et al., 1987; Webber & Marwan, 2015) that does not make any specific assumption on the mathematical structure of data, does not rely on assumptions of trends and does not even need to consider the studied data set as the output of a dynamical system. The importance of deriving a measure of the prosodic structuring of the text (in the sense of repetitions of sounds, words, and phrases irrespective of their meaning) could be crucial for the attainment of a standard 'style' of talking correspondent to a sort of 'synchronization' of the two speaking persons. This synchronization is a proxy for the information streams linking the two actors and the rhythms of their interaction. We can extract some relevant patterns of the dynamical structures in human interactions through the phonetic configuration of speech and its musicality.

We used RQA to measure the recurrence of patterns (how they repeat), their determinism (how predictable what will follow), and their entropy (the organization). Recurrence Plots (RP) were first introduced in physics by Eckmann, Kamphorst, and Ruelle (1987). Later, Webber, Zbilut, Giuliani, and Marwan enhanced this technique by defining nonlinear variables valid in the quantitative assessment of RPs, thus developing RQA. Since then, RQA has been used in different fields, ranging from molecular dynamics (Giuliani et al., 2002; Manetti et al., 1999) to physiology (Webber & Zbilut, 1994) and bioinformatics (Marwan, 2008; Webber & Marwan, 2015; Webber et al., 2009). The quantification of recurrences is obtained by many different 'counts' of recurrences disposition on the matrix. While testing the robustness of this methodology (Orsucci et al., 1997; 1999), we had to set to three (letters) the dimensional embedding as it maximized the sensitivity of the method by increasing the number of scored recurrences without interference. We noticed that a three-letter dimension is at the mesoscopic information level between single letters and whole words. This is the average length of *morphemes*, the smallest part of a word carrying meaning. We will see further relevant implications of this later. Our time series analysis used RQA and CRQA (cross-recurrence) to measure the coupling and synchronization of subjects during conversations as semiotic interactions. Such synchronization is related to a coexistent level of communication that is not coincident with the pure verbal information exchange mediated by the meaning of the words. This pre-verbal and infra-verbal (largely unconscious) communication channel could be highlighted by progressively similar information patterns of prosodic structures (stereotyped phrases, words, pauses) during dialogues between speakers.

During the same years, other independent centers started developing research on social and clinical interactions using a similar methodology based on recurrence analysis strategies to evaluate the shared activity between postural or verbal time series in a reconstructed phase space, studying interpersonal coordination during conversations (Shockley et al., 2009; Port et al., 1999; Fusaroli et al., 2014; Keller & Tschacher, 2007). All these studies usually took one type of time series at a time (i.e., movement, speech, or physiology) while not considering the mutual influence between different types of interaction. However, direct experience shows that human relations dynamics are naturally hybrid. One kind of interaction can influence the coupling or uncoupling of other streams:

motor, semiotic, or physiological. For example, movement can influence verbal communication, or emotions can influence motion and meaning in complex feedback loops.

5.3 Hybrid Couplings

Human interactions involve multiple streams (language, movement, emotions), coupling, decoupling, and synchronizing. These multiscale and hybrid interactions are better understood within the biosemiotic embodied mind framework that we defined as Mind Force (Orsucci, 2009). An empirical prototype of this approach was developed as a multidimensional analysis of the language and emotional responses of patients and therapists in psychotherapy (Orsucci et al., 2016). We had chosen GSR (galvanic skin response) and verbal prosody, as both variables reflect the expression of emotions in different streams (Koolagudi & Rao, 2012; Pichon & Kell, 2013). In our initial experiments, we considered four signals: the therapist's transcript, the patient's transcript, the therapist's GSR, and the patient's GSR as a marker of emotional reactions. We were mainly focused on how those four variables modulated, coupled, synchronized, or desynchronized. We considered the combinations and patterns of letters (representing phonemes) and morphemes (the minor portion of words able to convey meaning). The linguistic analysis methodology had already been validated in previous studies, which highlighted robust informational measures of entropy and determinism (Orsucci et al., 2006; 2013). We performed a RQA on the four variables in this new study. We first considered the synchronization of the two whole signals using the standard correlation coefficients of Principal Component Analysis (PCA); PCA helps simplify complex data by transforming it into a smaller set of summary indices. We clustered the interaction patterns between the four signals using K-means. K-means clustering is a widely used unsupervised machine learning algorithm that aims to partition a set of observations into distinct clusters based on their similarity. This procedure produced a seven-cluster model representing the phase space of the state transitions of this complex system. A different configuration of string parameters represented each state. Then, we used a Markov Transition Matrix to describe the probabilities of moving from one state to another in a dynamic system. In this way, we revealed the state transition probabilities within the system and the evolution of synchronization between linguistic and physiological signals.

In the Cross-Recurrence Plot of galvanic signals, we could find evidence that the therapist and patient synchronized their GSRs mainly at epoch 7. On the other hand, concerning language, we found a period of higher synchronization at the beginning (epoch 2) and in the third quarter of the session (epochs 8 and 9). Therefore, human dynamics coupling in terms of emotional and verbal synchronization stabilizes in epochs 7, 8, and 9. This happens in physiology/GSR at epoch seven and afterward in speech. As expressed by GSR, emotional synchronization comes first, while linguistic synchronization follows. This is consistent with a relevant corpus of psychotherapy and neuroscience research on the embodiment of the mind (Freeman, 1999; Stern, 2004). We will try to clarify the powerful results we retrieved in understanding the conversation dynamics.

Descriptively, this dyadic system is oscillating between two attractors. The first is at state 4, where the therapist may struggle with the patient. His oscillations between high and low galvanic recurrence rates, proxies for opposite emotional reactions, and medium determinism demonstrate this. On the other hand, the patient shows low values of galvanic recurrence and determinism rates, a sign of the high unpredictability in this specific session period. In terms of prosody, the therapist has high recurrence and determinism rates. Perhaps the therapist's repetitive linguistic patterns could be interpreted as an intellectual way to organize the patient's unpredictable emotional expression. The second attractor, instead, is at state 5 with a probability of recurrence with itself of $p = 0.33$. This state is characterized by a medium level of galvanic recurrence and determinism rates both for the patient and therapist. Regarding prosody, we observe medium recurrence and determinism rates for the therapist and low recurrence and determinism rates for the patient. Overall, this phase could be interpreted as a state in which the patient's physiological anxiety is becoming more manageable and his linguistic expression more connected with it. To summarize, while state 4 can be interpreted as an unpredictable phase of the therapeutic process in which the linguistic dimension seems independent from the patient's emotions, state 5 shows signs of a step towards verbal communication and elaboration of the emotions.

5.4 Chimera States in Human Interactions

This data analysis and mapping highlight how resonance and synchronization generate dynamic landscapes of mixed-coupling states, with synchronization, non-interaction, and areas drifting away in uncoupling. This also clarifies that the dynamical mapping of every interaction and synchronization changes over time, depending on the evolution of each human interaction. Yoshiki Kuramoto (1984b, 1984a) proposed a mathematical model used to describe these mixed synchronization dynamics, and it is a model for the behavior of a large set of coupled oscillators. The paper "Coexistence of Coherence and Incoherence in Nonlocally Coupled Phase Oscillators" by Kuramoto and Battogtokh (Kuramoto & Battogtokh, 2002; Smirnov et al., 2017) marks the commencement of intense research activities on a counter-intuitive phenomenon that has come to be known as a *chimera state*. In summary, a chimera can be a mythical monster, a biological hybrid, or a metaphorical concept representing fantastical creatures and unattainable aspirations. In this case, the definition primarily refers to mythical and biological hybrids. Kuramoto and Battogtokh observed the coexistence of coherence and incoherence in a network of nonlocally coupled complex Ginzburg-Landau oscillators. Later, Abrams and Strogatz (2004) named it a *chimera state* and introduced some theoretical explanations for the existence of such behavior. Initially, the chimera state was investigated in phase oscillators; later, it was also found in limit-cycle oscillators, chaotic oscillators, chaotic maps, and even neuronal systems. In the beginning, chimera patterns were observed in nonlocally coupled networks, but after that, these states were also found in globally and locally (nearest neighbor) coupled networks and in modular networks (Schöll et al., 2019; Wang & Liu, 2020). The usage of Markov chains for mapping couplings and chimera states has already been explored (Cavers & Vasudevan, 2015; Vasudevan et al., 2015). C. R. Laing analyzed chimera states in heterogeneous networks for which the natural frequencies of the oscillators are chosen from specific distributions. Depending on its form, heterogeneity affects the chimera states, and the influence of heterogeneous coupling strengths has been discussed. Of further interest in human dynamics is the emergence of chimera states in multiscale networks resulting from networking different networks (Laing, 2009; Makarov et al., 2019). The heterogeneous synchronization dynamical mapping highlighted in our studies indicates that we constantly have chimera states and inter-organ synchronization in our brains. Similar dynamics involving different brain areas related to emotional, motor, and verbal interactions co-occur. Cognitive tasks constantly require an intricate balance between segregated and integrated neural processing (Shine et al., 2015). The relative level of functional integration versus segregation of cognitive systems significantly affects cognitive performance. Highly segregated systems enable efficient computations in local, functionally specialized brain regions. In contrast, firmly integrated systems provide rapid consolidation of information across systems, necessary for coordinated cohesive performance of complex tasks. These crucial brain states are captured in the present framework simultaneously as metastable (segregated) and coherent (integrated) states and, perhaps the most critical for brain function, as the chimera state that describes partial synchrony across subsets of cognitive systems. Previous work has found that functionally segregated states tend to involve shorter, local connections (Liégeois et al., 2020), while integration largely relies on the global influence of subcortical regions and cortical hubs that have many diverse connections to other brain regions (Shine et al., 2018). Recognizing chimera dynamics in phase transitions and dynamic maps can help to clarify the hybrid complexity of synchronization in critical cognitive states where a balance between integration and segregation is required for adaptive cognition and social interactions (Chouzouris et al., 2018). Brain chimera dynamics might also be related to different neuronal interactions through electrical and chemical synapses in the nervous system. Further neural interactions involve neuromodulators and hormones, faster or slower action, and different synchronization time frames (Majhi et al., 2019). This is undoubtedly an additional factor in the emergence of chimera states in human hybrid synchronization (Makarov et al., 2019). As different regions dynamically interact to perform cognitive tasks, variable patterns of partial synchrony can be observed, forming chimera states. The spatial patterning of these states plays a fundamental role in the cognitive organization of the brain. It presents a cognitively informed, chimera-based framework to explore how large-scale brain architecture affects brain dynamics and function (Bansal et al., 2019).

5.5 From Determinism to Statistical Dynamics

Human dynamics are so complex and prone to indeterminacy and randomness that even deterministic chaos might be considered, in many cases, as a reductionist simplification. In deterministic models, the output is entirely determined by the parameter and initial values, whereas probabilistic (or stochastic) models incorporate randomness in their structure. A probabilistic model includes elements of randomness.

The previous study highlighted how bio-psycho-social dynamics are hybrid, discontinuous, and have many degrees of freedom. We also highlighted how cluster analysis and Markov states can help to clarify the dynamics. However, our knowledge of the state of the systems is always incomplete, and we must accept some uncertainty about the system's state. Ordinary dynamics only consider the behavior of a single state, but statistical dynamics introduce the statistical ensemble, which is a probability cloud of the system in its possible states (Kolmogorov, 1950). As usual for probabilities, the ensemble can be interpreted in two main ways:

a) The ensemble can be taken to represent the various possible states that a single system could be in (*epistemic probability*) or
b) Repeated experiments result in a set of possible states of the system (*empirical probability*).

Following this perspective, we used a probabilistic statistical dynamics approach to study empathy (Kleinbub et al., 2019). Empathy plays a significant role in changing the mind's configurations and establishing an empathic link between the therapists. The patient is a crucial component of a good therapeutic alliance and outcome. However, the definition of empathy and its aspects are still under debate, limiting the development of objective quantitative measures. Most authors agree that *resonance*, based on imitation, emotional response, attunement, and interpersonal regulation, is a core empathy factor. Following the growing literature on interpersonal physiology, we investigated the hypothesis that resonance should present significant physiological evidence. We applied a PCA on simultaneous electrodermal activity and heart rate variability signals from a patient-therapist dyad involved in a 16-session psychodynamic therapy. Confirming our expectations, PCA revealed a first 'shared' component correlated to both participants' signals and two 'individual' components separately correlating to the patients' and therapists' signals. We further investigated the shared component dynamic via a symbolic Markovian discrete model and cluster analysis, observing behavior that mirrors previously reported shared heart rate dynamics properties. In conclusion, the PCA extraction of the shared physiological activity is a data-driven procedure showing promising properties.

In the literature, there have been many examples aimed at finding coarse-grained descriptors able to explain the behavior of complex systems composed of several different elements. Statistical thermodynamics has emphasized the importance of focusing on the dynamics of the degree of order of a system. This approach can be extended to any scientific field, supposing we get a reliable measure of system autocorrelation.

In cognitive neuroscience, several studies (Freeman, 2000; Giuliani et al., 2018; Mojtahedi et al., 2016) established statistical dynamics in biological systems, focusing on the mutual correlations among system descriptors. This scientific stance takes the "middle-out" approach, focusing on a *mesoscopic level* (Giuliani, 2014), maximizing the correlations among system descriptors. In other words, this approach lies "in the middle" between pure "bottom-up" (the causally relevant layer is the microscopic one) and "top-down" (the causally relevant layer is where general laws are defined) approaches. The crucial role of mesoscopic dynamics was validated in our physiological analysis and semiotics, as highlighted by the robust evidence for embedding RQA at three information elements (letters). This is a level characterized by units defined in linguistics as *morphemes*: a term that refers to the minor component of a word that (a) seems to contribute some meaning or a grammatical function to the word to which it belongs and (b) cannot itself be decomposed into more minor morphemes. A morpheme is the smallest meaningful lexical item in a language. Morphemes can be considered as *semiotic quanta* of information in natural language. A morpheme is not necessarily the same as a word. The main difference between a morpheme and a word is that a morpheme sometimes does not stand alone, but a word, by definition, always stands alone. The field of linguistic study dedicated to morphemes is called *morphology*. Usually, a morpheme comprises more than one phoneme (and certainly by several letters or informational units). Every morpheme can be free or bound (Feldman, 1995; Talmy, 2019). Since the categories are mutually exclusive, a given morpheme will belong to exactly one of them. Free morphemes can function independently as words (e.g., town, dog) and appear within lexemes (e.g., town hall, doghouse). Bound morphemes appear only as parts of words, always in conjunction with a root and sometimes with other bound morphemes. For example, un-appears only accompanied by other morphemes to form a word. Most bound morphemes in English are affixes, particularly prefixes and suffixes. Examples of suffixes are -tion, -sion, -tive, -ation, -ible, and -ing. Bound morphemes that are not affixed are called cranberry morphemes.

Natural language and other symbolic systems, such as logic and mathematics, are combinatorial and compositional. A system where minimal symbols can be put together into more complex symbols systematically is combinatorial: in natural language, morphemes combine into words and words into phrases and sentences. A system in which symbols are combined also combines their meanings, again in systematic ways, which is compositional. Given a phrase or sentence, it is very often possible to assign a meaning that is a function of the meanings of the parts (e.g., the constituent words) and the structure of the whole expression. Meaning composition is remarkable among human mental capacities and behaviors because it does not appear to be adequately accounted for by statistical relationships or by associative processing alone (Martin & Baggio, 2020; Martinčić-Ipšić et al., 2016). This fact might be seen in contrast with the behavior of other perceptions–action and cognitive systems–which traditional or contemporary statistical or associative models can well predict. A further vexing conundrum lies in explaining how systems in the brain realize meaning composition within the bounds of neurophysiological computation, given that the human brain is a computational device whose primary remit is to learn from and capitalize upon the statistical structure of its environment.

Intra-individual and interpersonal relations were investigated as coevolution dynamics of hybrid couplings, synchronizations, and desynchronization. Clusters analysis and Markov chains produced evidence of chimera states and phase transitions. A probabilistic, non-deterministic approach can clarify properties of human dynamics, focusing on the mesoscopic scale and statistical dynamics. Theoretical models of human interactions should grasp the hybrid nature of human structural couplings.

5.6 Chimeras and Consciousness

The earliest and most elementary self might be a prokaryotic bacterial cell (Margulis et al., 2011). A cell shows all the properties of life: identity, communication, and community building. Their identity became more complex and adaptable through processes of symbiosis that produced internal organelles and generated chimeras as a successful merger of two or more distinct beings (Margulis, 1981). Our symbiogenesis is still represented in our *PsycheSoma* as a multiverse formed through the coordination and integration between multiple subsystems of different origins. We keep functioning as chimeras, as the brain is not only a combination of numerous sub-organs with different origins and functions. Our very nature is to combine neural plasticity with cognitive and cultural plasticity in a vital organization in community life. Humans are successful chimeras.

Chapter 6

Change

Teach me, dear creature, how to think and speak.
Lay open to my earthy-gross conceit,
Smother'd in errors, feeble, shallow, weak,
The folded meaning of your words' deceit.

William Shakespeare

6.1 Rupture and Repair

The *Comedy of Errors*, a five-act comedy by William Shakespeare, was written in 1589–94. It was based on *Menaechmi* by Plautus, with additional material from Plautus's *Amphitruo* and the story of *Apollonius of Tyre*. The play's comic confusions derive from the presence of twin brothers, unknown to each other, in the same town. Its plot twists provide suspense, surprise, expectation, and exhilaration and reveal Shakespeare's mastery of construction (Britannica, 1993). The phrase 'a comedy of errors' is often used to describe a situation of mistakes and problems that seems funny. However, errors, mistakes, misalignments, and misunderstandings regularly happen at any communication scale, from molecular to social, in our everyday lives. For example, errors can sometimes occur during the process of DNA replication. Nucleotide bases may incorrectly be inserted, deleted, or mismatched into the DNA strand. For this reason, biological systems need mechanisms to detect and repair these errors. Mismatch errors are relatively common in the new copy strand of DNA, but the repair mechanism can detect them by comparing them to the original strand. This system helps detect DNA helix distortions, distinguish between the two strands, and remove replication errors.

Imagine a world without methods to solve miscommunications. As we have seen, Heraclitus had already identified the problem when he wrote: "Though language is common, many live as if they had a wisdom of their own." (Kahn, 1981). In this world, if some coordination problem emerges during a joint activity, it can escalate to building a very tall tower of Babel; if it takes too long to resolve one problem, more problems will have time to escalate. Nothing that required any degree of mutual understanding and coordination would be possible. Although it may sometimes feel like we live in a confused and uncoordinated world, the evidence of our ability to engage in structured collaborative activities is all around us. Our highly complex systems for living, working, and sustaining relationships demonstrate the effectiveness of human communication. We must, therefore, have practical methods for maintaining joint coordination and understanding between individuals as an essential requirement of interaction. These methods enable us to fix problems faster than they can multiply.

Unsurprisingly, conversation analysis (CA) calls this area of research "repair" (Albert & De Ruiter, 2018). Within CA, studying repair involves observing and describing how people work to identify and resolve "troubles of speaking, hearing, and understanding" (Schegloff et al., 1977) as they emerge in interaction. Repairing conversations is part of our constant maintenance in all human collaborations at work, home, and anywhere. We are largely unaware of its relevance as it is a constant component of everyday life. Where interaction is delayed or derailed, people's attempts to fix the problem reveal how they have analyzed and understood it. The next question is which party takes responsibility for solving the problem by offering a "repair solution." The producer of a trouble source starts self-initiated repairs. The recipient of the trouble introduces other-initiated repairs. Since dealing with trouble in communication as speaking, hearing, or understanding may involve multiple parties, "self" and "other" here refer to shifting participation roles, which may be distributed between multiple persons involved in a conversation (Bolden, 2013). Rupture and repair can happen in all speech, emotional, and movement conversation domains. Not respecting turn-taking can be one of the most frequent disruption areas, as it is one of the foundations of conversation coordination.

A vast range of other hidden regulators potentially involved in human synchronizations generates implicit knowledge for coordination in relations. For example, subliminal messages make *every conversation an implicit musical* of singing and dance (Shockley et al., 2003). A relevant factor is the intrinsic musicality of spoken language, also called *prosody.* Voice tonality, accent, volume, cadence, flow, pressure, hue, sentence structure, grammar, vocabulary, conversation shifts, and breaks–all these linguistic variables express embodiment as studied in CA and clinical settings (Ryan, 2005). Many studies show how these signals, *hidden regulators,* are connected in hybrid synchronization with physiological functions, biological rhythms, and hormonal cycles (Hofer, 1981, 1994). We should also consider the role of the *olfactory system* in human interactions, with its direct impact on the entorhinal cortex (Freeman, 1998; Orsucci, 2000). The neural systems of mirroring and understanding called *mirror neurons* will concur with these hidden regulators (Rizzolatti & Arbib, 1998). Therefore, deep embodied human couplings can modify functional and organic pathologies (Orsucci, 1996).

Our research laboratory has contributed to studying prosodic structures and how prosodic resonances or dissonances can lead to coupling or decoupling during conversations, including the therapeutic process. We also developed complementary work on synchronizing physiological variables that indicate emotional responses between partners in psychotherapy (Orsucci, 2021). The pattern analysis we developed in *information analysis, recurrence plots, clusters analysis,* and *Markov chains* analysis showed how synchronization could happen partially or globally, symmetrically, and asymmetrically in multiple interconnected streams. Resonance and synchronization can generate dynamical landscapes of mixed states, where we might find areas of synchronization, areas of resonance, and areas incoherently drifting away from these coupling phenomena (Kuramoto & Battogtokh, 2002; Abrams & Strogatz, 2004). It would be helpful to differentiate the diachronic mixed states discovered by Kuramoto, later named *Chimera States.* In these states, synchronization is patchy and diachronic. These processes are interrelated with the synchronic hybrid dynamical mapping of subsystems organized in different dynamical structures, as highlighted in Schreiber's plots (Schreiber, 1999).

These intricate biosemiotic dynamics correlate to analog brain dynamics. Cognitive tasks constantly require an intricate balance between segregated and integrated neural processing (Shine et al., 2018). The relative level of functional integration versus segregation of cognitive systems significantly affects cognitive performance. Highly segregated systems enable efficient computations in local, functionally specialized brain regions. Integrated systems provide rapid consolidation of information across systems, necessary for the coordinated cohesive performance of complex tasks. These crucial brain states are captured in the present framework simultaneously as metastable (segregated) and coherent (integrated) states and, perhaps, the most critical for brain function, like the chimera state that describes partial synchrony across subsets of cognitive systems. Previous work has found that functionally segregated states involve shorter local connections (Liégeois et al., 2020). Integration, instead, largely relies on the global influence of subcortical regions and cortical hubs with many diverse connections to other brain regions (Shine et al., 2018). Recognizing chimera dynamics in phase transitions and dynamic maps can help clarify the hybrid complexity of synchronization in critical cognitive states where a balance between integration and segregation works for adaptive cognition and social interactions (Chouzouris et al., 2018).

6.2 Interpersonal Physiology

An excellent example of what we tried to describe is validated in clinical research. The processes of rupture and repair in communication have been specifically investigated in a cohort of therapies with borderline patients (Høgenhaug et al., 2024). Borderline Personality Disorder (BPD) is characterized by pervasive patterns of emotional instability, identity disturbance, lack of behavioral control, and interpersonal dysfunction (Gunderson, 2011). Difficulties in interpersonal functioning include sensitivity to perceived rejection, abandonment, and criticism (Waldinger & Gunderson, 1984). BPD is associated with insecure or disorganized attachment, emotional discordance, dysregulation, and impulsivity. Impaired mentalization (the ability to understand the mental states of self and others) and reduced epistemic trust (accepting social knowledge from others) have also been described (Fonagy & Luyten, 2009). In summary, BPD patients tend to have a higher rate of disruptions in social coordination, and their therapies' focus naturally gravitates to rupture and repair dynamics. These relational rupture-and-repair processes also apply to their inner Self dynamics. The final aim of the therapy is to establish natural maintenance of the relational and Self dynamics. However, the pathology of BPD may challenge the development, formation, and maintenance of the therapeutic alliance and treatment progress (McMain et al., 2015). Patients with high levels of personality disorder traits are more likely to have an unstable relationship with their therapists compared to patients with low levels of personality disorder traits (Muran et al., 2009; Fonagy et al., 2023). Emerging evidence shows a higher intensity and a more significant number of BPD treatment ruptures than those without BPD. The quality of the alliance is a specific focus of attention in all effective treatments for BPD. Ruptures can happen at different scales, from disorganized coordination to whole confrontation or withdrawal to acting out or the complete break-up of the therapeutic relationship. A constant repair and maintenance of the talking relationship can prevent the escalation of significant disruptions and ensure the gradual progress toward coordination and communication. This would eventually coincide with the therapeutic goals as positive playing linguistic games equates with regulating unstable expressions and behaviors. A growing interest has emerged in studying the alliance's more implicit aspects, including emotional communication and physiological synchronization between the patient and therapist, to deepen our understanding of alliance processes (Orsucci et al., 2016; Wiltshire et al., 2020). As we have seen, studying physiological synchronization is highly complex but fascinating (Orsucci, 2021). In a pilot study, Høgenhaug adopted the *interpersonal physiology* (IP) framework, broadly defined as a shared temporal organization of physiological signals of two or more interacting people (Palumbo, 2015; Palumbo et al., 2017). Understanding the concept of IP and its potential and clinical implications might become more comprehensive when viewed through a developmental lens of infant-caregiver co-regulation (Hofer, 1994; Trevarthen, 2009).

Studying the association between IP and rupture and repair episodes might allow bridging concepts like synchronization, emotion regulation, trust, safety, and learning and give more in-depth descriptions of the underlying mechanisms of alliance processes in BDP treatment (Schenk et al., 2021). A recent review examining the association between rupture repair processes and interpersonal coordination in psychotherapy found the relevance of synchronization between patients and therapists in different behavioral modalities of vocalization, facial expressions, movement, physiology, and hormones associated with rupture and repair processes (Høgenhaug et al., 2024). Interpersonal coordination was essential during rupture repair episodes, including mutual emotion regulation, sense-making, trust, and safety. However, high heterogeneity was identified regarding how interpersonal coordination was associated with rupture repair sequences, calling for further examination.

Large human gatherings and even crowds might also display signs of IP. Audience synchronies in live concerts illustrate the embodiment of the music experience and how shared experiences can eternally induce synchronization (Tschacher et al., 2023). A study of large audiences of classical concerts aimed to analyze audiences' physiological and motor responses. It was assumed that the music would induce synchronous physiology and movement in listeners (synchrony induction). There was clear evidence of physiological synchrony (heart rate, respiration rate, skin conductance response) and movement synchrony of the audience. Thus, the audiences of the three concerts resonated with the music; their music perception was embodied. Heart-rate synchrony was exceptionally high when listeners felt moved emotionally, inspired by a piece, and immersed in the music. Personality traits were also associated with individual contributions to induction synchrony.

6.3 Couplings

Coevolving living systems can establish relationships relevant to ecology and social sciences (Orsucci, 2002, 2013; Holstein & Gubrium, 2012; Margulis et al., 2011). A relevant feature of research on coupling between human systems is that, even if measurements are supposed to be objective, there is always some form of symmetry. The object is always a subject, which the experience can change. This is markedly different from other asymmetric couplings in empirical research. Freud recognized this specific order parameter when he discovered that *transference* mirrors *countertransference* (Laplanche & Pontalis, 1974). The therapist resonates with the patient in a *quasi-symmetric coupling and coevolution*. The therapist and the patient change each other in different forms of co-adaptation. Coevolution can take different routes while developing a system open to a broader ecosystem environment. The therapeutic ecosystem can follow the general coevolution dynamics of commensalism, parasitism, competition, or mutualism. *Commensalism* represents a class of relationships between two organisms where one benefits but is unaffected. It is perhaps the most unstable and challenging to recognize because it can easily slip into other types of relationships. *Parasitism* is a symbiotic relationship where one organism, the parasite, benefits at the host's expense. As a result, the parasite ends up hurting the vital capacity of the host for its benefit. *Competition* can be *cooperative or predatory*. *Cooperative competition* promotes the vital capacity of competitors, and it is a challenge that strengthens both parties. This kind of competition tends to fade quickly in mutualism. *Predatory competition* is a coevolutionary process of damaging or eliminating the rival system. In some cases, it looks like a *zero-sum game* where the winner takes all because the success of one of the competitors implies eliminating the other. However, total elimination of prey could starve predators, so more frequently, some coevolutionary balance settles before the zero-sum result. For example, *mutualism* is a *cooperative coevolution* in which each participant benefits from the interaction. Humans present this form of coevolution as the foundation of communities and the wider society.

Some questions about cooperative dynamics are still partially open. For example, why should an individual engage in a cooperative behavior that appears costly to perform but benefits others (Hamilton, 1964)? Benefits could be classified as direct or indirect fitness if linked to direct or indirect genetic benefits. However, these are not mutually exclusive, as, at times, they could be complementary (West et al., 2007b, 2007a). Nowak (2006, 2013) proposes five mechanisms for the evolution of cooperation:

kin selection, direct reciprocity, indirect reciprocity, network reciprocity, and group selection. He highlighted how having a theory that can only explain cooperation among relatives is unsatisfactory. We also observe cooperation between unrelated individuals or members of different species. There are other forms of human payoff beyond genetics — societal factors such as reputation, influence, and other material and immaterial benefits. Ethical and spiritual factors also have a relevant function in social welfare and cohesion, affecting the fitness of associated individuals. On some rare occasions, the therapeutic pathway can deviate from the dynamics of mutualism and cooperation to other potentially unhealthy domains. The clinical community recognized the risks of dynamic drifts. Searles (1979), for example, discussed the paradox of situations in which patients could take inverted roles, behaving as if therapeutic for the therapist.

Relationships of care should follow *mutualism,* which is *cooperation* that develops through structural coupling between partners. The therapist guides self-organized processes by keeping boundary conditions, endorsing positive rupture-repair practice, perturbing and accepting to be perturbed in controlled ways, and facilitating opportunities for change through new self-organization (Orsucci, 2015). Both partners in coevolution will change during this process. The structural coupling in psychotherapy creates what some authors define as an *inter-subjective bi-personal field* (Baranger & Baranger, 1985; Langs, 1976). This field includes *multiple semiotic, motor, and emotional variables* generated through various small reciprocal perturbations. It is a process of gentle "pushing and pulling," using a metaphor from the physics of coupling and synchronization (Carroll & Pecora, 1993; Dube & Despres, 2000; Pyragas, 2001; Strogatz, 2003). Alternate phases of coupling and decoupling, global or localized, as mentioned while discussing rupture and repair, punctuate the dynamic change process (Heagy et al., 1995).

6.4 Transformations

Semiotic projections through metaphors and metonymies rely on invariances and habits that root the Self systems in their continuity.

Invariance in transformations is a fundamental concept in both mathematics and physics. In mathematics, an invariant is a property of a system that remains unchanged under some transformation. For example, the fixed points of a transformation are the elements in the domain that are invariant under the transformation. Depending on the application, they may be called symmetric concerning that transformation. In physics, physical laws are said to be invariant under transformations when their predictions remain unchanged. This generally means that the form of the law (e.g., the type of differential equations used to describe the law) is unchanged in transformations so that no additional or different solutions are obtained. A specific example of invariance in transformations comes from classical mechanics. For a given system, there can be transformations for which the explicit equations of motion are the same for the old and new variables. Transformations for which the equations of motion are invariant are called invariant transformations. In summary, invariance in transformations allows us to see what stays the same when things change, providing deep insights into the structure and behavior of these systems.

There is a robust amount of literature on social rhythms and how they can synchronize social groups. Studies on commuting and its impact on nations' productivity and individuals' biorhythms exist. Historical studies are necessary on how the calendar and holidays can shape the identity of religions or nations (see the different choices of Sunday, Saturday, and Friday for the three monotheistic religions). At the same time, national revolutions tried to establish new social timings and define new calendars (Zerubavel, 1981).

Social timing is a powerful tool for social entrainment. In the same way, you can use timing to induce neuro-cognitive social synchronization and change, as shamans are well known for using tribal rhythms and dances. This is the same as in our social gatherings, clubs, discotheques, and parties (Freeman, 2001). Psychotherapies have been trying to do the same, and there is a relevant example of how Freud and followers from different schools tried to find the best timing techniques to induce entrainment. Elvio Fachinelli (2001) examined the relation between therapy as a crucial example of human change practice and time. He refers to three types of activity found in Freud's work, where he tried to address transformations, invariances, and the boundaries of change processes in different ways. First, the early treatments, whose duration was within the limited period of the illness, often went to cure in private or institutional environments. Then, semi-informal practice is based on 'friendly relationships,' such as his peripatetic conversations with Gustav Mahler. The third standardized practice, drawn from Freud's papers on technique, prescribes a strict setting of times and places, including abstinence from personal disclosures and contacts. The fourth, post-Freudian, as we might add, is the post-industrial practice of hundreds of different types of therapy based on the current multiple rhythms of social life. So many different types of psychotherapy exist that researchers cannot investigate all of them; they have generally concentrated on the most frequently used approaches. These include behavior therapy (altering unhealthy behaviors), cognitive therapy (altering maladaptive ways of thinking), psychodynamic therapy (resolving unconscious conflicts and adverse childhood experiences), interpersonal therapy (remedying unhealthy ways of interacting with others), systemic therapy (treating the family or other micro-social groups) and person-centered therapy (helping clients to find their solutions to life problems), and Gestalt-humanistic therapy (present-centered, contextual, holistic).

While the analytical work, as a first prototypical psychotherapy, became structured by acquiring organization, the apparatus seemed to necessitate a progressively more extended period because its aim became gradually less distinct, indefinite, and even potentially endless (Freud et al., 1991). Analytical therapeutic relations became monotonous and institutional, justifying themselves and following their own rules without concern for their end. The gradual bureaucratization of analytic therapy was epitomized by the classic "psychoanalytic technique and the creation of analytic patients" (Rothstein, 2018). In this book, the author presents a manualized approach to converting clients into suitable analytical patients, as if the patient would serve the therapy and not vice versa.

Freud used to complain that his therapeutic outcomes were better when he was younger, and his approach was less rigorous than after he developed his standard technique. This is well documented in books of histories from his patients (Albano, 1987; Borch-Jacobsen, 2021; Roazen, 2013), where we find the extraordinary variety of his approaches and discover that he was less Freudian than we would imagine. In his patients' memories, we can find that he tuned his attitude and technique to the patient's needs and used many different settings and timings. In other words, at the beginning of his practice, he personalized treatments and responded to patient feedback, adapting the boundaries of the therapeutic setting.

We should never forget that Anna O., the patient treated by Joseph Breuer, was the first to propose the "talking cure" definition, becoming virtually the patient zero of modern psychotherapies. While Freud never actually saw her as a patient, her case had a significant impact on the development of psychoanalysis. Freud was fascinated with her case and consulted with Breuer during the treatment (Breuer & Freud, 1956). One way or another, she self-organized her therapy and contributed to building a broad treatment model for all the following patients. A personalized attitude was further developed by Sandor Ferenczi, one of Freud's main partners in the early development of psychoanalysis. Ferenczi designed "technical experiments" focused on nonverbal language and a more interactive attitude of the analyst (Freud et al., 1919). Later, Kurt Eissler defined the *technical parameters* that could be adapted as qualitative and quantitative modifications of the basic model of the standard technique (Eissler, 1953).

A formal discussion on *common factors* in human change started in 1936 with a correspondence between Rosenzweig and Freud (Rosenzweig, 1936). However, Freud's technical experiments and the following ones led by Sandor Ferenczi were indeed antecedents. Saul Rosenzweig concluded after perusing the literature that one therapy works about as well as any other. At the time, many principal treatments fell roughly into the psychodynamic and behavioral categories, which are still widely used today. Rosenzweig introduced the metaphor of the Dodo Bird, after the feathered creature in Lewis Carroll's *Alice in Wonderland*, who declared that following a race, "everyone has won, and all must have prizes." (Carroll, 1865). The "Dodo Bird verdict" has since come to refer to the claim that all therapies are equivalent in their effects. This verdict gained traction in 1975 when Lester Luborsky and his colleagues (Luborsky, 1995) published a review of relevant research suggesting that most therapies work equally well. The common factors trend gathered momentum in 1997 when Bruce E. Wampold and his co-authors published a meta-analysis (quantitative review) of more than 200 scientific studies in which "bona fide" therapies were compared with no treatment. By bona fide, they meant treatments delivered by trained therapists based on sound psychological principles and described in publications. Wampold's team found the differences in the treatments' effectiveness minimal (and they were all better than no treatment) (Messer & Wampold, 2002).

One explanation for the *Dodo Bird effect* is that virtually all types of psychotherapy share certain core features. In a classic 1961 book, Jerome Frank argued that all effective therapies consist of clearly prescribed roles for the therapist and client (Frank & Frank, 1993). They present clients with a plausible theoretical rationale and provide specific therapeutic rituals. They also occur in a setting and protected environment, usually a comfortable office, associated with open dialogue and alleviating distress. Later, writers elaborated on Frank's thinking, asserting that effective therapies require empathy on the part of the clinician, close rapport between practitioner and client, and shared therapeutic goals. Today, many authors argue that these and other common elements are even more potent than the features that distinguish one therapy from another.

In reviewing about 50 years of research in psychotherapy, Horst Kachele (2001) concluded that the therapeutic alliance, intended as therapeutic cooperation, has become the most explored clinical concept. It is now evident that the construct of this alliance has both a direct and an indirect impact on the outcome, i.e., achieving the desired modifications. There is agreement that the therapeutic alliance is a multi-dimensional construct composed of four relatively independent dimensions:

a)   capacity to purposefully work in therapy;
b)   affective bond with the therapist;
c)   therapist's empathic understanding and involvement;
d)   agreement on treatment goals and tasks.

Kachele stressed that, beyond any technical consideration, a personal match between therapist and patient is a crucial predictor of outcome. That is important because we should start from the most favorable condition for cooperation, as many possible variables are beyond total control. The best therapeutic match corresponds to good preliminary conditions to facilitate structural coupling, synchronization dynamics, and establishing positive bipersonal fields. We assume that cognitive and emotional resonance between the candidates for joint explorations in the co-evolutionary landscapes are the markers of the possible collaboration to be developed in both directions. In other words, the T and P systems have some resonance that precedes and sets boundary conditions of a possible co-evolution. These preconditions for a favorable collaboration can be generalized to natural couplings in everyday life, as the clinical context represents a partially artificial subset of natural human relations.

The core of change is in the (therapeutic) relationship as a specialized gymnasium for communication games. The new interpersonal coupling generates a new system and partially reflects the history of the separated subsystems. We should consider the psychotherapeutic situation a specialized setting where coupling between human subjects evolves under partially artificial and controlled conditions for facilitating change. This protected environment allows a definition of boundary conditions and a partial reduction of the degrees of freedom in a coupled system. However, the way this coupling evolves still has multidimensional determinants.

6.5 Factors of Change

The process of human change can take different forms along a vast spectrum where, on one side, you might still find multiple degrees of freedom for self-organization. On the other hand, you can find simplified forms of psychosocial pedagogy. A recent article on the evidence of effectiveness for psychotherapies ironically asked if the dodo has grown enormous wings. The hypothesis was that their effectiveness does not depend pre-eminently on techniques but on common and shared factors: therapeutic alliance, complementarity with the therapist, secure environment, mirroring, and empathy have received validation (Duncan et al., 2010). Change directly caused by the treatment (including all the mentioned factors) might account for only 13% of the change process. At the core of change dynamics, 87% of client extra-therapeutic factors represent the patients' ability to regenerate and self-organize their resources and environment. The therapeutic environment facilitates and contains this process as an incubator for new self-organization. However, we can also consider that 13% is produced by psychotherapy from the point of view of complexity science. From the perspective of sensitivity to initial conditions, we can understand how such a small fraction may still be a potent trigger of change. Edward Glover (1958) noted that even the "most successful treatment is nothing more than a dent on the surface of a continent". A butterfly flap can potentially lead to eventful transformations by facilitating positive self-organization.

Therefore, we should consider the balance between therapists' and patients' roles in human change dynamics. How much is determined by direct therapeutic interventions, how much is caused by the definition of therapeutic boundaries, and how much is produced by the patients' self-organization. According to Jacobi et al. (2023), causal determinism is, roughly speaking, the idea that antecedent events, conditions, and the laws of nature cause any event. The idea is ancient but became subject to clarification and mathematical analysis in the 18th century. Determinism is deeply connected with our understanding of the physical sciences and their explanatory ambitions, on the one hand, and with our views about human free action on the other. In both general areas, there is no agreement over whether determinism is true (or even whether it can be known as true or false) and the import of human agency. Determinism is often contrasted with free will. Some philosophers, known as hard determinists, believe that determinism is incompatible with free will. On the other hand, soft determinists, also called compatibilists, believe that determinism and free will are compatible. They often achieve this reconciliation by subtly revising or weakening the common notion of free will. The extreme alternative to determinism is indeterminism, the view that at least some events have no deterministic cause but occur randomly or by chance. Research in quantum mechanics supports indeterminism to some extent, suggesting that some events at the quantum level are, in principle, unpredictable (and therefore random). These are complex philosophical concepts, and interpretations can vary. Pragmatic approaches can lead to different interventions, attitudes, and outcomes. Regarding human change dynamics, indeterminism and self-organization create more space for the expression of free will. One can interpret psychotherapy as a professional facilitation of self-change. The process also works the other way as the patient coaches the therapist, subtly and unconsciously, to implement practices and scenarios for personalizing recovery. Manuals' rigidity does not work unless manuals are used as toolboxes where the most valuable tools can be picked up at need. In this way, they might be considered toolboxes for initiating self-organization processes. The primary tool defines the setting as the boundary conditions, which are constraints or rules that define how a system interacts with its surroundings at its edges or boundaries. Understanding boundary conditions is crucial because they influence the system's response and behavior. The boundary conditions contain a system and interface it with its environment, shaping its dynamics and influencing emergent behaviors. The control parameters are the key variables that influence the dynamics of a complex system. They can be organized in patterns as order parameters characterizing a complex system's transition from one state to another.

6.6 Harmonious Couplings

Complexity science has accumulated evidence that it is possible to introduce optimal coupling between complex systems and, in this way, synchronize them. Synchronization, if properly harmonized, can lead to change in coupled systems. A well-tuned, harmonic perturbation from the driving system can resonate in optimal responses, leading to a consonant coevolution. The therapeutic system entrains the client system by using its response to an initial soft perturbation (Pecora & Carroll, 1990). This would create a process of convergence, entrainment, and synchronization. A co-evolving sequence of therapeutic conversations represents the sequential process of synchronization cascading between complex systems. In this process, communications change along scales of harmonic resonance in waves that usually trigger feedback loops into the therapeutic approach. The resulting method is a co-evolution. The psychotherapist can facilitate it by appropriately selecting the naturally rich variation of states. That is a way of playing co-evolution in psychotherapy. Several techniques have been proposed for *navigating synchronization and coevolution*. Most approaches are just developments of two basic ones: the *OGY (Ott-Grebogi and Yorke) method* (see Grebogi & Lai, 2006) and the *Pyragas method* (Pyragas, 1996). In the OGY method, small, wisely chosen, swift perturbations are applied to the system once per cycle to maintain and positively sustain it near the desired unstable periodic orbit (presentation, events). After the information and a formulation about the dynamical state have been gathered, the system can run and wait until it comes near a desired recurring condition. Next, the system is encouraged to remain in that recurring condition by reinforcing the appropriate parameter. One strength of this method is that it does not require a detailed model of the client system but only some information about its recurrence. This method's challenges are isolating the recurrence and establishing the perturbations necessary for stability. This method might have some analogies to Monte Carlo's algorithms for reinforcement learning and evolutionary selection of fit states.

The Pyragas method sends an appropriate continuous driving signal into the system. Its intensity is practically zero as it evolves close to the desired periodic orbit but increases when it drifts away from the desired trajectory.

A few complications come to mind when one considers the implementation of complexity navigation strategies:

- The presence of noise (dynamical or environmental) may induce loss of control or turbulence.
- Cascading can generate unforeseen feedback storms and lead to uncontrollable drifts in co-evolution.
- The drive system must be constantly re-split in an observing-controlling subsystem each time a feedback cascading happens to keep the compass of the navigation.

Introducing noise to the global system can sometimes foster synchronization, acting as *stochastic resonance*. This intriguing concept can be particularly beneficial for weak or unstable states, although it is essential to note that it can also lead to uncontrolled turbulences beyond a certain threshold. Coupling, in any case, increases the number of degrees of freedom of the resulting system and the possibility of new dynamical conditions. This is a powerful tool, even without specific control, in curing any dynamic disease in the client system. Fractal intermittency has been observed on the threshold of weak synchronizations, while strong synchronizations generate smoother landscapes. From a dynamical systems perspective, these methods represent a meta-explanation of several therapeutic techniques. They can be included in a guided self-organization toolbox, opening new possibilities for understanding and treatment.

Therapists and clients can usually recognize and consciously manage only a tiny portion of the broad communications stream. They could perceive this flow, mostly non-consciously or with some delayed reflective practice, as procedural communication, implicit memory, and knowledge. In these coupling and emerging cycles, transformations evolve towards new autopoietic beginnings (Orsucci, 2002). All therapeutic techniques would populate an enriched environment, fostering new self-organization. Reflective practices might work as temporary scaffolds until neuroplasticity can embed reflexive skills, reactions, habits, and relations. The new therapy-embedded attachment experiences are included in similar dynamics, gradually promoting new neurodynamics, relational patterns, and habits.

Relevant biosemiotic exchanges in therapeutic relations are a-conscious, i.e., different from the classical Freudian unconscious, which, in principle, could be verbalized (Etkin et al., 2005). Stern (2004) has extensively explained how implicit and procedural knowledge generates crucial therapeutic change processes. In his view, the therapeutic process is characterized by non-linear and sometimes unpredictable movements towards shared goals. Therapeutic landmarks can emerge from the experience of present moments in which participants create fields of implicit understanding and sharing in the *here and now*. These moments are emotionally charged, the experience of time duration seems to extend, and there is a strong sense of truth in what is happening.

The experience of having a genuine meeting is an emergent property of the bipersonal dynamic field. Emerging punctuations, de-couplings, and critical states of uncertainty and instability will announce a possible change. The flow of these events will create opportunities for changes in implicit memory. Explicit verbalizations of these states are optional and sometimes counterproductive. These states are related to the dynamical conditions otherwise defined as the free energy principle, with increased informational entropy.

Hidden regulators produce synchronizations, generating implicit knowledge. Every conversation is an implicit dance of subliminal messages (Fowler et al., 2008). Many studies document how these signals can lead to a deep attachment relationship, even to synchronizing physiological functions, biological rhythms, and hormone cycles (Hofer, 1975). At the same time, a psychotherapeutic treatment may change the evolution of critical physical pathologies. The neural functions of mirroring and arousal concur with these hidden regulators. The core of a change process is synchronization and co-evolution, generating dyadic states of expanded and shared consciousness. The therapeutic field reaches a state of self-organized criticality, causing cascades of openness for change. From a critical state of expectations and instabilities, waves of change can emerge.

A crucial factor in this process is the intrinsic musicality of spoken language, which is called prosody. The tone of voice, pitch, accent, volume, cadence of speech, flow, pressure, hue, sentence structure, grammar, vocabulary, conversation shifts, breaks, swing, and rhythm: all these linguistic variables are at the center of the expression of emotion and embodiment in the psychotherapeutic setting. However, the study of these components still needs to be developed, especially compared to the wealth of studies on semantic and explicit content. Our research group has made new contributions to studying prosodic structures and how prosodic resonances, or dissonances, can lead to coupling or decoupling during a therapeutic process (Orsucci et al., 2013; Orsucci, 2015).

Winnicott (1971) proposed that human change occurs when two areas of play and two living systems come together in a willing state of play. When play seems impossible, the therapist must help the patient get to a state where they can play. Psychotherapies provide specialized environments that allow people to play, free from the influences of aggression and sex. Play is a state of fusion where the boundaries between subjective and objective experience can dissolve. More than any other activity, it is likely that play can foster an extraordinary fitness landscape in mammals: Self-Organized Criticality. In playful activities and attitudes, we can find a sequence of intentions and cognitions with the highest degrees of freedom and the maximal amount of information. Creativity can be explored, and you can meet the Adjacent Possible (Kauffman, 1995).

In each session, it is essential to reach a playful atmosphere, the letting go and relaxation of a gentle and benevolent regression. Long regressions are usually exported from the protective environment and can trigger disruptions. Therefore, the therapist will establish a systemic closure of the bi-personal field at the beginning and end of each play session.

From this perspective, human change is making the other able to play and reach a critical state, and the most prominent therapy task would be creating a therapeutic environment. In this way, optimal boundary conditions would be ensured for self-organization. As play is human change, the primary test of a positive evolution is the subjective experience of the therapist and the patient enjoying playing.

In biophysical terms, all human encounters start with a possible entrainment. If this is effective, it might lead to synchronization, structural coupling, and the establishment of bi-personal, inter-subjective fields (Baranger & Baranger, 2008; Langs, 1976; Strogatz, 2004). The first stage of entrainment is triggered by sequences of mutual perturbations in verbal, prosodic, motor, and sensory communication. Only a tiny part of this immense amount of communication is consciously managed. Beyond the tip of the iceberg, the most significant portion of it is just procedural communication and implicit knowledge (Hofer, 1994; Stern, 2004; Etkin et al., 2005). This semiotic material is a-conscious and includes psychobiological hidden regulators (Hofer, 1994) and the implicit dance of coordination and corporal signs (Shockley et al., 2009). Many studies document the evidence of how these signals can lead to the synchronization of physiological functions, biological rhythms, and hormone cycles. The therapeutic process of change co-evolves cascading in punctuations of nonlinear singularities. They occur when participants share the *here and now* of implicit understanding. In these occasions, the phenomenological sense of time stretches, producing a strong sense of truth as an emergent property of the bi-personal field. This punctuation announces a change in implicit memory and knowledge, an event horizon (Stern et al., 1998). A verbal explanation of these states is only sometimes necessary and sometimes can be even counterproductive. Synchronization and co-evolution in the therapeutic relationship generate dyadic forms of extended and shared consciousness, constituting the engine of therapeutic change (Tronick et al., 1998). In this way, the therapeutic field reaches a relational critical state of maximum intensity, cascading into points of openness for change (Geary, 2009), where criticality finally generates state transitions (Bak, 1996).

6.7 Errors and Enchantments

As we started with *The Comedy of Errors*, we might conclude this chapter with considerations from another famous Shakespeare comedy, *A Midsummer Night's Dream*. In the former, humor, farcical situations, absurdity, and misunderstandings come from errors, while in the latter, they come from enchantments and phantasy characters. Both plays feature intricate plot structures with multiple interwoven subplots, which converge in a harmonious resolution at the end of the play. *The Comedy of Errors* concludes with the reunion of the separated twins and the resolution of misunderstandings, leading to a happy ending. In *A Midsummer Night's Dream*, the play ends with restoring harmony among lovers and resolving conflicts caused by the enchantments, with a sense of returning to reality after a dream-like adventure. Both misunderstanding and enchantment alter the perception of reality. Misunderstanding skews one's comprehension of events, words, or actions, leading to confusion or false beliefs. Similarly, enchantment, especially in the magical sense, manipulates perception through spells or charms, creating a distorted view of reality. They both create dramatic tension and ultimately contribute to the character's growth and the unfolding of the narrative. Both misunderstanding and enchantment can be part of a character's journey, leading to personal growth and transformation. Characters may emerge from misunderstandings or enchantments with greater self-awareness, wisdom, and a deeper understanding of themselves and others. In essence, misunderstanding and enchantment can be seen as metaphorical tools that Shakespeare and other writers use to explore themes of perception, reality, power, and transformation.

Chapter 7

Play

In playing, and perhaps only in playing, the child or adult is free to be creative.

D. W. Winnicott

7.1 Homo Ludens

Heraclitus created characteristic paradoxes by showing children as wiser and sharper than adults. In one of his most enigmatic aphorisms (Fr. 52), he represents the dynamism that propels and sustains us right through life as a child at play. Plato was interested in children and their play, and his no less paradoxical thesis in *The Laws* is that what, if anything, is solemn in human life is a playful activity conceived as participation in the ordered play of the gods. We see here an anticipation of Huizinga's thesis in *Homo Ludens* (Huizinga, 2014). In applying the concept of play lies the route to understanding not only children's games and the place of sport in the lives of adults but also all of what may be regarded as the higher forms of culture, law, and religious ritual. This includes all playful human interactions, such as humor, jokes, and creativity. He identifies the five crucial characteristics of play: it is not regular or natural (there is an element of illusion); it is distinct from ordinary activity for a duration; it creates its order; there is no material interest or profit. Unlike ordinary life, he also points out that play usually accompanies tension, joy, uncertainty, or surprise.

Huizinga's central thesis is that the play element is generative of culture. Culture bears the features of play in many aspects: law, war, science, poetry, religion, philosophy, and art. Play can operate below and above the level of seriousness. Their contrast is fluid and dynamic as they form a continuum. The most extraordinary human life is a blend of both, and the most extraordinary times in history, e.g., the Renaissance, are driven by both. The *Magic Circle* (virtual worlds and illusion) of play is secluded and limited in space and time. A temporary world within the ordinary world, dedicated to performing an act apart in which only the game's rules apply, and outsiders are excluded. This playground is identical in form to a sacred spot where rites are performed. Sometimes, the circle can be literal, while at other times, it can be virtual, encompassing exceptional experiences. Masks, impersonations, pretending, and avatars can evoke unique emotions, bringing ordinary life to a standstill and making things 'not real'. They express the plurality of the Self in impersonations of private and shared theatres (Colapietro, 1988). Avatar is the Sanskrit for incarnation, and even today, when we attach no religious emotion to a mask, it still conveys the power of mystery, taking us beyond ordinary life. Furthermore, it emphasizes the extraordinary nature of play, where the player transfigures into another being, playful and profound.

7.2 Language Plays

One of the master keys of Wittgenstein's evolved vision of language is that our communications are organized into *linguistic acts* (Wittgenstein, 1967). The original German *Sprachspiel* includes the English meaning of both play and game. The examples that Wittgenstein used often initially referred to board games (chess) and later to play (including theater scenes and children's fun). Martin Puchner suggested revising the usual English translation of *Sprachspiel* as a *"language play"* (Puchner, 2015). Early in the *Philosophical Investigations*, Wittgenstein lists various examples of *Sprachspiel*. Children's play, humor, irony, and jokes are more easily included in language plays than in chess and other formal board games.

Once one approaches Wittgenstein's conception of language through the notion of play, including "playing theater," one notices a drama current running through his entire late philosophy. First, many of Wittgenstein's examples, including those focused on language acquisition, gestures, and anthropological rituals, refer to a mode of behavior. It is more closely aligned with "playing theater" than "playing chess." Second, in developing his new understanding of language, Wittgenstein drew on a distinctly dramatic vocabulary that describes language as acts performed by actors in particular scenes and settings. Third, focusing on play allows a new approach to Wittgenstein's writing mode. Wittgenstein invented dramatic scenarios populated by characters (including Martians and animals) and centered on action sequences. Indeed, Wittgenstein's language plays, with their fat characters and minimal sets, resemble the theater of the absurd, and at least one representative of the absurd, Tom Stoppard, has incorporated Wittgenstein's dramatic examples into his plays. It is important to remember that Wittgenstein first introduced chess to explain not language but mathematics. The English translation of *Sprachspiel* hinges on the role and function of chess as a model for Wittgenstein's developing conception of language and, more particularly, on the claim that chess increasingly lost its power as Wittgenstein's primary model. His primary usage of chess as a model for language interactions started when he was still in Vienna, at the time of his *Tractatus* (Wittgenstein, 1961). It is influenced by his early models of language, which are based on logic and mathematics and related to the positivist logic school that included Schlick and Carnap. Language play conceptualization reflects much better the complexity and multidimensionality of linguistic interactions.

How important is it to negotiate play and agree that play is the name of the game? When animals play, behavior patterns are, for the most part, "borrowed" from other contexts, and individuals need to be able to tell one another that they do not want to eat, fight, or mate with the other individual(s). However, instead, they want to play with them. In most species in which play has been observed, specific actions have evolved that are used to initiate ("I want to play with you") or to maintain ("I still want to play with you regardless of what I just did to you or regardless of what I am going to do to you") play. These actions seem to function in negotiations between participants, which is that they foster an agreement to engage in play rather than to partake in aggression or predation, for example. There is no solid evidence that animals invite others to play and exploit them (Bekoff & Byers, 1998). Furthermore, self-handicapping and role reversals have also been observed, in which, for example, dominant individuals allow themselves to be dominated only in the context of play.

The participants must cooperate and negotiate agreements to participate in ongoing social play. After they agree to play, there seem to be social regulations and obligations to maintain the play's mood. Furthermore, data suggest that animals often seek permission to play with another animal by performing behavior patterns that indicate that play is desired and not another activity. For example, in self-handicapping (e.g., inhibited biting or clawing) and role-reversing (being chased rather than chasing), in which dominant animals engage to get more subordinate individuals to play, the dominant individuals are seeking permission to engage in play with animals who might otherwise avoid interacting with them. The result is that the two individuals agree to cooperate, with self-handicapping and role-reversing being a form of negotiating this agreement. These data are essential to consider in discussions of the evolution of cognition. They tell us that specific cognitive abilities must be present even before an individual has the linguistic sophistication of a human. While other animals might also cooperate, including those for whom we are hard-pressed to grant the presence of sophisticated cognitive abilities (e.g., cleaning fish), the flexibility of play, and the ease with which even two strange animals can play after only brief introductions to one another, lead to the conclusion that interactions between players are not merely the result of (somewhat hard-wired and inflexible) coevolved systems. They result from ongoing negotiations that require careful assessments throughout an encounter. It seems to be the flexibility of play that is important in allowing animals to negotiate the desired outcome. How are agreements reached in the context of social play? How do individuals accomplish turn-taking? In most species in which play has been described, play-soliciting signals appear to foster some cooperation between players so that they respond to the others in a way consistent with play and different from the responses the same actions would elicit in other contexts (Bekoff & Byers, 1998); play-soliciting signals help the receiver interpret other signals.

Winnicott (1971; 1971b) proposed that human creativity happens when there is a meeting between two areas of play and at least two persons willing to play together. Perhaps we could extend this to private theater, as a single individual could entertain playful interactions between the components of their Self as impersonations. This is what Peirce's framework for the Self also implies. When play is not possible, the therapist's task is to gently bring the other to a state in which being able to play. Play is a state of illusion in which the boundaries between subjective and objective experience can fade. Psychotherapies are specialized environments that allow people to play for change. Winnicott confirms the preconditions of playful activities defined by Huizinga as integral to the therapeutic setting. They constitute the boundary condition of a therapeutic system. Winnicott also recognized that "playing is inspiring" (Winnicott, 1971). Playing and gaming increase brain arousal and neuroplasticity, as confirmed directly and indirectly by research on enriched learning environments (LaFreniere, 2013; Nithianantharajah & Hannan, 2006; Reuderink et al., 2013). In the playing field, there is a chance of introducing enrichments. This is how we should consider some therapeutic techniques: Dialectical Behavioral Therapy (DBT) skills, Mentalization-based Treatment (MBT) reflective moments, Cognitive Behavioral Therapy (CBT) frames, slow-motion, psychodynamic clarifications, free associations, etc. Play is the golden pathway towards self-organization and neuroplasticity in therapy. It is sometimes a precarious way to be placed in the transitional area between subjective and objective reality. It is a creative activity in search of a rediscovery of the self. Psychotherapy is done by overlapping two play areas, that of the patient and that of the therapist. If the therapist cannot play, they cannot work as a therapist. If the patient cannot play, something must be done to enable them to play. This can be achieved in the trust and acceptance of a collaborative alliance, of a reliable, professional setting, defining the boundary conditions for new creative self-organization.

7.3 Contained Self-Organization

Play, a dynamic and creative activity, is intricately linked to self-organization. It operates on the edge of a self-organization fitness landscape, where a general arousal sparks tension, surprise, mystery, illusion, and fascination. The play experience is a sequence of intentions and cognitions with the highest degrees of freedom and the maximal amount of information. This connection between play and self-organization is a fascinating aspect of our world, occurring in physical, chemical, biological, robotic, and cognitive systems. Examples of self-organization include crystallization, thermal convection of fluids, chemical oscillation, animal swarming, and neural circuits. Self-organization, also known as spontaneous order in the social sciences, is a process where some form of overall order arises from local interactions between parts of an initially disordered system. The process can be spontaneous when sufficient energy is available, not needing control by any external agent. It is often triggered by seemingly random fluctuations, amplified by positive feedback. The resulting organization is wholly decentralized and distributed over all system components. As such, the organization is typically robust and able to survive or self-repair after substantial perturbation.

The history of the idea that the system's internal dynamics can lead to increasing its organization is long and rich. It possibly started with the early Atomists, such as Democritus and Lucretius, as both thought that an external intelligent agent, a demiurge, was unnecessary to create order in nature. Order, if given time and space, can emerge bottom-up by itself. Rene Descartes presented self-organization in the fifth part of his *Discourse on Method* and elaborated further in his unpublished *The World*. This historical development of the concept of self-organization provides a rich context for understanding its significance in various systems. (Descartes & Clarke, 1999). Immanuel Kant used the term in the *Critique of Judgment* to refer to human self-organization and free will. His philosophical perspective on self-organization adds a unique dimension to the concept, as it links it to free will (Kant & Bernard, 1951). The psychiatrist and engineer W. Ross Ashby introduced the term "self-organizing" to contemporary science in 1947 (Shannon et al., 1956). The cybernetician Heinz von Foerster took up the idea in 1960, organizing a conference on *The Principles of Self-Organization*, which led to a series of conferences on *Self-Organizing Systems* (Von Foerster, 2013). Norbert Wiener took up the idea in the second edition of his *Cybernetics* book (2019). Self-organization became commonplace in the recent scientific literature mainly thanks to Hermann Haken in physics as synergetics (Haken, 1983), Ilya Prigogine in chemistry as dissipative systems (Nicolis & Prigogine, 1977), Maturana and Varela in biology and sociology as autopoiesis (Maturana & Varela, 1980). Recently, the group led by Liane Gabora proposed an autocatalytic model of the therapeutic alliance based on autocatalytic networks following Stuart Kauffman's theory of self-organization (Ganesh & Gabora, 2022; Kauffman, 1993). There is a growing interest in the pre-subjective and undifferentiated phenomenal field from which the patient's and the therapist's experience co-emerges. The field is sometimes used as a metaphor (Baranger & Baranger, 2008; Langs, 1976), though it might have informational and network foundations (Orsucci, 2009; Orsucci et al., 2006). An explicit energy field has also been proposed (Friston, 2010). However, this definition leads mainly to a biosemiotic perspective as the thermodynamic implications are not yet compellingly evident (Park & Friston, 2013; Ramstead et al., 2020). General synchronization implies that when two free-information-minimizing agents, such as the therapist and the patient, are sensorily coupled, they share a phenomenal landscape. The uncertainty, dissonance, and information entropy levels depend on the fluctuations of synchronizations within their coupling fields. Therefore, their experiential possibilities are governed by a common relational field of free information gradients. The coupled therapist-patient organization tolerates transient states of increased entropy associated with unpredicted biosemiotic states, facilitating morphogenesis. Uncertainty and surprise might emerge, providing opportunities for new self-organizations and therapeutic change. These phase transitions are based on increasing informational entropy if surprise, dissonance, and disorganization can promote new consonant forms of internal and external self-organization. Recent work by Tschacher and Haken (2020) offers a compelling perspective on the core mechanism of psychotherapy based on the Fokker-Planck equation. Rooted within a systems science perspective, their main idea is that change in psychotherapy processes can be described in terms of two distinct dynamics. Therapeutic events are staged within a therapist-client relationship and become effectual by deterministic ('causation') and stochastic ('chance') forces. Deterministic processes might refer to defining the boundary conditions of the therapeutic system. Stochastic processes refer to a broader exploration of the field's states and possibilities. Thanks to stochastic dynamics, the therapeutic couple's conscious experience can escape being 'stuck' in a particular range of relational, perceptual, and affective experiences. Stochastic dynamics are related to the emergence of novelty, surprise, and playful humor (Tschacher & Haken, 2023).

Guided Self-Organization is situated within a similar framework (Gartner & Hu, 2021; Gershenson, 2020; Hamann et al., 2020). The regulation constrains a self-organizing process within a complex system by restricting local interactions between the system components rather than following a determinist control mechanism or a global design blueprint. The phenomenal and intentional field produced during communications, the linguistic play, would be affected by dysfunctionalities. Rupture and repair processes in this self-organizing system would be crucial to the fitness landscape of the developing therapy. Therefore, once the boundary conditions for linguistic play are in place, gradually, the self-organization will start unfolding. Boundary conditions are constraints or rules that define how a system interacts with its surroundings at its edges or boundaries. They provide essential information for solving boundary value problems in various domains. Understanding boundary conditions is crucial because they influence the system's response and behavior. As in the case of the starlings' murmuration and migration, self-organization ensures that new coordination patterns can occur combined with the boundary conditions, ensuring that safe navigation can be effectively achieved and the flock can find its route following the sky and geomagnetism. This is an effective combination of bottom-up and top-down forms of organization. Within this beneficial dynamic combination, we see the origins of an effective agency.

7.4 Maladaptive Self-organization

Self-organization is not always adaptive. Maladaptive self-organization plays a role in psychopathology. Complex systems have their own goals separate from our consciously set desires. An emergent structure of the Self may be appropriate for emotional survival within challenging boundary conditions at one point in life. However, it may lose effectiveness as we transition into new environments, becoming maladaptive. Lawrence

Heller's survival style is a prime example (Heller & Kammer, 2022). Adopting a survival style might help a child work through traumas and psychologically survive in a traumatic environment through deformation or fragmentation of the Self. However, these styles might interfere with functioning relationships as a child moves into other environments and adulthood. Siegel (2020) wrote that "self-regulation is fundamentally related to the modulation of emotion and self-organization." The goal of human biological complex systems, with feeling serving as the feedback loops, is often to emerge with properties that avoid discomforting emotions. We can do this in healthy and unhealthy ways. Often, the emergent properties represent themselves as defense mechanisms and coping skills.

Scott Kelso (2016) proposed that analysis and dynamical modeling of experiments on human infants suggest that the birth of agency is due to a eureka-like, pattern-forming phase transition in which the infant suddenly realizes it can make things happen in the world. The primary mechanism involves positive feedback: when the baby's initially spontaneous movements cause the world to change, their perceived consequences have a sudden and sustained amplifying effect on the baby's further actions. The baby discovers itself as a causal agent, which might give us insights into the PsycheSoma processes. Schrödinger wrote about the indisputable impression that the total of our experience and memory is unitary and distinct from any other person's (Schrödinger, 1959). We humans, for example, have no doubt that it is us, and us alone, who direct the motions of our bodies and foresee its effects. What is this '*I*'? (italics his) Schrödinger asks: Where do agency and directedness come from? How does the self as a causal agent come about? We proposed that self-organizing processes in living things must give rise to agency. The most fundamental kind of consciousness, the awareness of self, must spring from spontaneous self-organized activity. This experience lays the foundations of the self in eureka moments where conscious coordination seems definite (Piaget & Cook, 1952). These moments of vitality lay the foundations of being aware of oneself as a source of control, of doing something deliberately, as an inevitable consequence of active exchange with the environment (Stern, 2010; Kelso, 2016).

Complex systems play a significant role in relationships. Accordingly, a healthy relationship reorganizes around individual behaviors and emerges with new properties to integrate the differences. In unhealthy relationships, instead of reorganizing around the different properties, individuals bring to the relationship, try to extinguish differences and force the other to seamlessly fit into a preconceived notion of how they should act. The opposite of organization and cohesion is deformation or fragmentation. When events overwhelm our ability to cope, instead of organizing the experience by including it into current systems or adapting to it, the intense experience fragments standard organization.

Information flows continuously in both directions, from the body to the brain and the brain to the body, and social language plays a role. Similar loops exist within the brain's lower and higher structures, between the brain stem, limbic system, and cortex.

Complexity science-oriented therapy uses both top-down and bottom-up approaches. Top-down approaches emphasize adaptive cognitions and emotions as the primary focus and beneficial boundary conditions. Bottom-up approaches, on the other hand, focus on the body, the felt sense, and the instinctive responses as they are mediated through the brain stem toward higher levels of brain organization. Using both bottom-up and top-down orientations greatly expands therapeutic options. Complex systems-based therapies might be the way of working with the Mind and Life Force that facilitates the spontaneous movement in all of us toward connection and health. No matter how withdrawn and isolating we have become or how serious or cumulative the trauma we have experienced, on the deepest level, just as a plant spontaneously moves toward the sun, there is an impulse toward connection in each of us. Setting the boundary conditions and degrees of freedom for facilitating and containing self-organization is one of the crucial steps. It would be hasty to conclude that therapeutic techniques are unnecessary. Even at a minimal level, they help the therapeutic bipersonal field structure their work, and the setting rituals convey the focus of therapeutic goals, the feeling that something important is occurring, and the sacred space-time for play. The boundary conditions partially reduce the degrees of freedom and randomness of behaviors, balancing habit/structure and emerging new challenges. The patient can coach the therapist, subtly and unconsciously, to implement practices and scenarios facilitating recovery. One can interpret psychotherapy as professional coaching if self-directed change. Therapy manuals and handbooks do not work if rigidly implemented. They can be used as toolboxes where the most valuable tools can be picked up at need. Some therapeutic tools might be temporary scaffolds as seeds for triggering self-organization processes. Alliance, ruptures, and repairs are the necessary framework and attachment experience. From a dynamical systems perspective, they are part of transient chimeras of coupling and decoupling.

7.5 Repairing Biosemiotic Coordination

We examined how constantly we engage in multiple-level conversations. Our linguistic plays follow parallel verbal, emotional, and motor scripts. They regularly end up in micro or macro moments of miscommunication, hesitations, and disfluencies that conversation analysis explored (Albert & De Ruiter, 2018). We considered these dynamics from the point of view of complexity science in mapping synchronization dynamics and chimera states (Orsucci, 2021). If we look at how people talk in everyday life, it is surprising how much our communications require constant maintenance. Micro-rupture and repair procedures happen in every conversation and can affect all three main channels of communication, dealing with problems of speaking, hearing, and understanding as they emerge. The way everyday repair works is systematically organized and partially implicit. If there is an issue with understanding, it might be pointed out by the receiver and fixed by the speaker, while at times, it might be the opposite. Each of these types of repairs is organized differently. Self-initiated repairs might be based on restarting their talk by deleting, changing, adding, and rephrasing. Self-initiated other-repair is when the speaker identifies the problem and implicitly or explicitly asks the other for repair solutions. One of the most frequent ones is forgetting names. Other initiated self-repair is when the receiver notices a problem in the speaker's talk, including hearing and understanding issues. The last and least common is when the receiver notices a problem in the conversation and decides to fix it with a correction, clarification, or explanation. These verbal dynamics are more implicitly developed in the emotional and motor domains. This is well represented in the arts, such as drama and dance. Sometimes, misunderstandings or disagreements pass through conversations as forms of dissonance, additional entropy, and noise. The study of repair can provide an interface for cross-disciplinary research on communication between conversation analysis and other approaches to the study of human interaction. As we can see, all the repair interventions address the communication field. The therapeutic alliance is a great way to conceptualize this field in a therapeutic setting. Rupture and repair processes in therapy can magnify everyday conversational dynamics. The therapeutic process is a big game of rupture and repair, gradually progressing toward mainstream conversational dynamics. In this perspective, psychological or psychiatric symptoms represent disorders in communication. It might be helpful to consider that the miscommunication might be intra-subjective and inter-subjective.

In this direction, the later Wittgenstein works can guide us again towards healthy self-organization in linguistic play (Fischer, 2008). The problems he addresses result from misinterpretation and are driven by 'urges to misunderstand.' Such urges give rise to errors, misunderstandings, and failed repairs that aggravate the problems. Therapy, in this way, is re-establishing the harmonic simplicity of common sense. This consonance of senses and communications is "an experience supported by all the senses" (Bion & Bion, 1992). This involves tolerating the experience of going through disquiet of disharmony and using the dissonances for creative change. We might treat ourselves first from the urge to jump to premature conclusions that might disrupt harmonic self-organization. Premature conclusions might include determinist interventions in different therapeutic techniques: systemic paradoxes, cognitive restructuring or perturbations, analytic constructions, or interpretations. Other therapeutic interventions might be considered scaffolding, which needs to be removed at some stage for a healthy therapeutic return to common sense. Otherwise, the risks are exemplified by a relevant case of a well-known psychoanalyst. At the end of the treatment, the psychotic ideas of this patient were replaced by new delusions that included some of his psychoanalyst's interpretations. The scaffolding can become the new façade of a false self. Some common distortions of the repair processes can lead to psychopathology: attention biases and overvalued metaphorical or analogical thinking. Fischer (2008) defines this attitude as a "mentalist urge" to rush, ending cognitive dissonance (free energy) that might create disquiet, emotional tension, and free-floating arousal. These conditions equate with disrupted hybrid biosemiotic networks. Ill-motivated and ill-constructed attempts at reconciliation create disharmony and disorders. Proper therapeutic attitudes would re-establish and facilitate the pre-conditions and boundaries for linguistic play. This pathway would pave the way for a gradual dissolution superseding of the therapeutic approach.

7.6 A Musical Interlude

The biosemiotic and pragmatic information dynamics we examined could also be considered from the perspective of dissonance and consonance. Leon Festinger first proposed the theory of cognitive dissonance, centered on how people try to reach internal consistency. He suggested that people must ensure that their beliefs and behaviors are consistent. Inconsistent or conflicting beliefs lead to disharmony, which people strive to avoid (Morvan & O'Connor, 2017). Consonance, dissonance, and resonance are terms often used in music and acoustics, and they relate to how sounds interact with each other and the listener.

Consonance refers to a combination of notes that are in harmony and pleasing to the ear when played together. These combinations are perceived as stable and restful and do not require further resolution. For example, intervals like the perfect fifth or the octave are considered consonant. Dissonance, on the other hand, is the opposite of consonance. It involves combinations of harsh, tense, or unstable notes. This tension usually creates a musical expectation that the dissonance will resolve to a consonance. Dissonant intervals include the minor second or the tritone. Resonance is different as it is a physical phenomenon where an object vibrates at a particular frequency and can amplify sound waves at that same frequency. In a musical context, resonance can enhance the sound of an instrument or a voice. It is not about the harmony or tension between notes but the amplification and enrichment of sound. The similarity between these concepts is that they all deal with the perception and quality of sound. They are fundamental to the experience of music and sound, influencing the listener's emotional and psychological impact.

The difference lies in their function and effect: Consonance creates a sense of relaxation and satisfaction. Dissonance introduces tension and the need for resolution. Resonance enhances and sustains sound, affecting its loudness and timbre. In summary, while consonance and dissonance are about the relationship between pitches, resonance is about sound amplification. All three play crucial roles in shaping music's character and emotional expression (Morvan & O'Connor, 2017).

Composers use dissonance in their compositions as a powerful tool to create emotional depth, tension, and movement within a piece of music. Here is how they typically employ dissonance:

- *Creating Tension.* Dissonance introduces a sense of tension or instability that listeners instinctively want to be resolved. This tension can evoke emotions such as suspense, unease, or excitement.
- *Emotional Expression.* Different types of dissonance can express different emotions. For example, a composer might use a sharp, biting dissonance to convey anger or fear or a more subtle dissonance to suggest sadness or nostalgia.
- *Movement and Direction.* By resolving dissonant chords to consonant ones, composers create a sense of forward motion in the music. This resolution from tension to release can give the music a narrative quality, almost like telling a story through sound.
- *Contrast and Interest.* Dissonance can make a piece more interesting and dynamic. Just as a painter uses contrasting colors to make certain elements stand out, composers use dissonant sounds to highlight musical ideas or themes.
- *Structural Function.* In some musical forms, dissonance marks critical structural points, such as the climax of a piece or the transition between different sections.
- *Stylistic Characteristics.* Specific genres or styles of music, like jazz or modern classical music, often use dissonance as a defining feature to create a unique sound palette.

In essence, dissonance is about creating an effect that enhances the musical experience, whether it stirs emotions, provides contrast, or propels the music forward. Composers balance dissonance and consonance to shape the listener's journey through the piece (Morvan & O'Connor, 2017).

Many composers have used dissonance to add tension and color to their compositions. For example, Wolfgang Amadeus Mozart's "String Quartet No. 19 in C Major, K. 465" is nicknamed the *Dissonance Quartet* because of its unconventional and tense opening. It is one of the most famous examples where the dissonance is resolved into a more harmonious Allegro section. Ludwig van Beethoven's *Grosse Fuge, Op. 133* is another notable work that employs dissonance. This piece is known for its complex and dissonant counterpoint, which was quite ahead of its time. Igor Stravinsky's *The Rite of Spring* extensively uses dissonance to evoke primitive and ritualistic feelings. Its premiere famously caused a riot due to its avant-garde nature. Arnold Schoenberg's *Pierrot Lunaire, Op. 21* uses atonality and dissonance to create an eerie and expressionistic atmosphere. Béla Bartók's *String Quartet No. 4* is celebrated for using dissonance and folk influences, creating a unique and modern sound. These compositions showcase how dissonance can be a powerful expressive tool in music. They can convey various emotions and add depth to the musical narrative.

Jazz music is well known for its exciting dynamics between consonance and dissonance. In jazz and blues, a *blue note* is a note that, for expressive purposes, is sung or played at a slightly different pitch than standard. The alteration is typically between a quartertone and a semitone, but this can vary depending on the musical context. Blue notes are often used to add emotional expressiveness to a piece and are a defining characteristic of the blues genre. They are usually said to be the lowered third, lowered fifth, and lowered seventh scale degrees. For example, in the key of C major, the blue notes would be Eb (lowered third), Gb (lowered fifth), and Bb (lowered seventh). Blue notes give the music a slightly 'bent' or 'slurred' quality, which can evoke feelings of melancholy, soulfulness, or a deep emotional yearning. This microtonal bending of pitches is essential for many auditory activities, such as understanding speech and perceiving tonal music, as it derives directly from the harmonic series. Blue notes are a crucial element of jazz. They allow musicians to express a range of emotions and add depth to their music. They contribute to the distinctive sound of jazz and blues, making them stand out from other musical genres. Dissonance plays a significant role in jazz music, contributing to its distinctive sound and expressive depth (Morvan & O'Connor, 2017).

As jazz evolved, harmonies became more intricate. Jazz musicians often use minor and major 7th and extended and altered chords, introducing dissonance *for harmonic complexity*. Dissonance creates tension that can be resolved to consonance, providing a sense of release. This *tension-release cycle* is a critical element in jazz improvisation and composition.

Jazz musicians use dissonance to convey various *emotions*, from bluesy melancholy to exuberant joy. This allows for a more nuanced and personal expression in performance. Dissonance has been used to push the boundaries of traditional harmony, leading to the development of new jazz styles, such as bebop, characterized by fast tempos and complex chord progressions with dissonant harmonies. Dissonant chords are often used in syncopation with the rhythm, adding an element of *surprise* and keeping the listener engaged. In essence, dissonance in jazz serves as a tool for musicians to explore new harmonic landscapes, express emotions more vividly, and create a signature sound that distinguishes jazz from other musical genres. Dissonance has been a critical feature in many classic jazz songs, adding complexity and emotional depth to the music. Here are some classic jazz pieces that make use of dissonance:

- *Mood Indigo* by Duke Ellington is known for its lush harmonies and subtle use of dissonance, creating a melancholic and introspective mood.
- *Round Midnight* by Thelonious Monk, dissonance and unconventional harmonies are a hallmark of this iconic jazz standard.
- *Giant Steps* by John Coltrane presents rapid chord changes and intervallic leaps in this composition, creating masterfully resolved dissonant tensions.
- *Bitches Brew* by Miles Davis is a groundbreaking album featuring dissonant harmonies that helped define the jazz fusion genre.

These songs are just a few examples of how jazz musicians have creatively used dissonance to enrich their compositions and create a unique sound that has become synonymous with the genre. Play in human change and music have many features in common. Style and some coordinates define the place and time for playing. Playing has always provided opportunities for creation and improvisation. Music originated as improvisation and is still extensively improvised in the West and the East. Many great classical composers, such as Bach, Mozart, Beethoven, and Chopin, were celebrated performers. The amount of improvisation and creativity in Western classical music has been gradually reduced, while individual creativity is partially relegated to personal interpretation. In jazz, the role of improvisation and creativity is still quite relevant. The history of jazz has been defined by great improvisers such as Charlie Parker, John Coltrane, and Miles Davis. Similar relevance can be seen in classical Indian ragas, such as Ravi Shankar, Hariprashad Chaurasia, and Zakir Hussain. The role of dissonances, consonances, and resonances tend to be relevant in the improvised parts. In psychotherapy, as a form of human change practice, we can notice the relevance of the balance between the framework of a setting, codified and manualized components, and creative improvisation is equally essential. It is also relevant to consider how the manualized component tends to be more pedagogical and predictable, while the creative component is usually more personalized and unpredictable.

In music, dissonance evokes tension, suspense, horror, or sadness. It is an essential tool for composers looking to create a truly memorable musical experience. However, the optimal frequency of dissonance in music can vary greatly depending on the context and the desired effect (Morvan & O'Connor, 2017).

The dissonant intervals are the minor second, the major second, the minor seventh, the major seventh, and particularly the tritone, which is the interval between the perfect fourth and perfect fifth. These intervals are all considered to be somewhat unpleasant or tension-producing. In tonal music, chords containing dissonances are considered "unstable"; when we hear them, we expect them to move on to a more stable chord.

However, as defined by the *Wundt Curve*, there must be a balance between predictability and complexity. Both extremes are not preferred. The sweet spot between the two is usually governed by an inverted U-shaped curve that peaks in the middle. The peak position may vary based on individual perceptions, but the pattern remains consistent for most listeners. In summary, the optimal frequency of dissonance in music is not a fixed value but rather a balance that depends on the context, the composer's intentions, and the listener's perceptions (Klempe, 2022; Kraus, 2020).

7.7 Biosemiotic Orchestration

The sheer complexity of internal and interpersonal alignment, synchronization, and communication dynamics makes it like listening to and studying a musical symphony. Even part of the terminology used comes from the musical dictionary. Therefore, a better understanding of these highly complex dynamics can be facilitated if we look further at the orchestration (Kennan & Grantham, 2024). Orchestrating a piece of music involves arranging and assigning musical ideas to different instruments within an ensemble. Some relevant factors are involved in orchestrating a melody with harmony and rhythm. For example, we might consider the famous orchestration examples from Mozart's diaries, now freely available in his handwritten musical score on the British Library website. The score contains all the parts for the singers, the leading instruments, the accompaniment parts, and melodies for the orchestra. As we can see, some instruments synchronize, not playing in unison but in a distributed harmony. Other instruments do not synchronize and wait for their turn to enter the musical flow. Human hybrid synchronization impressively resembles this orchestration with multiple chimera states, ruptures, and repairs. In complex human synchronization networks, we alternate, like in musical orchestration, complex scripts of couplings and de-couplings between different physiological, motor, and semiotic streams. Full synchronization in music, just as in life, would be tedious or overwhelming. An excess of decoupling and de-synchronization would result in noise, disturbing dissonances, or just silence (with its musical and life forms). Some dissonances and manageable ruptures could make listening (and life) more attractive, possibly pleasant, and resilient. Therefore, musical orchestration might alternate synchronically and diachronically, coupling and decoupling rhythms, pitches, and volumes.

In a series of studies on rodents and primates, Myron Hofer and other developmental biologists demonstrated many hidden regulatory mechanisms (Hofer, 1984; Hofer, 1994b). These hidden multiple pre- and intra-emotional factors act on different sensorial channels: nutritional, olfactory, tactile, thermal, visual, and vestibular. For example, the importance of bodily contact and tactile stimulation was demonstrated by the finding that a decrease in the growth hormone levels in separated rat pups can be prevented by stroking their skins with a brush. Also, a 30% reduction in heart rate following separation could be prevented by providing the pups with a feeding. The body temperature of infant rats, primarily determined by the mother's body temperature, has been shown to regulate levels of brain peptides, nucleic acids, and neuro-amines. All of them are reduced if the young rats are prematurely separated from their mother. Olfactory stimuli are also involved in regulating crucial aspects. For example, infant rats are unable to locate the nipple in the absence of a pheromone secreted from the mother's areolar glands, whose secretion is stimulated by the suckling (interesting learning recurrence).

There is evidence of a multiplicity of regulatory mechanisms. Most remain hidden from a passive third observer outside the "nursing couple" and can only be discovered in experimental contexts. They continue in adulthood, and their functioning is intermingled with other emotional, cognitive, and social factors. They play an essential role in growth and health. Margaret Mahler's (1968; 1975) works on the vicissitudes of human symbiosis and the contributions of Bowlby, Winnicott, Searles, Gaddini, and Kohut can provide a general framework for these findings. The interactions between the self and its self-objects (also known as transitional objects or sensation objects) regulate the psychosomatic balance. Various interpersonal relationships and social demands can trigger synchronizations and de-synchronizations of biological rhythms in individuals and groups. Everyday life evidence of one of these hidden psychobiological mechanisms is related to the well-known synchronization of menstrual cycles of women living in the same environment as, for example, roommates in a college. Streams of biosemiotic entities form the musical interactions in our everyday lives, with their rhythms, pitch, resonance, dissonance, and harmony, and we are unaware of most of them. They act on our minds and bodies. They form a matrix that probably starts from our pre-birth fetal life and forms a biosemiotic universe. It is a natural symphony with its multidimensional script.

Because we know that synchronization is associated with positive relational traits (e.g., empathy; Marci et al., 2007), it is frequently assumed that the more synchronization, the better. Various findings point toward a more sophisticated scenario. For instance, research on couples and mother-infant dyads reports that a balance between moments of rupture and synchronization is optimal (Jaffe et al., 2001; Timmons et al., 2015; Beebe et al., 2015). This is consistent with the qualitative analysis reported in our running examples. While we observed clear descriptions of the patients' experience and expression of their feelings associated with heightened synchronization, we also saw that these moments were often preceded (and even prepared) by passages of lower synchronization, where the patient provided background information to ensure mutual understanding. Changes in topic and expression of disagreement from the patient and the therapist seemed similarly associated with lower physiological synchronization in the analyzed session. We assume that providing context, introducing new topics, and even dissenting from the therapist's interpretations are crucial aspects of a collaborative relationship (Safran & Muran, 2000). A coregulation where the dyad can flexibly enter and exit synchronous states by adapting and negotiating to the partner's various lags and speed, such as in the data we observed, may be beneficial and even necessary to form clinical relationships that genuinely support change. Following our musical interludes, the metaphors of a musical script for multiple instruments might be even more appropriate. As we have seen, the components and dimensions of synchronizing sources are multiple and hybrid. In multiple chimeric configurations, they synchronize, desynchronize, or stay silent depending on context and occasion. The way they might modulate creates dynamic patterns of harmony and dissonance. Stochastic resonance is a technique of purposefully adding noise to the global system to foster synchronization between weak attractors. However, it comes with a risk of inducing uncontrolled turbulences beyond a certain threshold. Coupling, in any case, increases the degrees of freedom of the resulting system. Besides any specific control, this is very useful for curing any dynamical disease in the system. Fractal intermittency has been observed on the threshold of weak synchronizations, while strong synchronizations generate smoother landscapes (Pikovsky et al., 2001). Kauffman (Kauffman, 1993; Palombo, 1999) suggested that no general law is likely to govern all possible non-equilibrium systems; the central aim is to define the general conditions that allow evolution and co-evolution to assemble complex systems. Not all complex systems can be assembled by an evolutionary process. The general character of fitness landscapes of co-evolutionary processes is where the adaptive moves of one agent deform the fitness landscapes of its partners and tries to show that an endogenous co-evolutionary process allows agents, each adapting for its selfish fitness, to tune the couplings and ruggedness of their fitness landscapes such that the entire system achieves a specific self-organized critical state. The frequency, amplitude, and type of conversation ruptures and repairs can significantly influence a conversation's biosemiotic harmony and effectiveness. Recognizing and addressing all the biosemiotic factors involved can improve all language plays.

7.8 The Mozart Orchestrations

On April 23, 1764, eight-year-old Wolfgang Amadeus Mozart arrived in London with his father Leopold, mother Anna Maria, and sister Maria Anna (aka Nannerl). The visit formed part of an ambitious European tour in which the Mozart children were presented as musical prodigies in public concerts and to private patrons. Their visit to London, which would last for 15 months, has special significance for the British Library since Mozart may be counted as the first in an illustrious line of composers to have presented manuscripts to the Library. This event occurred during the family's visit to the British Museum in July 1765. On that occasion, Mozart deposited a copy of his first composition (and the only one in English text) and copies of two sets of keyboard sonatas published the previous year in Paris. The most spectacular single acquisition came in 1986, with the donation by Stefan Zweig's heirs of his collection of musical and literary autographs, which contained, among other treasures, 12 Mozart manuscripts, including some of his orchestrations. Most notable among these is the thematic catalog that Mozart maintained from 1784 till his death in 1791, in which he noted, among other details, the date, title, and first few bars of music for each work.

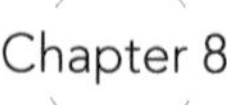

Nostos

We shall not cease from exploration
And the end of all our exploring
Will be to arrive where we started
And know the place for the first time.

Thomas S. Eliot

8.1 Nostos

Nostos is a theme in Ancient Greek literature and revolves around an epic return home. In this case, we are the heroes as we have explored human change's complexities. One of the most famous portrayals of nostos appears in Homer's *The Odyssey*. The protagonist, Odysseus, contests various challenges on his way home after the Trojan War. His encounters with the Sirens and the Lotus-eaters test his determination. Giving in to these temptations would have meant certain death and failure to return home. Interestingly, James Joyce weaves the theme of nostos into his novel *Ulysses*. The novel's final part, during which Leopold Bloom returns home, is named Nostos. In this section, Bloom's experiences mirror Odysseus' trials, albeit within a single day in Dublin. Joyce's portrayal of ordinary life, complete with frustrations, joys, and small triumphs, aligns with a modern essence of nostos. Notably, Bloom's relationship with his wife, Molly Bloom, diverges from the faithful Penelope of the original Odyssey. In T. S. Eliot, quoted in this chapter's exergo, the theme of nostos resonates around identity and time. The *Four Quartets* present stages of the poet's journey. In the first quartet, *Burnt Norton* presents the person, the poet, meditating on the concrete present of actualities and unchosen possibilities, that is, on existence in the flow of time. The second quartet, *East Coker*, broadens the poet's meditation on existence by introducing its temporal layers of family and cultural heritage, social and technological change, and the depths of history. The third, *Dry Salvages*, is the nature poem that deepens the existential meditation further, shifting the focus from the historical community to the individual's consciousness of both the world of nature as the human habitat and of the pervasive immediacy of death, as well as of a universe of nature and history. Finally, in *Little Gidding*, world, history, and cultural heritage are all presented as transfigured through the intense consciousness and meditation on human existence as the intersection of eternity with time comes nostos. The *Four Quartets* is a meditation on the human destinies of permanence through the impermanence of constant changes. It is a magnum opus of reflections on the systems we are made of and share.

Nostos continues to resonate in literature, bridging ancient and modern narratives and inviting the exploration of the complexities of homecoming and identity. We reconsidered human change from a complexity science perspective and returned home with a new, fresh, and different view. We can now realize that established views and practices can be dealt with in new ways and with the evidence of extraordinary scientific advancements, applications, and validations.

8.2 Core

We explored emotions' central role in overcoming Cartesian dualism on mind and body, *res cogitans*, and *res extensa*. They naturally bridge and unify, making the *PsycheSoma* an integrated system of systems composed of heterogeneous synergic dynamic elements. The Autonomic Nervous System activation is an example of the circular relationship between mind and body addressed by the embodiment perspective: mental arousal or relaxation has the consequence of bodily arousal or relaxation, whereas the reverse is also true, as the mind becomes alerted by sympathetic physiological activation or relaxed by parasympathetic activation. In analogy to the reciprocal relationship of physiological and mental activation, there is also an interchange between body movement and so-called body language. Emotional responses always integrate at least three systems: a) neurophysiological autonomic and endocrine systems, b) motor and expressive behavioral systems, and c) cognitive and experiential systems. Automatic and reflective processes are not mutually exclusive but frequently mix on a continuum. Emotional expression and recognition can involve a combination of both. Reflective processes may follow initial reflexive responses as individuals become aware of their emotions, consider their implications, and choose how to respond or interpret them. Similarly, reflective processes can inform and shape future reflexive responses through learning and socialization. Cultural, individual, and contextual factors can influence the balance between automatic and reflective emotional processes. For example, cultural norms and upbringing can impact how individuals express or suppress their emotions reflexively or engage in more reflective emotional regulation. Similarly, individuals with high emotional intelligence or those who have undergone emotional self-reflection may rely more on reflective processes for emotional expression and recognition.

The Self is a biosemiotic pattern of patterns emerging within a web of interactions. The process has biological origins but, in the human case, is strongly influenced by the world of cultural meaning, and this influence grows as selfhood. The human PsycheSoma seems predisposed to achieve selfhood. Our primary relations and community upbringing facilitate the establishment of a Self (Johnston & Malabou, 2013; Stern, 1985). Primitive feelings appear to lie at the core of our beings, and the neural mechanisms that generate such states may constitute an essential foundation for the evolution of other rational forms of consciousness.

At present, abundant evidence indicates that affective states arise from the intrinsic neurodynamics of primary self-centered emotional and motivational systems situated in subcortical regions of the brain. The roots of the Self go back to specific mesencephalic and diencephalic sensory-motor action circuits within the mammalian brain, which can generate a primitive sort of intentionality (action readiness) and primitive forms of psychic coherence (global affective states of the brain) by interacting with various emotional and attentional circuits that encode fundamental biological values (Panksepp, 1998a). The self-pattern is coherent, changing, invariant, flexible, and stable. The general parameters of a more significant part of the self-pattern remain intact, even if modified, with friends and strangers. These changes may lead to small changes in some other aspects of the self-pattern, but the overall arrangement and set of relations hold steady. Scott Kelso proposed that coordination is ubiquitous in all living things. It occurs by informational coupling among components and processes (Kelso, 2021). It can be specific (as when cells in the brain resonate with signals in the environment) or non-specific (as in generic brain arousal or when simple diffusion creates a source-sink dynamic for gene networks). This dynamical integration of patterns will include fast and slow synchronization dynamics. For example, regarding emotions and moods, there will be fast physiological reactions in movement, neuro mediators, breathing and heart rate, and slow reactions for neurotrophic factors, hormones, and attachment dynamics. Disorder-order transitions, multistability, order-order phase transitions, and especially metastability are shown prominently on multiple levels of description, suggesting fundamental coordination dynamics (synchronization) that operate on all scales. The complex dynamical systems theory of the Self attempts to capture the plurality of factors involved in it and their related dynamical structure. The multi-layered hypernetworks of the Self can be modeled and empirically validated in human change dynamics, narratives, artifacts, clinical settings, and psychopathology (Freeman, 2012; Lindahl & Arhem, 1994; Orsucci, 2009). Mapping the changes across different configurations should reveal a set of underlying dynamics that get disrupted or adjusted as one change impacts the whole pattern. Suppose the pattern is, in fact, a dynamical gestalt. In that case, we expect to find isolated symptoms affecting one aspect alone and readjustments (disruptions or compensatory adjustments) in other aspects (Gallagher & Daly, 2018).

8.3 Accord

Sharing and playing forms of life are joining common sense (Bion, 2014). The term "common sense" has a rich and varied philosophical pre-history, beginning with Aristotle and continuing with the Romans. Descartes and others then took it up in early modern Europe. Wittgenstein (Wittgenstein et al., 1969) uses the expression "healthy human understanding" as the German equivalent of the English term "common sense." The concept extends the semantics of "common sense" to what is understood in Bion's terms as "common to the senses" (Bion, 2014). That is the coordinated and consensual functioning of the senses and relations acquired at any stage of life and the common sense as trust shared in a community. Bion and Sullivan appear to concur on *consensus* as both internal embodiment integration and a sense of community sharing (Bion, 2014; Bromberg, 1980; Lincourt & Olczak, 1974). Limanowski and Blankenburg (2013) argue that the minimal and pre-reflective experiential elements of the bodily self, including the first-person perspective and the senses of agency and ownership, all of which depend on multisensory integration, including interoception, can be mapped onto a dynamical model of the Self. This process may constitute the foundations of higher-level, cognitive forms of self-narrative. Beyond minimal experiential aspects of the self, multisensory integration on the predictive processing model can also explicate connections to affective factors and solve problems of self-recognition, which may involve recognition of the self-as-object, for example, mirror self-recognition. The notion of a dynamical complex system of the Self is, in biophysical terms, parsimonious and accurate. The embodied system predicts and integrates exteroceptive and interoceptive multisensory variations probabilistically as we perceive, move, and experience. This cross-modal, self-correcting interoceptive, proprioceptive, efferent/afferent, and exteroceptive integration generates a self-model manifested phenomenologically in a body-centered spatial frame of reference. This suggests a dynamical integration between the embodied and experiential aspects of the self-pattern and the extended and normative elements, understanding the environment to be social/cultural as well as physical. Some dynamical configurations of the Self have been historically defined in psychopathology. Historically, there has been a slow evolution from deterministic paradigms challenged by the high complexity of this field and non-deterministic paradigms following fluid dynamics, the multiplicity of configurations, and personal differences.

The weaving, warp, and weft of the highly complex fabric of the Self can be damaged or deformed for different bio-psycho-social reasons. The psychopathology of human dynamics has identified forms and processes and defined dimensions and categories. Working on ruptures and repair develops through new couplings and new transient chimeras. Some new couplings can be biological or environmental, as considered in ecological psychology (Gibson, 1979).

Some can be new forms of activity and general care of the Self. Other forms can be specific forms of therapy, general or specifically designed to address the disrupted patterns of the Self. All these forms of care for the Self can be temporary scaffolding in a reconstruction, allowing the repairing practice to occur. Practicing rupture and repair exercises within the therapeutic context helps reestablish regular routines of internal and relational repairing habits. As an orthopedic structure and additional intellectual mind, this part of the therapeutic work might temporarily help the natural PsycheSoma to re-establish a good enough balance. Later, the scaffolding as an orthopedic cast might be removed.

8.4 Orience

Charles Sanders Peirce used the concept of *Orience* to address "the inexhaustibly lush and diverse aspect of reality" (Peirce & Fisch, 1982). In this, he resonated with John Dewey (Moore, 1961), who called Orience the sheer totality and unity of quality in everything experienced, whether it be an odor of freshly made bread at the bakery or the *madeleines* celebrated by Marcel Proust in his *Recherche* (Proust, 2006). In a colorful essay, Fernando Andacht enquires about "the habit-taking journey of the Self: between freewheeling orience and the inveterate habits of effete mind" (Andacht, 2016). The certainty of humans of always being themselves, always the same person, despite the overtly evolving nature of the Self. Intriguingly, what epitomizes the regular and predictable nature of habit and habit-taking centrally involves the incidence of the most volatile element in Peirce's theory, namely, Orience ("free originality"), spontaneity. Orience describes the emergence of change in identities construed in processes of habit-taking. How fundamental is the role of the imagination in shaping habits in his account? The operation of change in the realm of human identity is construed as habit-taking, a semiosis process that comes about through fleeting flashes of originality, the manifestations of what Peirce called *Orience*, namely, the genesis of meaning in "irresponsible, free originality" (Peirce & Fisch, 1982). Interestingly, in the development of what seems to be the epitome of regularity and predictability, namely habit, Peirce's account attaches a decisive weight to a wholly unpredictable element of play, wit, freewheeling spontaneity, thus positing a tension between the tendential habits and beliefs, as the closure of doubts, and the light imaginary flights that bring about slight or appreciable departures from rule-like behavior.

This is Peirce's unique contribution to solving an age-old paradox: the indispensable permanence inseparable from the unavoidable, constant change in human identity. At times, the Self sets off in the sheer qualities of Firstness as Orience, the coming into being, or the emergence of absolute "feeling," a notion distinct from the embodied physiological "emotion." We find a verbal novelty matching habit change and new beliefs; "considering some wonder in one of the Universes" (Peirce & Fisch, 1982). To construe the mind as "lively matter" (Hausman, 1993) entails thinking of it as consisting of patterns that are sufficiently organized to be efficient modes of conduct but also flexible enough to allow for spontaneity, for chance to come into the picture and bring about change, the adaptation to new circumstances, no matter how surprising they may be. "The soul may contain several personalities and is as complex as the brain itself, and that the faculties, while not exactly definable and not fixed, are as real as the different convolutions of the cortex," as he impressively wrote long before modern cognitive neuroscience (Peirce & Fisch, 1982). The lack of a fixed identity defined in absolute terms forever is essential for habit-taking to serve as an adaptation mechanism; the Ship of Theseus will be ready for you.

8.5 Descartes Redux

Most representational theories of mind imply some privacy of mental contents. This position is significant in philosophy, linguistics, psychology, and epistemology (Baker, 1998; Kripke, 1982). Wittgenstein's private language paradox is relevant because the possibility of a private language is a vague assumption of standard theories of knowledge and philosophy of mind from Plato to Descartes and most of the cognitive science of the late 20th century. Wittgenstein dedicated his investigations to "healing grammar diseases" and "infections" from conceptual confusion. Similarly, early Freud's attention went to all the anomalies that jut out of speech — puns, slips of the tongue, and narrative of dreams, regarded as rebuses or cryptic texts needing deciphering. Freud was not immune to rationalism as he notoriously wrote, "Where the Id was, there the Ego shall be," and added, "It is the work of culture — not unlike the draining of the Zuider Zee." (Freud, 1927). For Wittgenstein, language is not intrinsically misleading or deviant. On the contrary, Wittgenstein seems to find the cause of "linguistic disorders" in a metaphysical desire to "[run] its head up against the limits of language" (Wittgenstein, 1967).

Language develops in a coordinated flow of interactions, not in single gestures, sounds, words, or attitudes extracted from the communication streams. Inner and outer streams constantly merge or diverge. Language is a manner of living together in a flow of consensual behaviors (Maturana & Varela, 1980). Language evolves as a form of structural coupling in which living systems interact, engage, and affect each other. The concept of coupling between systems is present both in physics and biology. Coupling can facilitate the entrainment in synchronization (Pikovsky et al., 2001) and coevolution (Durham, 1992; Lumsden et al., 1981). In this perspective, following the pathways traced by Wittgenstein (1967), language can be considered a tool for cognition and social interaction. Language can produce the weaving of presentations between agents in distributed cognitive systems. Language is "a skillful, joint activity through which interlocutors attune to each other and the task at hand co-constructing a shared cognitive niche" (Fusaroli et al., 2014; Fusaroli & Tylén, 2016). A language is a form of joint action through multiple attunement/coupling dynamics of cognitive and motor processes (Tschacher & Bergomi, 2015).

The standard approaches to social cognition rarely emphasize intersubjective interaction, and even when they mention interaction, they frame the problem in terms of two minds communicating across a gap (Gallagher, 2001, 2013). In the theory of mind, inference about what is going on in others' minds bridges the grey area gap between minds. The theory of mind bridging inference is a simulation that will permit a form of mind-reading, also called "mentalizing." However, we do not usually take that detached observational stance in everyday social life with others. As agents and partners of the situation, we directly interact with our own verbal, motor, and emotional systems. Developmental studies prove this active process, which developmental psychologist Colwyn Trevarthen calls primary intersubjectivity (Trevarthen, 1998). By the end of the first year of life, the infant develops a non-mentalistic, perceptually based, embodied understanding of the intentions and dispositions of another person. These capabilities mature and become more sophisticated (see Dittrich et al., 1996), as shown in a micro-analysis of people's postures, movements, gestures, gazes, and facial expressions as they engage in a novel task. Communication among them is intrinsic to the actions that they take. This *primary intersubjectivity* is supplemented and enhanced by secondary intersubjectivity and cognitive scaffolding (Trevarthen, 2012). We start later to notice and critically reflect on how others interact with the world in expressions, intonations, gestures, and movements, and the bodies manifest in different contexts. As Gibson's (1979) theory of affordances suggests, we see things in our interactions and never as disembodied observers.

Dynamical system theory can be an excellent toolbox for understanding the synergy between symbolic and dynamic aspects of language (Elman, 1996; McWhinney, 1999; Orsucci, 2002; Rączaszek-Leonardi & Kelso, 2008). Human language evolved — through a series of intermediate stages of mimetic culture — due to pressure for increasingly sophisticated means of socio-cultural coordination and cooperation (Orsucci, 2008). The main features deriving from the dynamical system nature of language are: (1) higher balance of dynamical synchronization between interlocutors, increased stability, and complexity of collectively evolved symbolic patterns, (2) better coordination and, therefore, higher synergy performance in everyday tasks, and (3) emerging symbolic patterns of trans-subjective cultural repositories of collective knowledge. Semiotic patterns come to constitute communal cognitive niches structuring and coevolving with coordinative dynamics. Semiotics can be considered a tool for social and ecological harmonization. Synchronization in complex heterogeneous networks produces the emergence of semantic patterns from indexes, icons, and symbols (Orsucci et al., 2013; 2015; 2016). These studies of complex intersubjective dynamics are the evidence-based alternative to the idealism of monologue-based monadic rationalism — the same rationalism of the cognitivist approaches to language, such as Generative grammar.

8.6 Pattern Dynamics

Therapeutic interactions can offer a setting for in-depth studies as a magnifying lens on human couplings and transitions between different self-pattern configurations (Tschacher et al., 1998; Orsucci, 1998, 2002; Schiepek, 2003). There is a growing interest in the dyadic phenomenal field from which the patient's and the therapist's experience co-emerges. The field is sometimes used as a metaphor (Baranger & Baranger, 2008; Langs, 1976), though it has dynamical systems foundations (Orsucci et al., 2006; Orsucci, 2009). An explicit energy field has also been proposed as a free energy principle related to information entropy (Friston, 2010; Park & Friston, 2013; Ramstead et al., 2020). Recently, the group led by Liane Gabora proposed an autocatalytic model of dyadic collaboration based on autocatalytic networks following Stuart Kauffman's theory of self-organization (Ganesh & Gabora, 2022; Kauffman, 1993).

General synchronization in therapeutic interactions implies that when two free-information-minimizing agents share a phenomenal landscape, such as the therapist and the patient, they are in a biosemiotic coupling. The uncertainty, consonance, and information entropy levels depend on the fluctuations of synchronizations within their coupling fields. Pattern formation, transitions, and creative destruction and reconstruction form cycles of hybrid, multiscale, couplings, and de-couplings (Høgenhaug et al., 2024). These transitions test the systemic flexibility and resilience of the Self. Depending on its capacity to absorb systemic stressors and maintain pattern formation processes, the Self might be considered fragile, robust, or antifragile (Axenie et al., 2024; Kiefer & Pincus, 2023; Taleb, 2014).

Phase transitions between patterns release free information entropy until a new organization coalesces into new patterns. The coupled inter-subjective organization tolerates transient states of increased entropy associated with decoupling or pattern dissolution and transitions facilitating new morphogenesis. Uncertainty, dissonance, distress, or surprise might emerge, providing opportunities for new self-organizations and possible therapeutic changes. Recent work by Tschacher and Haken (2020) offers a compelling perspective based on the Fokker-Planck equation. The relationship is affected by deterministic (causation) and stochastic (chance) forces. Deterministic processes might refer to defining the boundary conditions of the therapeutic system. Stochastic processes refer to a broader exploration of states and possibilities in the bipersonal field state space. The therapeutic couple's experience can escape being trapped in a particular range of disharmonic relational, perceptual, and affective experiences thanks to stochastic dynamics. Stochastic dynamics are related to the emergence of uncertainty, dissonance, distress, novelty, surprise, and sometimes playful humor (Tschacher & Haken, 2023).

Guided and contained Self-Organization channels the self-organizing process by restricting local interactions between the system components. This contrasts with a direct determinist control mechanism or a top-down global design blueprint. Pattern formation, rupture, and repair processes in this self-organizing system are crucial to the fitness landscape of the developing relationship. Once the boundary conditions for biosemiotic play are in place, the self-organization will unfold. Boundary conditions are constraints or rules that define how a system interacts with its surroundings at its edges or boundaries. They provide essential information for solving boundary value problems in various domains. Understanding boundary conditions in a bipersonal setting is crucial because they influence the system's response and behavior. The fascinating experience of starlings' murmuration offers a clear example of contained self-organization. As in the case of the starlings' murmuration and migration, self-organization ensures that new coordination patterns can occur combined with the environment boundary conditions, ensuring that safe navigation can be effectively achieved and the flock can find its route following the sky reference points and geomagnetism. This is an effective combination of bottom-up and top-down forms of organization. Within this beneficial dynamic combination, we see the origins of an effective agency. Harmonic functioning in highly complex systems is based on coordinating intricate dynamics. The dynamical Self hyper-structure results from networks of synchronized oscillators coupled in fields spanning heterogeneous biosemiotic domains (Freeman, 2012; Orsucci, 2009). Order phase transitions, multistability, and metastability are evident on multiple levels, suggesting fundamental coordination dynamics operating on all scales. Patterns form and dissolve in the streams of the Self relations and are repaired or reformed similarly yet differently. It is a natural orchestration of manifold lines in the multiscale weaving tapestry of highly complex scripts.

8.7 Beyond Rationalism

In a deep and, at times, elusive paper, D. W. Winnicott outlined a post-rationalist foundation in which the mind does not exist as a separate entity but as a function of an integral PsycheSoma (Winnicott, 1954). He clarified that in the study of a developing individual, the mind is often found to be developing a false entity and a false localization. The psyche is not localized in the brain; the nervous system is distributed in the embodiment. Therefore, a separate mind function develops as a prosthetic overgrowth to deal with environmental challenges and control relational stressors. Mentalizing is part of these processes, which can be transitional or temporary. However, they sometimes crystallize in intellectual overgrowths not reintegrated into the PsycheSoma. Winnicott mentions one of his patients who managed to accept the reintegration of her ectomorphic mind systems through a deep mindful regression of physiological sensations: "For the first time, she was able to have a psyche, an entity of her own, a body that breathes and, in addition, the beginning of fantasy belonging to the breathing and other basic physiological functions." (Winnicott, 1954). The mind is frequently a false localization in the head, while the Self PsycheSoma is distributed in full embodiment. Winnicott noticed that impingements and challenges trigger the mind's prosthetic existence. Micro or macro traumas could strengthen the PsycheSoma, make it more robust, or even anti-fragile (Axenie et al., 2024; Taleb, 2014).

However, the impingements will continue as they are a natural part of life. Therefore, the process of formation of the mind "ectoplasm" and its reabsorption in the PsycheSoma can be a natural dialectic. It is when the mind becomes sclerotized as intellect that we start drifting towards forms of system pathologies.

The PsycheSoma is, in fact, a form of life, a set of implicit and tacit knowledge embedded in the natural existence of individuals and relations.

Wittgenstein explicitly identifies the similarities of aims and methods with Goethe's morphology when he defines his perspective on human forms of life in a consonant way (Kelley, 2007). This moment, coinciding with the introduction of the concept of *forms of life,* marks a turning point in Wittgenstein's trajectory, confirming the significance of this notion (Boncompagni, 2022). Why did Wittgenstein abandon "culture" in favor of "form of life"? Piero Sraffa and Alan Turing influenced Wittgenstein's focus on implicit human relational morphogenesis patterns. Regarding the first mention of *Lebensformen* in Wittgenstein's work, this notion replaced the concept of culture; it was meant to capture the embeddedness of language in the activities and practices of life, and it signaled anthropological attention to how language and logic are practiced in everyday contexts. Sraffa and Turing were most likely relevant for developing Wittgenstein's ideas on this subject, as language games or plays are activities embedded in patterns and forms of life. Agreements, coordination, and synchronizations in human relationships are not just epistemic trust in opinions but sharing life forms. Sharing forms of life is vital to playing in complex orchestrations. It is a creative expression of vitality (Stern, 2010).

8.8 Probabilities

As we have seen, human interactions are essentially based on the hybrid synchronization dynamics of embodied communications. They are also essentially intermittent and punctuated by discontinuities, ruptures, and repairs, from steps in conversations to meetings and emotional reactions. Time series are coarse-grained and discontinuous. Also, synchronization can vary from initial entrainments and chimera states to phase transitions into episodes of full merger synchronization (like plasma or Bose condensate) on specific domains. The continuity of time series in human dynamics should be reconsidered in favor of the quantum field approaches based on fundamental principles (Orsucci, 2020):

1. Granularity. An elementary structure of the world is emerging, generated by swarms of quantum events, where time and space do not exist independently. Quantum fields draw space, time, matter, and light, exchanging information between one event and another. Reality is a network of granular events; the dynamic that connects them is probabilistic; between one event and another, space, time, matter, and energy melt in clouds of probability (Munkhammar, 2011; Rovelli, 2005)

2. Relationality. The second cornerstone of quantum mechanics is the relational aspect of things. Things exist when they interact, producing events. They materialize in a place when they collide with something else. The quantum leaps constitute their way of existence as each particle is a combination of events from one interaction to another. Events exist only in interactions at all scale levels.

3. Indeterminacy. The theory also gives information on which value of the spectrum will manifest itself in the next interaction, but only in the form of probabilities. We do not know with certainty where the event will appear, but we can compute the probability that it will appear here or there. This is a radical change from Newton's theory, where it is possible, in principle, to predict the future with certainty. Quantum mechanics brings probability to the heart of the evolution of things. This indeterminacy is the third cornerstone of quantum mechanics.

4. Relational time. If what matters is not how things are but how they interact, space as an amorphous container of things disappears. Things (the quanta) do not inhabit space; they dwell one over the other, and space is the fabric of their neighboring relations. Similarly, as we abandon the idea of space as an inert container, we must abandon the idea of time as an inert flow along which reality unfurls. Just as the idea of the space continuum containing things disappears, so does the idea of a flowing continuum of 'time' during which phenomena happen. Time counts interactions and emerges from quantum fields (Lisi, 2006; Van Fraassen, 2010). We might follow Dirac's quantum mechanics, which allows us to do two things. The first is to calculate which values

a physical variable may assume. This is called the 'calculation of the spectrum of a variable'; it captures the granular nature of things (Khalkhali & Pagliaroli, 2022). When an object (atom, electromagnetic field, molecule, pendulum, stone, star, and so on with individual and social events) interacts with something else, the values computed are those that its variables can assume in the interaction (relationality). The second thing that Dirac's quantum mechanics allows us to do is to compute the probability that this or that value of a variable appears at the next interaction. This is called the 'calculation of an amplitude of transition.' Probability expresses the third feature of the theory: indeterminacy — the fact that it does not give unique predictions, only probabilistic ones. Following this approach, time becomes relational and purely based on interactions and their rhythms. Topological phase transitions are one of the consequences. Einstein (Przibram et al., 1967) had a unique capacity to imagine how the world might be constructed, to 'see' it in his mind. The equations, for him, came afterward; they were the language with which to make concrete his visions of reality. For Einstein, the theory of general relativity is not a collection of equations but a mental image of the world arduously translated into equations.

The idea behind the theory is that the best way to understand a universe at any scale is not to 'see it from the outside' but to describe what happens when moving within it. Gauss's method, developed by Hoffman & Osserman (1980) to describe curved surfaces and generalized by Riemann (Feigenbaum, 1994; Willmore, 1988) to describe the curvature of spaces in three or more dimensions, amounts to Brunetto Latini's way (Latini, 1839; Carmody, 1935). Brunetto Latini was an Italian philosopher, scholar, notary, politician, and statesman. He was a teacher and friend of Dante Alighieri. The idea is to describe what may be experienced within that space by somebody moving and always remaining within it. All the variables 'fluctuate' continually, as if everything constantly vibrates at a miniature scale. This might become a good start for our future journey.

Mozart wrote in his diaries, "The music is not only in the notes but in the silence between."

Modeling Human Dynamics

As a dynamic duo, synchronization and pattern formation are crucial in emerging new structures in the embodied Self. Modern research in synchronization and pattern formation can lay the ground for robust models of the embodied Self. Synchronization refers to the coordinated behavior of multiple individual components. Synchronization can also be a driver of pattern formation, as synchronized activity can lead to the emergence of new patterns. Pattern formation, the process of creating organized structures from initially disorganized systems, often acts as a foundation for further dynamics, with patterns usually providing further framework for synchronization. Neurons can fire synchronously, forming oscillatory patterns underlying cognitive functions like memory and perception. The connectivity patterns within neural networks influence new emerging patterns (Edelman, 1985, 1987, 1988). For example, the coordinated movement of cells during development can contribute to the formation of complex structures, such as the synchronization of neural networks. Understanding pattern formation and transformation in phase transitions is essential in various fields, including materials science, condensed matter physics, chemistry, ecology, biophysics, neuroscience, and biosemiotics. At the same time, patterns in individual subjects involve embodied complex multidimensional networks (Wu, 2007). Patterns in language are involved in scaling synchronization dynamics. A language's sounds are organized into patterns known as phonemes, expressed in morphemes. These patterns can be analyzed in terms of their features, such as voice, place, and manner of articulation. Morphemes form patterns of informational structures analyzed in information combinatorics (Orsucci et al., 2006). Syntactic patterns of word combinations to form sentences follow specific syntactic rules. These rules can be analyzed in terms of phrase structure, dependency relations, and grammatical categories. Words and sentences' meaning is determined by their semantic relationships, which can be interpreted in terms of semantic features, fields, and networks. The body's physiological processes, such as heart rate, breathing, and hormone levels, exhibit rhythmic or cyclical patterns, coupling and decoupling, sync and desync, alternating in different yet connected streams.

Kelso proposed that unified coordination dynamics could be seen as the partnership of well-known small- and large-scale synchronization models. The former is based on synergetics and nonlinear dynamics concepts, such as the extended Haken–Kelso–Bunz or HKB (Kelso, 2021), and the latter on the statistical mechanics in ensembles of many oscillators (Kuramoto, 1984b). Most research supporting the extended HKB model has involved coordinating two interacting components, whether two joints of a single limb or two persons interacting.

$$\Phi = \delta\omega - \alpha\sin\phi - 2b\sin2\phi$$

In contrast, Kuramoto captured the statistical mechanics features of large-scale coordination among many oscillators. Kuramoto's model, in the hands of mathematical biologists like Steven Strogatz (2004) and Art Winfree (2001), soon became a paradigm for large-scale coordination in complex living systems that ranged from the flashing of fireflies to heart cells and neurons to the concert audiences composed of human beings (Tschacher et al., 2024). This modeling and empirical work suggested that the integrated patterns sustain a dynamic structure of synchronization and coordination, multistability, and metastability

$$\frac{d\theta_i}{dt} = \omega_i + \frac{K}{N}\sum_{j=1}^{N}\sin(\theta_j - \theta_i),\ i=1....N,$$

The system comprises N limit-cycle oscillators with phase θ_i, and coupling K describes their coupling strength (how strongly they interact with each other). ω_i is the natural frequency of the i-th oscillators at time t. Over time, various extensions and generalizations of the original Kuramoto model have been developed to account for more complex dynamics, such as oscillators that may have different coupling strengths and other oscillators (non-uniform coupling), or those that have different intrinsic frequencies and coupling strengths (non-identical oscillators). The effects of noise or random fluctuations can also be included to model real-world phenomena more accurately.

Later, Kuramoto and Battogtokh (2002) observed that their previous model was based on ideal homogeneous forms of synchronization in large ensembles. In empirical research, we can frequently observe the coexistence of coherence and incoherence even in a network of identical, nonlocally coupled, complex Ginzburg–Landau oscillators. Coupled non-identical oscillators were already known to exhibit mixed complex behavior (frequency locking, phase synchronization, partial synchronization, and incoherence). Identical oscillators were supposed to either synchronize in phase or incoherently drift. They showed that oscillators that were identically coupled with similar natural frequencies could behave differently from one another for specific initial conditions. Some could synchronize, while others remained incoherent in a stable state.

$$\frac{\partial}{\partial t}\phi(x,t)=\omega(x)-\int G(x-x')\sin(\phi(x,t)-\phi(x',t)+\alpha)dx'$$

where $\omega(x) = \omega$ for all x. Note that if $G(x, x') = \exp(-|x - x'|)$, the kernel decays exponentially with the distance between x and x', defining stronger coupling for nearby oscillators.

Abrams and Strogatz (2004) named this mixed synchronization a *chimera state* from the mythological Greek creature made up of parts of different animals and introduced some theoretical clarifications for such behavior. Chimera states are everywhere; coupling, synchronization, and patterns come and go, with gaps in between. Chimera states were later found in limit-cycle oscillators, chaotic oscillators, chaotic maps, and neuronal systems. In the beginning, chimera patterns were observed in nonlocally coupled networks, but afterward, these states were also found in globally and locally (nearest neighbor) coupled networks and in modular networks. The usage of Markov chains for mapping couplings and chimera states was also explored. C. R. Laing studied chimera states in heterogeneous networks, analyzing the influence of heterogeneous coupling strengths. Of further interest for human dynamics is the emergence of chimera states in multiscale networks that result from coupling different networks (Laing, 2009), as usual in biosemiotic dynamics. The dynamic Self hyper-structure results from networks of synchronized oscillators coupled in fields spanning heterogeneous biosemiotic domains (Freeman, 2012; Orsucci, 2009). A simplified general mathematical model for heterogenous mixed chimera networks can be expressed as follows (Orsucci & Zimatore, 2025):

$$\frac{dx_i}{dt} = F_i(x_i) + \sum_j K_{ij} G_{ij}(x_j, x_i)$$

where:

x_i is the state vector of the i-th oscillator;

$F_i x_i$ is the intrinsic dynamics of the i-th oscillator, which can differ for different oscillators;

K_{ij} is the coupling strength between the i-th and j-th oscillators;

$G_{ij}(x_j, x_i)$ is the coupling function between the i-th and j-th oscillators, which can also differ for different oscillators.

This equation is a Coupled Differential Equation or Interaction-based Differential Equation. More specifically, it represents a generalized form of a Coupled Nonlinear Dynamical System. The general structure suggests a system where each component evolves due to its internal dynamics while simultaneously being influenced by interactions with other components in the system. The coupling allows interaction between multiple variables. Variables are interconnected and influence each other, though each variable has independent dynamics. The change rate depends on the variable's intrinsic behavior and interactions with different variables (Omel'chenko, 2018; Schöll, 2016).

The ubiquity of chimera mapping of synchronization and its different typologies extended its original definition to areas that might include human non-identical coupling oscillators in hybrid networks and multiscale networking of networks already known to present chimera-like dynamics before this definition started to be used (Orsucci, 2021). In essence, while hybrid chimera networks focus on the diversity of coupling within a single type of oscillator, heterogenous mixed-nodes chimera networks explore the complex interplay between oscillators of different types. The dynamical integration of patterns will include fast and slow synchronization dynamics. For example, there will be fast physiological reactions in emotions, movement, neuro mediators, breathing, and heart rate, and slow reactions in neurotrophic factors, hormones, and attachment dynamics. Speech and cognition might be fast, moderate, or slow, ideally placed in a mesoscopic dynamic area (Kahneman, 2011). Chimeras represent a unique class of complex dynamical systems characterized by coexisting coherent (synchronized) and incoherent (desynchronized) regions. This hybrid or mixed state bridges deterministic and stochastic behaviors, offering a rich landscape for understanding information processing and system dynamics. Combining multidisciplinary expertise in human dynamics is crucial to making meaningful progress in this new frontier of dynamical systems studies (Orsucci, 2021; Orsucci & Zimatore, 2025). The very nature of complex adaptive systems is that they must remain flexible and responsive to environmental changes over time. A system that becomes too rigidly optimized and reaches a very low entropy may become vulnerable to disruption or the "creative destruction" of its existing patterns. As a system approaches this critical state of low entropy and high coordination, it becomes increasingly rigid, fragile, and sensitive to external influences or internal fluctuations. These critical fluctuations can trigger a phase transition, in which the system abandons its current optimal patterns and undergoes a period of creative destruction, exploring new organizational possibilities (Krakovská et al., 2024; Scheffer et al., 2018; Speranza et al., 2014).

Complex systems often operate near a critical point or phase transition, where small perturbations can lead to large-scale reorganization of the system's structures and dynamics. When the system's current patterns become insufficient or inflexible, the free energy principle may drive it to explore new organizational possibilities, even temporarily increasing its entropy. This cycle of optimization, rigidity, and creative destruction can be seen as a fundamental feature of complex adaptive systems that strive to maintain their structural and functional integrity over time.

Chimera states demonstrate a unique form of resilience through their inherent structural flexibility. The coexistence of synchronized and desynchronized regions allows the system to maintain partial functionality, even when some components are disrupted. This partial synchronization acts as a dynamic buffer against complete system breakdown. The mixed synchronization pattern enables robust information transfer across different system components. Synchronized clusters can maintain coherent communication, while desynchronized regions provide adaptive pathways for alternative signal routing.

Unlike completely synchronized or random systems, chimera states occupy an intermediate complexity zone with dynamic flexibility. This intermediate state enhances resilience by allowing the localized stabilization of relevant system components. Due to their unique balance between determinism and stochasticity, chimera states result in distributed response mechanisms and graceful degradation under perturbation. The resilience of chimera states relies on their unique network architecture. Different coupling strengths, network connectivity patterns, and node characteristics significantly modulate the system's ability to maintain coherence under systemic stress.

Chimera states can dynamically reconfigure their synchronization patterns in response to external perturbations. This adaptive capacity allows the system to redistribute energy, information, or computational resources in real time. Chimeras exhibit a distinctive information transfer mechanism, where synchronized regions maintain coherent, predictable information flows, while desynchronized regions introduce probabilistic information pathways. This creates a multi-scale information processing architecture. The coexistence of ordered and disordered regions generates unique entropy characteristics. Synchronized clusters reduce local entropy, and desynchronized (decoupled) regions increase local entropy.

The result is a complex information landscape with mixed predictability. Synchronized regions follow predictable, rule-based interactions and demonstrate precise coupling mechanisms. Desynchronized regions introduce randomness, allow for adaptive, flexible system responses, and enable the exploration of alternative dynamical configurations. Synchronization-breaking mechanisms and parametric perturbations can produce pattern destruction processes. Noise introduction, coupling strength modifications, or topological network changes can trigger pattern destructions and creative transformations. This information entropy dynamics have interdisciplinary relevance in cognitive neuroscience, ecosystems, and biophysics. Related morphogenetic perspectives apply in patterns of embodied cognitive processes, structural coupling between organisms and environments, and information gradients driving developmental dynamics. Variability is more indicative of systemic health and flexibility than simple average.

References

Abrams, D. M., & Strogatz, S. H. (2004). Chimera states for coupled oscillators. *Physical Review Letters, 93*(17), 174102.

Adloff, F. (2016). *Gifts of Cooperation, Mauss, and Pragmatism*. Routledge.

Adolph, D., Tschacher, W., Niemeyer, H., & Michalak, J. (2021). Gait patterns and mood in everyday life: a comparison between depressed patients and non-depressed controls. *Cognitive Therapy and Research, 45*(6), 1128–1140.

Adornetti, I., & Ferretti, F. (2015). The pragmatic foundations of communication: an action-oriented model of the origin of language. *Theoria et Historia Scientiarum, 11*, 63–80.

Aftab, A., & Ryznar, E. (2021). Conceptual and historical evolution of psychiatric nosology. *International Review of Psychiatry, 33*(5), 486–499.

Ainsworth, M. (1990). Epilogue. In *Attachment in the Preschool Years* (pp. 463–488). Chicago University Press.

Ainsworth, M. D., Blehar, M. C., Waters, E., Wall, S., et al. (1978). *Patterns of Attachment: Assessed in the Strange Situation and at Home*. Erlbaum.

Albano, L.. (1987). *Il divano di Freud*. Pratiche Editrice.

Albert, S., & De Ruiter, J. P. (2018). Repair: the interface between interaction and cognition. *Topics in Cognitive Science, 10*(2), 279–313.

Alexander, R., Aragón, O. R., Bookwala, J., Cherbuin, N., Gatt, J. M., Kahrilas, I. J., Kästner, N., Lawrence, A., Lowe, L., & Morrison, R. G. (2021). The neuroscience of positive emotions and affect: Implications for cultivating happiness and wellbeing. *Neuroscience & Biobehavioral Reviews, 121*, 220–249.

Allport, G. (1998). *Personality: A Psychological Interpretation*. Holt.

Almkvist, G., Van Enckevort, C., Van Straten, D., & Zudilin, W. (2005). Tables of Calabi--Yau equations. *arXiv preprint math/0507430*.

Andacht, F. (2016). The Habit-Taking Journey of the Self: Between Freewheeling Orience and the Inveterate Habits of Effete Mind. In *Consensus on Peirce's Concept of Habit* (Vol. 31, pp. 341–359). Springer.

Anderson, D. J., & Adolphs, R. (2014). A framework for studying emotions across species. *Cell, 157*(1), 187–200.

Andreasen, N. C., & Grove, W. M. (1986). Thought, language, and communication in schizophrenia: diagnosis and prognosis. *Schizophrenia Bulletin, 12*(3), 348.

Apps, M. A., & Tsakiris, M. (2014). The free-energy self: A predictive coding account of self-recognition. *Neuroscience & Biobehavioral Reviews, 41,* 85–97.

Aragona, M. (2014). Epistemological reflections about the crisis of the DSM-5 and the revolutionary potential of the RDoC project. *Dialogues in Philosophy, Mental and Neuro Sciences, 7*(1), 11-20.

Arecchi, F. T., Farini, A., & Musso, P. (1997). Lexicon of complexity. *Epistemologia, 20*(1), 188–189.

Aristotle, & Bostock, D. (1994). *Aristotle Metaphysics.* Clarendon Press.

Aristotle, & Irwin, T. (1999). *Nicomachean Ethics 2nd ed.* Hackett Pub. Co.

Aristotle, & Telford, K. A. (1985). *Aristotle's Poetics: Translation and Analysis.* University Press of America.

Attar, F. al-Din, Davis, D., & Darbandi, A. (1984). *The Conference of the Birds.* Penguin Books.

Axenie, C., López-Corona, O., Makridis, M. A., Akbarzadeh, M., Saveriano, M., Stancu, A., & West, J. (2024). Antifragility in complex dynamical systems. *Npj Complexity, 1*(1), 12.

Baas, N. A. (1994). *Emergence, Hierarchies, and Hyperstructures.* Addison-Wesley.

Bacon, R. (1983). *The Cure of Old Age, and Preservation of Youth.* Tho. Flesher and Edward Evets.

Bak, P. (1996). *How Nature Works is the Science of Self-Organized Criticality.* Copernicus.

Bak, P., & Sneppen, K. (1993). Punctuated equilibrium and criticality in a simple model of evolution. *Physical Review Letters, 71*(24), 4083–4086.

Baker, G. (1998). The private language argument. *Language and Communication, 18*(4), 325–356.

Balbi, J. (1996). What is a person? Reflections on the domain of psychology from an ontological and post-rationalist perspective. *Journal of Constructivist Psychology, 9*(4), 249–261.

Balbi, J. (2015). Adolescence, order through fluctuations and psychopathology. A post-rationalist conception of mental disorders and their treatment on the grounds of chaos theory. *Chaos and Complexity Letters, 9*(2), 85.

Ban, T. A. (2013). Neuropsychopharmacology and the forgotten language of psychiatry. *Risskov: International Network for the History of Neuropsychopharmacology.*

Bansal, K., Garcia, J. O., Tompson, S. H., Verstynen, T., Vettel, J. M., & Muldoon, S. F. (2019). Cognitive chimera states in human brain networks. *Science Advances*, 5(4), eaau8535.

Barabasi, A. (2003). *Linked: The New Science of Networks.* Basic Books.

Baranger, M., & Baranger, W. (1985). La situation analytique comme champ dynamique. *Revue Française de Psychanalyse.*

Baranger, M., & Baranger, W. (2008). The analytic situation as a dynamic field. *The International Journal of Psychoanalysis*, 89(4), 795–826.

Barley, K., & Cherif, A. (2011). Stochastic nonlinear dynamics of interpersonal and romantic relationships. *Applied Mathematics and Computation*, 217(13), 6273–6281.

Barlow, M. (1986). The Voynich Manuscript-By Voynich? *Cryptologia*, 10(4), 210–216.

Barrett, F. S., Robins, R. W., & Janata, P. (2013). A brief form of the affective neuroscience personality scales. *Psychological Assessment*, 25(3), 826.

Bateson, G. (1979). *Mind and Nature: A Necessary Unity.* Dutton.

Bateson, G. (1987). *Steps to an Ecology of Mind: Collected Essays in Anthropology, Psychiatry, Evolution, and Epistemology.* Aronson.

Bausani, A. (1974). *Le lingue inventate: Linguaggi artificiali, linguaggi segreti, linguaggi universali.* Ubaldini.

Beebe, B., Jaffe, J., & Lachmann, F. M. (2015). A Dyadic Systems View of Communication. In *Relational Perspectives in Psychoanalysis* (pp. 61–81). Routledge.

Bekoff, M., & Byers, J. A. (1998). *Animal Play: Evolutionary, Comparative, and Ecological Perspectives.* Cambridge University Press.

Bernecker, S. L., Levy, K. N., & Ellison, W. D. (2014). A meta-analysis of the relation between patient adult attachment style and the working alliance. *Psychotherapy Research*, 24(1), 12–24.

Berridge, K. C., & Kringelbach, M. L. (2008). Affective neuroscience of pleasure: Reward in humans and animals. *Psychopharmacology*, 199(3), 457–480.

Berridge, K. C., & Kringelbach, M. L. (2013). Neuroscience of affect: Brain mechanisms of pleasure and displeasure. *Current Opinion in Neurobiology*, 23(3), 294–303.

Berridge, K. C., & Kringelbach, M. L. (2015). Pleasure systems in the brain. *Neuron*, 86(3), 646–664.

Berrios, G. E. (1999). Classifications in psychiatry: a conceptual history. *Australian & New Zealand Journal of Psychiatry*, 33(2), 145–160.

Berrios, G. E., & Hauser, R. (1988). The early development of Kraepelin's ideas on classification: A conceptual history. *Psychological Medicine, 18*(4), 813–821.

Bertolaso, M., Capolupo, A., Cherubini, C., Filippi, S., Gizzi, A., Loppini, A., & Vitiello, G. (2015). The role of coherence in emergent behavior of biological systems. *Electromagnetic Biology and Medicine, 34*(2), 138–140.

Bick, C., & Martens, E. A. (2015). Controlling chimeras. *New Journal of Physics, 17*(3), 033030.

Bick, C., Goodfellow, M., Laing, C. R., & Martens, E. A. (2020). Understanding the dynamics of biological and neural oscillator networks through exact mean-field reductions: A review. *The Journal of Mathematical Neuroscience, 10*(1), 1–43.

Bingman, V. P., & Able, K. P. (2002). Maps in birds: Representational mechanisms and neural bases. *Current Opinion in Neurobiology, 12*(6), 745–750.

Bion, W. R. (1983). *Transformations*. J. Aronson.

Bion, W. R. (2014). *The Complete Works of WR Bion*. Karnac Books.

Bion, W. R., & Bion, F. (1992). *Cogitations*. Karnac Books.

Biro, D., Sasaki, T., & Portugal, S. J. (2016). Bringing a time-depth perspective to collective animal behavior. *Trends in Ecology & Evolution, 31*(7), 550–562.

Bizzarri, M., Naimark, O., Nieto-Villar, J., Fedeli, V., & Giuliani, A. (2020). Complexity in biological organization: Deconstruction (and subsequent restating) of key concepts. *Entropy, 22*(8), 885.

Black, I. B. (1994). *Information in the Brain: A Molecular Perspective*. MIT Press.

Blackmore, S. J. (2000). *The Meme Machine*. Oxford University Press.

Boccaletti, S., Pecora, L., & Pelaez, A. (2001). Unifying framework for synchronization of coupled dynamical systems. *Physical Review E, 63*(6), 66–78.

Bolbecker, A. R., Hong, S. L., Kent, J. S., Klaunig, M. J., O'Donnell, B. F., & Hetrick, W. P. (2011). Postural control in bipolar disorder: Increased sway area and decreased dynamical complexity. *PloS One, 6*(5), e19824.

Bolden, G. B. (2013). Unpacking "self": repair and epistemics in conversation. *Social Psychology Quarterly, 76*(4), 314–342.

Boncompagni, A. (2022). *Wittgenstein on Forms of Life*. Cambridge University Press.

Borch-Jacobsen, M. (2021). *Freud's Patients: A Book of Lives*. Reaktion Books.

Borges, J. L. (1937). The analytical language of John Wilkins. *Other Inquisitions, 1952*, 101–105.

Borges, J. L. (1964). *Labyrinths: Selected Stories & Other Writings* (Augmented ed.). New Directions Pub. Corp.

Borges, J. L. (1968). *Other Inquisitions: 1937–1952*. Simon and Schuster.

Bowlby, J. (1978). Attachment theory and its therapeutic implications. *Adolescent Psychiatry, 6*, 5–33.

Bowlby, J. (1982). Attachment and loss: Retrospect and prospect. *American Journal of Orthopsychiatry, 52*(4), 664–678.

Brennan, K. A., & Shaver, P. R. (1995). Dimensions of adult attachment, affect regulation, and romantic relationship functioning. *Personality and Social Psychology Bulletin, 21*(3), 267–283.

Brentano, F. (2012). *Psychology from an Empirical Standpoint*. Routledge.

Breuer, J., & Freud, S. (1956). *Studies on Hysteria*. Hogarth Press.

Brier, S. (2015). Can biosemiotics be a "science" if its purpose is to be a bridge between the natural, social, and human sciences? *Progress in Biophysics and Molecular Biology, 119*(3), 576–587.

Britannica, E. (1993). *Encyclopædia Britannica*. University of Chicago.

Bromberg, P. M. (1980). Sullivan's concept of consensual validation and the therapeutic action of psychoanalysis. *Contemporary Psychoanalysis, 16*(2), 237–248.

Brumbaugh, R. S. (1975). The solution of the Voynich 'Roger Bacon' Cipher. *Yale Library Gazette, 49*, 347–355.

Brumbaugh, R. S. (1978). *The Most Mysterious Manuscript: The Voynich "Roger Bacon" Cipher Manuscript*. Southern Illinois University Press.

Bryant, F. (2003). Savoring Beliefs Inventory (SBI): A scale for measuring beliefs about savouring. *Journal of Mental Health, 12*(2), 175–196.

Burns, S., MacKeith, J., & Graham, K. (2008). Using the Outcomes Star: Impact and good practice. https://www.outcomesstar.org.uk/wp-content/uploads/Q_ Outcomes-Star-Impact-and-good-practice.pdf

Calabi, E. (1954). The space of Kähler metrics. In *Proceedings of the International Congress of Mathematicians* (Vol. 2, pp. 206–207). Amsterdam.

Canacott, L., Moghaddam, N., & Tickle, A. (2019). Is the Wellness Recovery Action Plan (WRAP) efficacious for improving personal and clinical recovery outcomes? A systematic review and meta-analysis. *Psychiatric Rehabilitation Journal, 42*(4), 372.

Cannon, W. B. (1987). The James-Lange theory of emotions: A critical examination and an alternative theory. *The American Journal of Psychology, 100*(3/4), 567–586.

Carmody, F. J. (1935). The revised version of Brunetto Latini's" Tresor". *Italica, 12*(2), 146.

Carroll, L. (1865). *Alice's Adventures in Wonderland*. Broadview Press 2011.

Carroll, T. L., & Pecora, L. M. (1993). Stochastic resonance and crises. *Physical Review Letters, 70*(5), 576–579.

Cavers, M., & Vasudevan, K. (2015). Spatio-temporal complex Markov Chain (SCMC) model using directed graphs: Earthquake sequencing. *Pure and Applied Geophysics, 172*(2), 225–241.

Cherif, A., Barley, K., Xiu-Lian, X., Chun-Hua, F., Ai-Fen, L., Da-Ren, H., Helbing, D., Johansson, A., Szabo, G., & Szolnoki, A. (2009). Stochastic nonlinear dynamics of interpersonal and romantic relationships. *ArXiv Preprint ArXiv:0911.0013*. http://my.arxiv.org/arxiv/FilterServlet/pdf/0911.0013

Chouzouris, T., Omelchenko, I., Zakharova, A., Hlinka, J., Jiruska, P., & Schöll, E. (2018). Chimera states in brain networks: Empirical neural vs. modular fractal connectivity. *Chaos: An Interdisciplinary Journal of Nonlinear Science, 28*(4), 045112.

Clark, A., & Chalmers, D. J. (1998). The extended mind. *Analysis, 58*(1), 7–19.

Cloninger, C. R. (1994). Temperament and personality. *Current Opinion in Neurobiology, 4*(2), 266–273.

Cohn, J. F., Kruez, T. S., Matthews, I., Yang, Y., Nguyen, M. H., Padilla, M. T., Zhou, F., & De la Torre, F. (2009). Detecting depression from facial actions and vocal prosody. *Affective Computing and Intelligent Interaction and Workshops*, 1–7.

Colapietro, V. M. (1988). *Peirce's Approach to the Self: A Semiotic Perspective on Human Subjectivity*. State University of New York Press.

Condray, R., Steinhauer, S. R., van Kammen, D. P., & Kasparek, A. (2002). The language system in schizophrenia: Effects of capacity and linguistic structure. *Schizophrenia Bulletin, 28*(3), 475.

Cornford, F. M. (1957). *From Religion to Philosophy: A Study of the Origins of Western Speculation*. Harper.

Cross, S. E., & Madson, L. (1997). Models of the self: Self-construals and gender. *Psychological Bulletin, 122*(1), 5.

Crow, T. J. (2000). Schizophrenia as the price that Homo sapiens pays for language: A resolution of the central paradox in the origin of the species. *Brain Research Reviews, 31*(2–3), 118–129.

Cuccio, V., & Gallese, V. (2018). A Peircean account of concepts: Grounding abstraction in phylogeny through a comparative neuroscientific perspective. *Philosophical Transactions of the Royal Society B: Biological Sciences, 373*(1752), 20170128.

D 'Imperio, M. E. (1978). *The Voynich Manuscript: An Elegant Enigma*. Aegean Park.

Daly, A., & Gallagher, S. (2019). Towards a phenomenology of self-patterns in psychopathological diagnosis and therapy. *Psychopathology, 52*(1), 33–49.

Damasio, A. R. (1998). Emotion in the perspective of an integrated nervous system. *Brain Research Reviews, 26*(2–3), 83–86.

Damasio, A. R. (2003). Mental self: The person within. *Nature, 423*(6937), 227.

Damasio, A. R. (2006). *Descartes' Error*. Random House.

Damasio, A., & Carvalho, G. B. (2013). The nature of feelings: Evolutionary and neurobiological origins. *Nature Reviews Neuroscience, 14*(2), 143–152.

Danesi, M. (2017). Visual rhetoric and semiotic. In *Oxford Research Encyclopaedia of Communication*. https://doi.org/10.1093/acrefore/9780190228613.013.43

Darwin, C. R. (1972). *The Expression of the Emotions in Man and Animals*. AMS Press.

Darwin, C. R. (1977). *The Collected Papers of Charles Darwin*. University of Chicago Press.

Davidson, R. J. (2001). Toward a biology of personality and emotion. *Annals of the New York Academy of Sciences, 935*(1), 191–207.

Davis, K. L., & Panksepp, J. (2018). *The Emotional Foundations of Personality: A Neurobiological and Evolutionary Approach*. W. W. Norton & Company.

Davis, K. L., Panksepp, J., & Normansell, L. (2003). The affective neuroscience personality scales: Normative data and implications. *Neuropsychoanalysis, 5*(1), 57–69.

Dawkins, R. (2006). *The Selfish Gene*. Oxford University Press.

Dehaene, S. (2011). *The Number Sense: How The Mind Creates Mathematics*. Oxford University Press.

DeLisi, L. E. (2001). Speech disorder in schizophrenia: Review of the literature and exploration of its relation to the uniquely human capacity for language. *Schizophrenia Bulletin, 27*(3), 481.

Dennett, D. C. (1991). *Consciousness Explained*. Little, Brown and Co.

Descartes, R. (2001). *Discourse on Method, Optics, Geometry, and Meteorology: Revised ed.* Hackett Pub.

Descartes, R., & Clarke, D. M. (1999). *Discourse on Method and Related Writings*. Penguin Books.

Diels, H. (1912). *Die fragmente der Vorsokratiker Griechisch und Deutsch*. Weidmannsche Buchhandlung.

Diener, E., Thapa, S., & Tay, L. (2020). Positive emotions at work. *Annual Review of Organizational Psychology and Organizational Behavior, 7*(1), 451–477.

Diener, M. J., & Monroe, J. M. (2011). The relationship between adult attachment style and therapeutic alliance in individual psychotherapy: A meta-analytic review. *Psychotherapy, 48*(3), 237.

Dittrich, W. H., Troscianko, T., Lea, S. E. G., & Morgan, D. (1996). Perception of emotion from dynamic point-light displays represented in dance. *Perception, 25*(6), 727–738.

Dixon, R. M. W. (1997). *The Rise and Fall of Languages.* Cambridge University Press.

Doidge, N. (2007). *The Brain That Changes Itself: Stories of Personal Triumph from the Frontiers of Brain Science.* Penguin.

Dube, J., & Despres, P. (2000). The control of dynamical systems — recovering order from chaos. In *The Physics of Electronic and Atomic Collisions.* American Institute of Physics.

Duncan, B. L., Miller, S. D., Wampold, B. E., & Hubble, M. A. (2010). *The Heart & Soul of Change: Delivering What Works in Therapy.* American Psychological Association.

Dupré, J. A., & Nicholson, D. J. (2018). A Manifesto for a Processual Philosophy of Biology. In *Everything Flows: Towards a Processual Philosophy of Biology* (pp. 3–46). Oxford University Press.

Durham, W. H. (1992). *Coevolution: Genes, Culture, and Human Diversity.* Stanford University Press.

Eckmann, J.-P., Kamphorst, S. O., & Ruelle, D. (1987). Recurrence plots of dynamical systems. *Europhysics Letters, 4*(9), 973.

Eco, U. (1976). *A Theory of Semiotics.* Indiana University Press.

Eco, U. (1989). *The Open Work.* Harvard University Press.

Edelman, G. M. (1985). Molecular determinants of animal form. Proceedings of the UCLA symposium held at Park City, Utah, March 30-April 4, 1985. A.R. Liss.

Edelman, G. M. (1987). *Neural Darwinism: The Theory of Neuronal Group Selection.* Basic Books.

Edelman, G. M. (1988). *Topobiology: An Introduction to Molecular Embryology.* Basic Books.

Eissler, K. R. (1953). The effect of the structure of the ego on psychoanalytic technique. *Journal of the American Psychoanalytic Association, 1*(1), 104–143.

Ekman, P. (1999). Basic emotions. *Handbook of Cognition and Emotion, 98*(45–60), 16.

Ekman, P. (2006). *Darwin and Facial Expression: A Century of Review Research.* Ishk.

Ekman, P. (2009). Darwin's contributions to our understanding of emotional expressions. *Philosophical Transactions of the Royal Society B: Biological Sciences, 364*(1535), 3449–3451.

Eliot, T. S. (2011). *The Complete Poems and Plays of TS Eliot.* Faber & Faber.

Elman, J. L. (1996). *Rethinking Innateness: A Connectionist Perspective on Development.* MIT Press.

Elowitz, M. B., Levine, A. J., Siggia, E. D., & Swain, P. S. (2002). Stochastic gene expression in a single cell. *Science, 297*(5584), 1183–1186.

Elsasser, W. M. (1987). *Reflections on a Theory of Organisms: Holism in Biology.*

Emmeche, C. (2003). Causal Processes, Semiosis, and Consciousness. In *Process Theories* (pp. 313–336). Springer.

Engstrom, E. J., & Kendler, K. S. (2015). Emil Kraepelin: icon and reality. *American Journal of Psychiatry, 172*(12), 1190–1196.

Etkin, A., Pittenger, C., Polan, H. J., & Kandel, E. R. (2005). Toward a neurobiology of psychotherapy: basic science and clinical applications. *Journal of Neuropsychiatry and Clinical Neurosciences, 17*(2), 145–158.

Fachinelli, E. (2001). Freud's clock. On time in psychoanalysis. *Journal of European Psychoanalysis, 12/13.*

Feigenbaum, M. J. (1994). Riemann Maps and World Maps. In *Trends and Perspectives in Applied Mathematics* (Vol. 100, pp. 55–71). Springer.

Feighner, J. P., Robins, E., Guze, S. B., Woodruff, R. A., Winokur, G., & Munoz, R. (1972). Diagnostic criteria for use in psychiatric research. *Archives of General Psychiatry, 26*(1), 57–63.

Feldman, J. A. (2006). *From Molecule to Metaphor: A Neural Theory of Language.* The MIT Press.

Feldman, L. B. (1995). *Morphological Aspects of Language Processing.* Lawrence Erlbaum.

Ferrari, H. (2006). Psychodynamic Diagnostic Manual, PDM. *Vertex (Buenos Aires, Argentina), 17*(69), 356–361.

Feynman, R. P. (1949). The theory of positrons. *Physical Review, 76*(6), 749–759.

Fido, D., Kotera, Y., & Asano, K. (2020). English translation and validation of the Ikigai-9 in a UK sample. *International Journal of Mental Health and Addiction, 18*(5), 1352–1359.

Fischer, E. (2008). Wittgenstein's 'non-cognitivism' — explained and vindicated. *Synthese, 162*(1), 53–84.

Fisher, A. J., & Newman, M. G. (2016). Reductions in the diurnal rigidity of anxiety predict treatment outcome in cognitive behavioral therapy for generalized anxiety disorder. *Behaviour Research and Therapy, 79*, 46–55.

Fónagy, I., & Fonagy, P. (1995). Communication with pretend actions in language, literature, and psychoanalysis. *Psychoanalysis and Contemporary Thought, 18*(3), 363–418.

Fonagy, P. (1999). Memory and therapeutic action. *International Journal of Psycho-Analysis, 80*(2), 215–223.

Fonagy, P. (2002). *Affect Regulation, Mentalization, and the Development of the Self.* Other Press.

Fonagy, P., & Luyten, P. (2009). A developmental, mentalization-based approach to the understanding and treatment of borderline personality disorder. *Development and Psychopathology, 21*(4), 1355–1381.

Fonagy, P., Campbell, C., & Luyten, P. (2023). Attachment, mentalizing and trauma: Then (1992) and now (2022). *Brain Sciences, 13*(3), 459.

Fonagy, P., Gergely, G., & Jurist, E. L. (2004). *Affect Regulation, Mentalization, and the Development of the Self.* Karnac Books.

Foucault, M. (1971). *The Order of Things: An Archaeology of the Human Sciences.* Pantheon Books.

Foucault, M. (1973). *Madness and Civilization: A History of Insanity in the Age of Reason.* Vintage Books.

Fowler, C., Richardson, M., Marsh, K., & Shockley, K. (2008). Language Use, Coordination, and the Emergence of Cooperative Action. In *Coordination: Neural, Behavioral and Social Dynamics* (pp. 261–279). Springer.

Franck, I. (1986). Psychology as a Science. In *The Individual Subject and Scientific Psychology* (pp. 17–36). Springer.

Frank, J. D., & Frank, J. B. (1993). *Persuasion and Healing: A Comparative Study of Psychotherapy.* JHU Press.

Fredrickson, B. L. (1998). What good are positive emotions? *Review of General Psychology, 2*(3), 300–319.

Freeman, W. (1975). *Mass Action in The Nervous System: Examination of the Neurophysiological Basis of Adaptive Behavior through the EEG.* Academic Press.

Freeman, W. J. (1995). *Societies of Brains: Study in the Neuroscience of Love and Hate.* Lawrence Erlbaum Associates.

Freeman, W. J. (1998). The neurobiology of multimodal sensory integration. *Integrative Psychological and Behavioral Science, 33*(2), 124–129.

Freeman, W. J. (1999). *How Brains Make Up Their Minds*. Weidenfeld & Nicolson.

Freeman, W. J. (2000). Mesoscopic neurodynamics: from neuron to brain. *Journal of Physiology Paris, 94*(5–6), 303–322.

Freeman, W. J. (2001). *How Brains Make Up Their Minds*. Columbia University Press.

Freeman, W. J. (2012). On the nature and neural mechanisms of mind force. *Chaos and Complexity Letters, 6*(1/2), 7.

Freeman, W. J., & Orsucci, F. (2017). Semiotic dynamics: Conversations and reflections at Trinity College. *Chaos and Complexity Letters, 11*(1), 183–192.

Freud, S. (1927). *The ego and the id*. L. & Virginia Woolf at the Hogarth press, and the Institute of psycho-analysis.

Freud, S. (1966). Project for a Scientific Psychology (1895). In *The Standard Edition of the Complete Psychological Works of Sigmund Freud, Volume I (1886–1899): Pre-Psycho-Analytic Publications and Unpublished Drafts*. Allen & Unwin.

Freud, S., & Fliess, W. (1954). *The Origins of Psycho-Analysis Letters to Wilhelm Fleiss: Drafts and Notes, 1887–1902*. Imago Pub. Co.

Freud, S., Riviere, J., & Strachey, J. (1959). *Collected Papers: Authorized Translation under the Supervision of Joan Riviere*. Basic Books.

Freud, S., Sandler, J., & International Psycho-Analytical Association. (1991). *On Freud's 'Analysis Terminable and Interminable'*. Yale University Press.

Freud, S., Strachey, J., Freud, A., Rothgeb, C. L., & Scientific Literature Corporation. (1919). *The Standard Edition of the Complete Psychological Works of Sigmund Freud*. Hogarth Press.

Friston, K. (2010). The free-energy principle: A unified brain theory? *Nature Reviews Neuroscience, 11*(2), 127–138.

Fulford, K. W. M., & Sartorius, N. (2009). *A Secret History of ICD and the Hidden Future of DSM*. In *Psychiatry as Cognitive Neuroscience: Philosophical Perspectives* (pp. 29–48). Oxford University Press.

Fusaroli, R., & Tylén, K. (2016). Investigating conversational dynamics: Interactive alignment, interpersonal synergy, and collective task performance. *Cognitive Science, 40*(1), 145–171.

Fusaroli, R., Rączaszek-Leonardi, J., & Tylén, K. (2014). Dialog as interpersonal synergy. *New Ideas in Psychology, 32*, 147–157.

Gallagher, S. (2001). The practice of mind: Theory, simulation, or primary interaction? *Journal of Consciousness Studies, 8*(5–6), 83–108.

Gallagher, S. (2013). The socially extended mind. *Cognitive Systems Research, 25*, 4–12.

Gallagher, S., & Daly, A. (2018). Dynamical relations in the self-pattern. *Frontiers in Psychology, 11*(9), 664.

Gallese, V. (2005). Embodied simulation: From neurons to phenomenal experience. *Phenomenology and the Cognitive Sciences, 4*, 23–48.

Gallese, V. (2018). Embodied simulation and its role in cognition. *Reti, Saperi, Linguaggi, 1*, 31–46.

Gallese, V., & Lakoff, G. (2005). The brain's concepts: The role of the sensory-motor system in conceptual knowledge. *Cognitive Neuropsychology, 22*(3–4), 455–479.

Ganesh, K., & Gabora, L. (2022). A dynamic autocatalytic network model of therapeutic change. *Entropy, 24*(4), 547.

Gartner, Z. J., & Hu, J. L. (2021). Guiding tissue-scale self-organization. *Nature Materials, 20*(1), 2–3.

Gatt, J. M., Burton, K. L., Schofield, P. R., Bryant, R. A., & Williams, L. M. (2014). The heritability of mental health and wellbeing defined using COMPAS-W, a new composite measure of wellbeing. *Psychiatry Research, 219*(1), 204–213.

Gavrilova, L., & Zawadzki, M. J. (2023). Testing the associations between state and trait anxiety, anger, sadness, and ambulatory blood pressure and whether race impacts these relationships. *Annals of Behavioral Medicine, 57*(1), 38–49.

Gazzaniga, M. S. (2011). *Who is in Charge?: Free Will and the Science of the Brain.* Ecco.

Geary, D. H. (2009). *The Legacy of Punctuated Equilibrium.* Oxford University Press.

Gelo, O. C. G., & Salvatore, S. (2016). A dynamic systems approach to psychotherapy: A meta-theoretical framework for explaining psychotherapy change processes. *Journal of Counseling Psychology, 63*(4), 379.

George, A. (1990). Whose language is it anyway? Some notes on idiolects. *The Philosophical Quarterly, 40*(160), 275–298.

Gershenson, C. (2020). Guiding the self-organization of cyber-physical systems. *Frontiers in Robotics and AI, 7*, 41.

Gibson, J. J. (1979). *The Ecological Approach to Visual Perception.* Houghton Mifflin.

Gilden, D. L., & Hancock, H. (2007). Response variability in attention-deficit disorders. *Psychological Science, 18*(9), 796–802.

Giuliani, A. (2014). Networks as a privileged way to develop mesoscopic level approaches in systems biology. *Systems, 2*(2), 237–242.

Giuliani, A., Benigni, R., Zbilut, J. P., Webber, C. L., Sirabella, P., & Colosimo, A. (2002). Nonlinear signal analysis methods in the elucidation of protein sequence-structure relationships. *Chemical Reviews, 102*(5), 1471–1492.

Giuliani, A., Tsuchiya, M., & Yoshikawa, K. (2018). Self-organization of genome expression from embryo to terminal cell fate: single-cell statistical mechanics of biological regulation. *Entropy, 20*(1), 13.

Glass, L. (2001). Synchronization and rhythmic processes in physiology. *Nature, 410*(6825), 277–284.

Glazer, T. (2017). The semiotics of emotional expression. *Transaction of the Charles S. Peirce Society, 53*(2), 189–215.

Glover, E. (1958). *The Technique of Psycho-Analysis.* International Universities Press.

Goekoop, R., & Goekoop, J. G. (2014). A network view on psychiatric disorders: Network clusters of symptoms as elementary syndromes of psychopathology. *PloS One, 9*(11), e112734.

Goethe, J. W. von. (1962). *Elective Affinities: A Novel.* F. Ungar.

Goldstein, J. (2004). Embracing the random in the self-organizing psyche. *Nonlinear Dynamics, Psychology, and Life Sciences, 1*(3), 181–202.

Goleman, D. (1997). *Healing Emotions: Conversations with the Dalai Lama on Mindfulness, Emotions, and Health.* Shambhala.

Gould, S. J., & Eldredge, N. (1977). Punctuated equilibria: the time and mode of evolution reconsidered. *Paleobiology, 3*(2), 115–151.

Grebogi, C., & Lai, Y. C. (2006). Controlling Chaos. In *Handbook of Chaos Control* (pp. 1–20). John Wiley & Sons.

Greenberg, L. S. (2015). *Emotion-Focused Therapy: Coaching Clients to Work Through Their Feelings.* American Psychological Association; 2nd edition.

Greenfield, P. M., & Cocking, R. R. (1994). Effects of interactive entertainment technologies on development. *Journal of Applied Developmental Psychology, 15*(1), 1–2.

Grotstein, J. S. (1994). Projective identification reappraised: part I. *Contemporary Psychoanalysis, 30*(4), 708–746.

Guan, X., & Liu, Y. (2023). Appreciation of color-field paintings through reception theory: a case study of Mark Rothko. *Art and Performance Letters, 4*(13), 25–30.

Guidano, V. F. (1987). *Complexity of the Self.* Guilford Press.

Guidano, V. F. (1991). *The Self in Process: Toward a Post-Rationalist Cognitive Therapy.* Guilford Press.

Guidi, M. E. (2007). Jeremy Bentham's quantitative analysis of happiness and its asymmetries. *Handbook on the Economics of Happiness, 23*, 68–94.

Gunderson, J. G. (2011). A BPD Brief. *NEABPD (National Education Alliance Borderline Personality Disorder).* https://on-bpd.ca/sites/default/files/file_attach/bpd_brief.pdf

Haken, H. (1983). *Advanced Synergetics: Instability Hierarchies of Self-Organizing Systems and Devices.* Springer.

Haken, H. (1985). Complex systems: operational approaches in neurobiology, physics, and computers. In *Proceedings of the International Symposium on Synergetics.* Springer.

Haken, H., & Stadler, M. (1990). Synergetics of cognition. In *Proceedings of the International Symposium on Synergetics.* Springer.

Hallisey, C. (1988). Review of *Nāgārjuna: The Philosophy of the Middle Way, Mūlamadhyamakārikā* by David J. Kalupahana. *The Journal of Asian Studies, 47*(2), 402–403.

Hallisey, C. (2022). Buddhist Ethics: Trajectories. In *Encyclopedia of Religious Ethics* (pp. 623–632). John Wiley & Sons.

Hamann, H., Schranz, M., Elmenreich, W., Trianni, V., Pinciroli, C., Bredeche, N., & Ferrante, E. (2020). Designing Self-Organization in the Physical Realm. *Frontiers in Robotics and AI, 7,* 597859.

Hamilton, W. D. (1964). The genetic evolution of social behaviour. II. *Journal of Theoretical Biology, 7*(1), 17–52.

Harris, K. M., Gottdiener, J. S., Gottlieb, S. S., Burg, M. M., Li, S., & Krantz, D. S. (2020). Impact of mental stress and anger on indices of diastolic function in patients with heart failure. *Journal of Cardiac Failure, 26*(11), 1006–1010.

Heagy, J. F., Carroll, T. L., & Pecora, L. M. (1995). Desynchronization by periodic orbits. *Physical Review E, 52*(2), R1253–R1256.

Heft, H. (1989). Affordances and the body: An intentional analysis of Gibson's ecological approach to visual perception. *Journal for the Theory of Social Behaviour, 19*(1), 1–30.

Heidegger, M., & Fink, E. (1993). *Heraclitus Seminar.* Northwestern University Press.

Heisenberg, W., & Hayes, F. (1952). *Philosophic Problems of Nuclear Science.* Faber and Faber.

Heller, L., & Kammer, B. J. (2022). *The Practical Guide for Healing Developmental Trauma: Using the Neuroaffective Relational Model to Address Adverse Childhood Experiences and Resolve Complex Trauma.* North Atlantic Books.

Higginbotham, J. (2006). Languages and Idiolects: Their Language and Ours. In *The Oxford Handbook of Philosophy of Language* (pp. 140–150). Oxford University Press.

Hilbe, C., Šimsa, Š., Chatterjee, K., & Nowak, M. A. (2018). Evolution of cooperation in stochastic games. *Nature, 559*(7713), 246–249.

Hildenbrandt, H., Carere, C., & Hemelrijk, C. K. (2010). Self-organized aerial displays of thousands of starlings: A model. *Behavioral Ecology*, *21*(6), 1349–1359.

Hippius, H., & Müller, N. (2008). The work of Emil Kraepelin and his research group in München. *European Archives of Psychiatry and Clinical Neuroscience*, *258*(S2), 3–11.

Hizanidis, J., Kouvaris, N. E., Zamora-López, G., Díaz-Guilera, A., & Antonopoulos, C. G. (2016). Chimera-like states in modular neural networks. *Scientific Reports*, *6*(1), 19845.

Hofer, M. A. (1975). Parent-infant interaction. Summing up. *Ciba Foundation Symposium*, (33), 309–313.

Hofer, M. A. (1981). *The Roots of Human Behavior: An Introduction to the Psychobiology of Early Development*. Freeman.

Hofer, M. A. (1984). Relationships as regulators: A psychobiologic perspective on bereavement. *Psychosomatic Medicine*, *46*(3), 183–197.

Hofer, M. A. (1994a). Hidden regulators in attachment, separation, and loss. *Monographs of the Society for Research in Child Development*, *59*(2–3), 192–207.

Hofer, M. A. (1994b). Early relationships as regulators of infant physiology and behavior. *Acta Paediatrica*, *397*, 9–18.

Hoffman, D. A., & Osserman, R. (1980). *The Geometry of the Generalized Gauss Map* (Vol. 236). American Mathematical Society.

Hoffmeyer, J. (1997). Biosemiotics: towards a new synthesis in biology. *European Journal for Semiotic Studies*, *9*(2), 355–376.

Hoffmeyer, J. (2008). *Biosemiotics: An Examination into the Signs of Life and the Life of Signs*. University of Chicago Press.

Hofstadter, D. R. (1985). *Metamagical Themas: Questing for the Essence of Mind and Pattern*. Basic Books.

Høgenhaug, S. S., Steffensen, S. V., Orsucci, F., Zimatore, G., Schiepek, G. K., Kongerslev, M. T., Bateman, A., & Kjaersdam Telléus, G. (2024). The complexity of interpersonal physiology during rupture and repair episodes in the treatment of borderline personality disorder: a proof-of-concept multimethod single case study of verbal and non-verbal interactional dynamics. *Frontiers in Psychology*, *15*, 1408183.

Holstein, J. A., & Gubrium, J. F. (2012). The Self We Live By: Narrative Identity in a Postmodern World. Oxford University Press.

Holton, G. J. (2000). *Einstein, History, and Other Passions: The Rebellion Against Science at the End of the Twentieth Century*. Harvard University Press.

Huizinga, J. (2014). *Homo ludens ils 86*. Routledge.

Husserl, E. (1980). *Collected Works*. The Hague.

Hutchins, E. (2020). The Distributed Cognition Perspective on Human Interaction. In *Roots of Human Sociality* (pp. 375–398). Routledge.

Insel, T. R. (2014). The NIMH Research Domain Criteria (RDoC) project: precision medicine for psychiatry. *American Journal of Psychiatry, 171*(4), 395–397.

Jacobi, F. H., Livieri, P., & di Giovanni, G. (2023). *Stanford Encyclopedia of Philosophy*. https://plato.stanford.edu/entries/friedrich-jacobi/

Jacobson, E. (1964). *The Self and the Object World*. International Universities Press.

Jaffe, J., Beebe, B., Feldstein, S., Crown, C. L., Jasnow, M. D., Rochat, P., & Stern, D. N. (2001). Rhythms of dialogue in infancy: Coordinated timing in development. *Monographs of the Society for Research in Child Development, 66*(2), 1–132.

James, W. (1985). *Psychology: Briefer Course*. Harvard University Press.

James, W., & McDermott, J. J. (1967). *The Writings of William James: A Comprehensive Edition*. Random House.

Jaspers, K. (1953). *Lionardo als Philosoph*.

Jaspers, K. (1997). *General Psychopathology* (Vol. 2). Johns Hopkins University Press.

Jayawickreme, E., Meindl, P., Helzer, E. G., Furr, R. M., & Fleeson, W. (2014). Virtuous states and virtuous traits: How the empirical evidence regarding the existence of broad traits saves virtue ethics from the situationist critique. *Theory and Research in Education, 12*(3), 283–308.

Jennings, H. D., & Pessoa, F. (2019). *Fernando Pessoa, The Poet with Many Faces: A Biography and Anthology [Excerpt & Bibliography]*. Tinta-da-China.

Johnston, A., & Malabou, C. (2013). *Self and Emotional Life: Philosophy, Psychoanalysis, and Neuroscience*. Columbia University Press.

Jones, H. (2020). *Piet Mondrian's Stylistic Development*. https://digitalcommons.jsu.edu/ce_jsustudentsymp_2020/27/

Jovanović, G. (2018). A revival of Wundt's heritage: Searching for the philosophical foundations of psychology from an historical perspective. *Theory & Psychology, 28*(6), 847–854.

Jung, C. G., & Pauli, W. (1955). *The Interpretation of Nature and the Psyche*. Pantheon Books.

Jurgens, H. A., & Johnson, R. W. (2012). Environmental enrichment attenuates hippocampal neuroinflammation and improves cognitive function during influenza infection. *Brain, Behavior, and Immunity, 26*(6), 1006–1016.

Kabat-Zinn, J. (2003a). Mindfulness-based interventions in context: past, present, and future. *Clinical Psychology: Science and Practice, 10*(2), 144–156.

Kabat-Zinn, J. (2003b). Mindfulness-based stress reduction (MBSR). *Constructivism in the Human Sciences, 8*(2), 73.

Kachele, H. (2001). Are there 'pillars of therapeutic wisdom' for psychoanalytic therapy? *Journal of European Psychoanalysis, 12/13*.

Kahn, C. H. (1981). *The Art and Thought of Heraclitus: A New Arrangement and Translation of the Fragments with Literary and Philosophical Commentary.* Cambridge University Press.

Kahneman, D. (2011). *Thinking: Fast and Slow.* Farrar, Straus and Giroux.

Kahr, B. (2005). The fifteen critical ingredients of good psychotherapy. *How Does Psychotherapy Work* (pp. 1–14). Routledge.

Kandel, E. R. (2004). The molecular biology of memory storage: A dialog between genes and synapses. *Bioscience Reports, 24*(4–5), 475–522.

Kant, I., & Bernard, J. H. (1951). *Critique of Judgment.* Hafner Pub. Co.

Kantz, H., & Schreiber, T. (1997). *Nonlinear Time Series Analysis.* Cambridge University Press.

Kaplan, M., & Kaplan, N. (1991). The self-organization of human psychological functioning. *Systems Research & Behavioral Science, 36*(3), 161–178.

Kauffman, S. A. (1993). *The Origins of Order: Self Organization and Selection in Evolution.* Oxford University Press.

Kauffman, S. A. (1995). *At Home in the Universe: The Search for Laws of Self-Organization and Complexity.* Oxford University Press.

Keller, E., & Tschacher, W. (2007). Prosodic and gestural expression of interactional agreement. In *Verbal and Nonverbal Communication Behaviours* (pp. 85–98). Springer.

Kelley, T. (2007). *Goethe's Plant Morphology: The Seeds of Evolution.* https://philpapers.org/rec/KELQPM

Kelso, J. A. S. (1995). *Dynamic Patterns: The Self-Organization of Brain and Behavior.* MIT Press.

Kelso, J. A. S. (2021). The Haken–Kelso–Bunz (HKB) model: From matter to movement to mind. *Biological Cybernetics, 115*(4), 305–322.

Kelso, J. A. S., Mandell, A. J., Shlesinger, M. F., Haken, H., & Florida Atlantic University. (1988). *Dynamic Patterns in Complex Systems.* World Scientific.

Kelso, J. S. (2016). On the self-organizing origins of agency. *Trends in Cognitive Sciences, 20*(7), 490–499.

Kendler, K. S., Muñoz, R. A., & Murphy, G. (2010). The development of the Feighner criteria: a historical perspective. *American Journal of Psychiatry, 167*(2), 134–142.

Kennan, K., & Grantham, D. (2024). *The Technique of Orchestration*. Taylor & Francis.

Kernberg, O. F. (1993). *Severe Personality Disorders: Psychotherapeutic Strategies*. Yale University Press.

Khalkhali, M., & Pagliaroli, N. (2022). Spectral statistics of Dirac ensembles. *Journal of Mathematical Physics, 63*(5), 053504.

Kiefer, A. W., & Pincus, D. (2023). Nonlinear Biopsychosocial Resilience: Self-Organization as the Basis for a Common Framework. In *The Routledge International Handbook of Changes in Human Perceptions and Behaviors* (pp. 424–436). Routledge.

Kierkegaard, S. (2013). *Kierkegaard's Writings, VIII, Volume 8: Concept of Anxiety: A Simple Psychologically Orienting Deliberation on the Dogmatic Issue of Hereditary Sin* (Vol. 18). Princeton University Press.

Kitayama, S., & Markus, H. R. (1994). Introduction to Cultural Psychology and Emotion Research. In *Emotion and Culture: Empirical Studies of Mutual Influence* (pp. 1–19). American Psychological Association.

Klein, J. T. (1997). Advancing Interdisciplinary Studies. In *Handbook of the Undergraduate Curriculum: A Comprehensive Guide to Purposes, Structures, Practices, and Change*. John Wiley & Sons.

Klein, J. T. (2008). Evaluation of interdisciplinary and transdisciplinary research: A literature review. *American Journal of Preventive Medicine, 35*(2), S116–S123.

Kleinbub, J. R., Palmieri, A., Orsucci, F. F., Andreassi, S., Musmeci, N., Benelli, E., … de Felice, G. (2019). Measuring empathy: A statistical physics grounded approach. *Physica A: Statistical Mechanics and Its Applications, 526*, 120979.

Klempe, S. H. (2022). The Understanding of Music in Early Psychology and Musicology. In *Sound and Reason* (pp. 17–52). Springer.

Knezevic, E., Nenic, K., Milanovic, V., & Knezevic, N. N. (2023). The role of cortisol in chronic stress, neurodegenerative diseases, and psychological disorders. *Cells, 12*(23), 2726.

Kolmogorov, A. N. (1950). *Foundations of Probability Theory*. Dover Publications.

Kono, S., & Walker, G. J. (2020). Theorizing ikigai or life worth living among Japanese university students: a mixed-methods approach. *Journal of Happiness Studies, 21*(1), 327–355.

Koolagudi, S. G., & Rao, K. S. (2012). Emotion recognition from speech: a review. *International Journal of Speech Technology, 15*(2), 99–117.

Kotera, Y., Kaluzeviciute, G., Garip, G., McEwan, K., & Chamberlain, K. (2021). Health Benefits of Ikigai: A Review of Literature. *Ikigai: Towards a*

Psychological Understanding of a Life Worth Living. Concurrent Disorders Society Publishing.

Kotov, R., Krueger, R. F., Watson, D., Achenbach, T. M., Althoff, R. R., Bagby, R. M., Brown, T. A., Carpenter, W. T., Caspi, A., & Clark, L. A. (2017). The Hierarchical Taxonomy of Psychopathology (HiTOP): A dimensional alternative to traditional nosologies. *Journal of Abnormal Psychology, 126*(4), 454.

Krakovská, H., Kuehn, C., & Longo, I. P. (2024) Resilience of dynamical systems. *European Journal of Applied Mathematics, 35*, 155–200.

Kraljic, T., Brennan, S. E., & Samuel, A. G. (2008). Accommodating variation: Dialects, idiolects, and speech processing. *Cognition, 107*(1), 54–81.

Kramer, U. (2020). Individualizing psychotherapy research designs. *Journal of Psychotherapy Integration, 30*(3), 440.

Kraus, N. (2020). The joyful reduction of uncertainty: Music perception as a window to predictive neuronal processing. *Journal of Neuroscience, 40*(14), 2790–2792.

Krause, M., & Behn, A. (2022). Case formulation as a bridge between theory, clinical practice, and research: A commentary. *Journal of Clinical Psychology, 78*(3), 454–461.

Kripke, S. A. (1982). *Wittgenstein on Rules and Private Language: An Elementary Exposition*. Harvard University Press.

Kuramoto, Y. (1984a). Chemical Turbulence. In *Chemical Oscillations, Waves, and Turbulence* (pp. 111–140). Springer.

Kuramoto, Y. (1984b). Cooperative dynamics of oscillator community a study based on lattice of rings. *Progress of Theoretical Physics Supplement, 79*, 223–240.

Kuramoto, Y., & Battogtokh, D. (2002). Coexistence of coherence and incoherence in nonlocally coupled phase oscillators. *arXiv Preprint Cond-Mat/0210694*.

Lacan, J. (1966). *Ecrits*. Editions du Seuil.

Lacan, J. (1978). *The Four Fundamental Concepts of Psycho-Analysis:* W. W. Norton & Company.

LaFreniere, P. (2013). Children's play as a context for managing physiological arousal and learning emotion regulation. *Psihologijske Teme, 22*(2), 183–204.

Laing, C. R. (2009). Chimera states in heterogeneous networks. *Chaos: An Interdisciplinary Journal of Nonlinear Science, 19*(1), 013113.

Lakoff, G., & Johnson, M. (1980). *Metaphors We Live By*. University of Chicago Press.

Lakoff, G., & Johnson, M. (1999). *Philosophy in the Flesh: The Embodied Mind and its Challenge to Western Thought*. Basic Books.

Lalande, A. (1962). *Vocabulaire technique et critique de la philosophie.* Presses Universitaires de France.

Lama, H. R. H., & Muyzenberg, L. van den. (2011). *The Leader's Way: Business, Buddhism and Happiness in an Interconnected World.* Nicholas Brealey Publishing.

Lanczik, M., & Keil, G. (1991). Carl Wernicke's localization theory and its significance for the development of scientific psychiatry. *History of Psychiatry, 2*(6), 171–180.

Landini, G. (2001). Evidence of linguistic structure in the Voynich manuscript using spectral analysis. *Cryptologia, 25*(4), 275–295.

Lange, K. (1894). *Apperception: A Monograph on Psychology and Pedagogy.* DC Heath & Company.

Langs, R. (1976). *The Bipersonal Field.* J. Aronson.

Laplanche, J., & Pontalis, J. B. (1974). *The Language of Psychoanalysis.* W. W. Norton & Company.

Latini, B. (1839). *Il tesoro* (Vol. 1). Company'tipi del Gondoliere. https://books. google.co.uk/books?hl=en&lr=&id=B0xQAAAAcAAJ&oi=fnd&pg=PA34& dq=brunetto+latini%27s+tesoro&ots=Pm69cARxJ_&sig=VzSGb3FO7YUUq hjkLZfUBdZzg3Y

LeDoux, J. E. (1996). *The Emotional Brain: The Mysterious Underpinnings of Emotional Life.* Simon & Schuster.

LeDoux, J. E. (2002). *Synaptic Self: How Our Brains Become Who We Are.* Viking.

Leiman, M. (1994). Projective identification as early joint action sequences: A Vygotskian addendum to the procedural sequence object relations model. *British Journal of Medical Psychology, 67*(2), 97–106.

Lewin, K. (2014). Psychological Ecology. In *The People, Place, and Space Reader* (p. 17). Routledge.

Lewin, R. (1999). *Complexity: Life at the Edge of Chaos* (2nd ed). University of Chicago Press.

Li, B., & Saad, D. (2017). Chimera-like states in structured heterogeneous networks. *Chaos: An Interdisciplinary Journal of Nonlinear Science, 27*(4), 043109.

Li, L., Gow, A. D. I., & Zhou, J. (2020). The role of positive emotions in education: a neuroscience perspective. *Mind, Brain, and Education, 14*(3), 220–234.

Liao, X., & Ran, J. (2007). Hopf bifurcation in love dynamical models with nonlinear couples and time delays. *Chaos, Solitons & Fractals, 31*(4), 853–865.

Liégeois, R., Santos, A., Matta, V., Van De Ville, D., & Sayed, A. H. (2020). Revisiting correlation-based functional connectivity and its relationship with structural connectivity. *Network Neuroscience, 4*(4), 1235–1251.

Limanowski, J., & Blankenburg, F. (2013). Minimal self-models and the free energy principle. *Frontiers in Human Neuroscience, 7*, 547.

Lincourt, J. M., & Olczak, P. V. (1974). C. S. Peirce and H. S. Sullivan on the human self. *Psychiatry, 37*(1), 78–87.

Lindahl, B. I., & Arhem, P. (1994). Mind as a force field: Comments on a new interactionistic hypothesis. *Journal of Theoretical Biology, 171*, 111–122.

Lingiardi, V., & McWilliams, N. (2015). The psychodynamic diagnostic manual–2nd edition (PDM-2). *World Psychiatry, 14*(2), 237.

Lipsitz, L. A., & Goldberger, A. L. (1992). Loss of complexity and aging. *JAMA: The Journal of the American Medical Association, 267*(13), 1806–1809.

Lisi, A. G. (2006). Quantum mechanics from a universal action reservoir (arXiv:physics/0605068). arXiv. https://doi.org/10.48550/arXiv.physics/0605068

Lorenz, E. N. (1993). *The Essence of Chaos.* University of Washington Press.

Lorenzer, A. (1977). *Sprachspiel und Interaktionsformen: Vorträge und Aufsätze zu Psychoanalyse, Sprache und Praxis.* Suhrkamp Frankfurt a. M.

Lotman, Y. M. (1990). *Universe of the Mind: A Semiotic Theory of Culture.* Indiana University Press.

Luborsky, L. (1995). Are common factors across different psychotherapies the main explanation for the Dodo Bird verdict that "everyone has won so all shall have prizes"? *Clinical Psychology: Science and Practice, 2*(1), 106–109.

Lumsden, C. J., Wilson, E. O., & Osborne, E. (1981). *Genes, Mind, and Culture: The Coevolutionary Process.* Harvard University Press.

Lv, G., Zhang, N., Ma, K., Weng, J., Zhu, P., Chen, F., & He, G. (2021). Functional brain network dynamics based on the Hindmarsh–Rose model. *Nonlinear Dynamics, 104*(2), 1475–1489.

Mahler, M. S. (1968). *On Human Symbiosis and the Vicissitudes of Individuation.* International Universities Press.

Mahler, M. S., Bergman, A., & Pine, F. (1975). *The Psychological Birth of the Human Infant Symbiosis and Individuation.* Basic Books.

Mainzer, K. (1994). *Thinking in Complexity: The Complex Dynamics of Matter, Mind, and Mankind.* Springer.

Majhi, S., Bera, B. K., Ghosh, D., & Perc, M. (2019). Chimera states in neuronal networks: A review. *Physics of Life Reviews, 28*, 100–121.

Makarov, V. V., Kundu, S., Kirsanov, D. V., Frolov, N. S., Maksimenko, V. A., Ghosh, D., Dana, S. K., & Hramov, A. E. (2019). Multiscale interaction promotes chimera states in complex networks. *Communications in Nonlinear Science and Numerical Simulation, 71*, 118–129.

Mandelbrot, B. B. (1977). *Fractals: Form, Chance and Dimension*. W. H. Freeman and Co.

Manetti, C., Ceruso, M. A., Giuliani, A., Webber, C. L., & Zbilut, J. P. (1999). Recurrence quantification analysis in molecular dynamics. *Annals of the New York Academy of Sciences, 879*, 258–266.

Mansilla, V. B. (2006). Assessing expert interdisciplinary work at the frontier: An empirical exploration. *Research Evaluation, 15*(1), 17–29.

Marchionne, A., Ditlevsen, P., & Wieczorek, S. (2018). Synchronization vs. resonance: Isolated resonances in damped nonlinear oscillators. *Physica D: Nonlinear Phenomena, 380*, 8–16.

Marci, C. D., Ham, J., Moran, E., & Orr, S. P. (2007). Physiologic correlates of perceived therapist empathy and social-emotional process during psychotherapy. *The Journal of Nervous and Mental Disease, 195*(2), 103–111.

Margulis, L. (1981). *Symbiosis in Cell Evolution: Life and its Environment on the Early Earth*. W. H. Freeman and Co.

Margulis, L., Asikainen, C. A., & Krumbein, W. E. (2011). *Chimeras and Consciousness: Evolution of the Sensory Self*. MIT Press.

Marks-Tarlow, T. (1999). The self as a dynamical system. *Nonlinear Dynamics, Psychology, and Life Sciences, 3*, 311–345.

Markus, H. R., & Kitayama, S. (1994). The Cultural Construction of Self and Emotion: Implications for Social Behavior. In *Emotion and Culture: Empirical Studies of Mutual Influence* (pp. 89–130). American Psychological Association.

Marmarosh, C. L., Kivlighan Jr, D. M., Bieri, K., LaFauci Schutt, J. M., Barone, C., & Choi, J. (2014). The insecure psychotherapy base: Using client and therapist attachment styles to understand the early alliance. *Psychotherapy, 51*(3), 404.

Martin, A. E., & Baggio, G. (2020). Modeling meaning composition from formalism to mechanism. *Phil. Trans. R. Soc. B, 375*, 20190298.

Martinčić-Ipšić, S., Margan, D., & Meštrović, A. (2016). Multilayer network of language: A unified framework for structural analysis of linguistic subsystems. *Physica A: Statistical Mechanics and Its Applications, 457*, 117–128.

Martinet, J. (1989). The Semiotics of Luis Jorge Prieto. In *The Semiotic Web* (pp. 89–108). De Gruyter Mouton.

Marwan, N. (2008). A historical review of recurrence plots. *The European Physical Journal Special Topics, 164*(1), 3–12.

Matelli, E. (2019). The Living Body as a Model of Systemic Organization in Ancient Thinking. In *The Systemic Turn in Human and Natural Sciences* (pp. 149–170). Springer.

Maturana, H. (2002). Autopoiesis, structural coupling and cognition: a history of these and other notions in the biology of cognition. *Cybernetics & Human Knowing, 9*, 3–4.

Maturana, H. R., & Varela, F. J. (1980). *Autopoiesis and Cognition: The Realization of the Living*. D. Reidel Pub. Co.

Maturana, H. R., & Varela, F. J. (1992). *The Tree of Knowledge: The Biological Roots of Human Understanding*. Shambhala.

Mauss, M. (2000). *The Gift: The Form and Reason for Exchange in Archaic Societies*. W. W. Norton & Company.

Mayes, R., & Horwitz, A. V. (2005). DSM-III and the revolution in the classification of mental illness. *Journal of the History of the Behavioral Sciences, 41*(3), 249–267.

McMain, S. F., Boritz, T. Z., & Leybman, M. J. (2015). Common strategies for cultivating a positive therapy relationship in the treatment of borderline personality disorder. *Journal of Psychotherapy Integration, 25*(1), 20.

McWhinney, B. (1999). The Emergence of Language from Embodiment. In *The Emergence of Language*. Psychology Press.

Meadows, D. H. (2008). *Thinking in Systems* (Illustrated edition). Chelsea Green Publishing.

Menken, S., & Keestra, M. (2016). *An Introduction to Interdisciplinary Research: Theory and Practice*. Amsterdam University Press.

Merleau-Ponty, M. (1945). *Phenomenologie de la Perception*. Gallimard.

Merleau-Ponty, M. (1960). *Signes*. Gallimard.

Merleau-Ponty, M. (1962). *Phenomenology of Perception*. Humanities Press.

Merleau-Ponty, M. (1966). *Sens et non-sens*. Nagel.

Merleau-Ponty, M. (1973). *The Prose of the World*. Northwestern University Press.

Messer, S. B., & Wampold, B. E. (2002). Let's face facts: Common factors are more potent than specific therapy ingredients. *Clinical Psychology: Science and Practice, 9*(1), 21–25.

Metzinger, T. (2004). *Being No One: The Self-Model Theory of Subjectivity*. MIT Press.

Michalak, J., Rohde, K., & Troje, N. F. (2015). How we walk affects what we remember: Gait modifications through biofeedback change negative affective memory bias. *Journal of Behavior Therapy and Experimental Psychiatry, 46*, 121–125.

Mojtahedi, M., Skupin, A., Zhou, J., Castaño, I. G., Leong-Quong, R. Y., Chang, H., & Huang, S. (2016). Cell fate decision as high-dimensional critical state transition. *PLoS Biology, 14*(12), e2000640.

Monteleone, M. (2014). De ira. In *Brill's Companion to Seneca* (pp. 127–134). Brill.

Moore, E. C. (1961). *American Pragmatism: Peirce, James and Dewey*. Columbia University Press.

Morawetz, C., Riedel, M. C., Salo, T., Berboth, S., Eickhoff, S. B., Laird, A. R., & Kohn, N. (2020). Multiple large-scale neural networks underlying emotion regulation. *Neuroscience & Biobehavioral Reviews, 116*, 382–395.

Moriyama, I. M., Loy, R. M., Robb-Smith, A. H. T., Rosenberg, H. M., & Hoyert, D. L. (2011). *History of the Statistical Classification of Diseases and Causes of Death*. https://stacks.cdc.gov/view/cdc/5928

Morvan, C., & O'Connor, A. (2017). *An Analysis of Leon Festinger's A Theory of Cognitive Dissonance*. Macat Library.

Munkhammar, J. (2011). Canonical relational quantum mechanics from information theory. *arXiv Preprint arXiv*:1101.1417.

Muran, J. C., Safran, J. D., Gorman, B. S., Samstag, L. W., Eubanks-Carter, C., & Winston, A. (2009). The relationship of early alliance ruptures and their resolution to process and outcome in three time-limited psychotherapies for personality disorders. *Psychotherapy: Theory, Research, Practice, Training, 46*(2), 233.

Nagel, E. (1961). *The Structure of Science: Problems in the Logic of Scientific Explanation*. Harcourt, Brace & World.

Nagel, T. (1974). What is it like to be a bat? *The Philosophical Review, 83*(4), 435–450.

Nagel, T. (2007). What is the Mind-Body Problem? In *Ciba Foundation Symposium: Experimental and Theoretical Studies of Consciousness* (pp. 1–7). John Wiley & Sons.

Nandam, L. S., Brazel, M., Zhou, M., & Jhaveri, D. J. (2020). Cortisol and major depressive disorder — Translating findings from humans to animal models and back. *Frontiers in Psychiatry, 10*, 974.

Nardi, B., & Bellantuono, C. (2008). A new adaptive and evolutionary conceptualization of the Personal Meaning Organization (PMO) framework. *European Psychotherapy, 8*(1), 5–16.

Nardi, B., Rezzonico, G., & Bellantuono, C. (2010). Toward a scientific framework for the Personal Meaning Organization (PMO) paradigm: neuroimaging and genetic studies. *Quaderni Italiani Di Psichiatria, 29*(3), 81–88.

Neisser, U. (1988). Five kinds of self-knowledge. *Philosophical Psychology, 1*(1), 35–59.

Neisser, U. (1993). *The Self Perceived.* Cambridge University Press.

Nelder, J. A., & Wedderburn, R. W. (1972). Generalized linear models. *Journal of the Royal Statistical Society Series A: Statistics in Society, 135*(3), 370–384.

Newell, W. H. (2001). A theory of interdisciplinary studies. *Issues in Integrative Studies, 19,* 1–25.

Newell, A., & Simon, H. A. (1972). *Human Problem Solving.* Prentice-Hall.

Newen, A., De Bruin, L., & Gallagher, S. (2018). *The Oxford Handbook of 4E Cognition.* Oxford University Press.

Newen, A., Welpinghus, A., & Juckel, G. (2015). Emotion recognition as pattern recognition: the relevance of perception. *Mind & Language, 30*(2), 187–208.

Newman, M. (2006). *The Structure and Dynamics of Networks.* Oxford University Press.

Nicolis, G., & Prigogine, I. (1977). *Self-Organization in Nonequilibrium Systems: From Dissipative Structures to Order through Fluctuations.* John Wiley & Sons.

Nijhof, S. L., Vinkers, C. H., van Geelen, S. M., Duijff, S. N., Achterberg, E. M., Van Der Net, J., Veltkamp, R. C., Grootenhuis, M. A., van de Putte, E. M., & Hillegers, M. H. (2018). Healthy play, better coping: The importance of play for the development of children in health and disease. *Neuroscience & Biobehavioral Reviews, 95,* 421–429.

Nithianantharajah, J., & Hannan, A. J. (2006). Enriched environments, experience-dependent plasticity and disorders of the nervous system. *Nature Reviews Neuroscience, 7*(9), 697–709.

Norris, S. (2006). Multiparty interaction: A multimodal perspective on relevance. *Discourse Studies, 8*(3), 401–421.

Norris, S., & Maier, C. D. (2014). *Interactions, Images and Texts: A Reader in Multimodality.* Walter de Gruyter GmbH & Co KG.

Nowak, M. A. (2006). *Evolutionary Dynamics.* Harvard University Press.

Nowak, M. A. (2013). *Evolution, Games, and God.* Harvard University Press.

Olthof, M., Hasselman, F., Maatman, F. O., Bosman, A., & Lichtwarck-Aschoff, A. (2020). Adaptive dynamic pattern theory (ADAPT) of psychopathology. *Preprint, 10.*

Olthof, M., Hasselman, F., Aas, B., Lamoth, D., Scholz, S., Daniels-Wredenhagen, N., Goldbeck, F., Weinans, E., Strunk, G., & Schiepek, G. (2023). The best of both worlds? General principles of psychopathology in personalized assessment. *Journal of Psychopathology and Clinical Science, 132*(7), 808.

Oltvai, Z. N., & Barabási, A.-L. (2002). Life's complexity pyramid. *Science, 298*(5594), 763–764.

Omel'chenko, O. E. (2018). The mathematics behind chimera states. *Nonlinearity*, *31*(5), R121.

Orsucci, F. (1981a). Structural analysis of schizophrenic language. *Neuropsychiatric Work*, *68*(1–2), 57–65.

Orsucci, F. (1981b). Linguistic sign in neurosis and psychosis. *Neuropsychiatric Work*, *68*(1–2), 66–78.

Orsucci, F. (1996). Behçet's disease and psychosomatic patterns of thinking. *Psychotherapy and Psychosomatics*, *65*(2), 112–114.

Orsucci, F. (1998). *Nonlinear Dynamics in Language and Psychobiological Interactions*. In *Chaos Fractals Models*. Italian University Press.

Orsucci, F. (1998). *The Complex Matters of the Mind*. World Scientific.

Orsucci, F. (2000). *Olfaction: New Frontiers for Cognitive Sciences*. World Scientific.

Orsucci, F. (2001). Happiness and deep ecology: On noise, harmony, and beauty in the mind. *Nonlinear Dynamics, Psychology, and Life Sciences*, *5*(1), 65–76.

Orsucci, F. (2002). *Changing Mind: Transitions in Natural and Artificial Environments*. World Scientific.

Orsucci, F. (2006). The paradigm of complexity in clinical neurocognitive science. *The Neuroscientist*, *12*(5), 390–397.

Orsucci, F. (2008). *Reflexing Interfaces: The Complex Coevolution of Information Technology Ecosystems*. IGI.

Orsucci, F. (2009). *Mind Force: On Human Attractions*. World Scientific.

Orsucci, F. (2013). Coevolution and linguistic creation. *Journal of Experiential Psychotherapy/Revista de Psicoterapie Experiential*, *16*(3).

Orsucci, F. (2015). Towards a meta-model of human change, from singularity to event horizon. *Chaos and Complexity Letters*, *9*(2), 107.

Orsucci, F. (2016). *Human Dynamics: A Complexity Science Open Handbook*. Nova Science Publishers.

Orsucci, F. (2020). Towards integrating semiotic and physiological dynamics: from nonlinear dynamics to quantum fields. In *Selbstorganisation — ein Paradigma für die Humanwissenschaften* (pp. 153–175). Springer.

Orsucci, F. (2021). Human synchronization maps — the hybrid consciousness of the embodied mind. *Entropy*, *23*(12), 1569.

Orsucci, F., & Tschacher, W. (2022). Complexity science in human change: research, models, clinical applications. *Entropy*, *24*(11), 1670.

Orsucci, F., & Zimatore, G. (2025). Information entropy in chimera states of human dynamics. *Entropy*, *27*(2), 98.

Orsucci, F., Giuliani, A., Webber, C., Mazza, M., & Fonagy, P. (2006). Combinatorics and synchronization in natural semiotics. *Physica A: Statistical Mechanics and its Applications, 361*(2), 665–676.

Orsucci, F., Musmeci, N., Aas, B., Schiepek, G., Reda, M. A., Canestri, L., de Felice, G. (2016). Synchronization analysis of language and physiology in human dyads. *Nonlinear Dynamics, Psychology, and Life Sciences, 20*(2), 167–191.

Orsucci, F., Petrosino, R., Paoloni, G., Canestri, L., Conte, E., Reda, M. A., & Fulcheri, M. (2013). Prosody and synchronization in cognitive neuroscience. *EPJ Nonlinear Biomedical Physics, 1*(1), 1–11.

Orsucci, F., Walter, K., Giuliani, A., Webber Jr, C. L., & Zbilut, J. P. (1997). Orthographic structuring of human speech and texts: Linguistic application of recurrence quantification analysis. *ArXiv Preprint* Cmp-Lg/9712010. https://arxiv.org/abs/cmp-lg/9712010

Orsucci, F., Walter, K., Giuliani, A., Webber, C. Jr, & Zbilut, J. (1999). Orthographic structuring of human speech and texts: linguistic application of recurrence quantification analysis. *International Journal of Chaos Theory and Applications, 4*, 2–12.

Ott, E., & Antonsen, T. M. (2008). Low dimensional behavior of large systems of globally coupled oscillators. *Chaos: An Interdisciplinary Journal of Nonlinear Science, 18*(3), 037113.

Ott, E., & Antonsen, T. M. (2009). Long-time evolution of phase oscillator systems. *Chaos: An Interdisciplinary Journal of Nonlinear Science, 19*(2), 023117.

Ott, E., Grebogi, C., & Yorke, J. A. (1990). Controlling chaotic dynamical systems. In *Chaos: Soviet-American Perspective on Nonlinear Science* (pp. 153–172). American Institute of Physics.

Palombo, S. R. (1999). *The Emergent Ego: Complexity and Coevolution in the Psychoanalytic Process*. International Universities Press.

Palomero-Gallagher, N., & Amunts, K. (2022). A short review on emotion processing: A lateralized network of neuronal networks. *Brain Structure and Function, 227*(2), 673–684.

Palumbo, R. V. (2015). *Interpersonal Physiology: Assessing Interpersonal Relationships Through Physiology*. University of Rhode Island.

Palumbo, R. V., Marraccini, M. E., Weyandt, L. L., Wilder-Smith, O., McGee, H. A., Liu, S., & Goodwin, M. S. (2017). Interpersonal autonomic physiology: a systematic review of the literature. *Personality and Social Psychology Review, 21*(2), 99–141.

Panksepp, J. (1998a). *Affective Neuroscience. The Foundations of Human and Animal Emotions*. Oxford University Press.

Panksepp, J. (1998b). The periconscious substrates of consciousness: Affective states and the evolutionary origins of the self. *Journal of Consciousness Studies*, 5(5–6), 566–582.

Panksepp, J. (1999). Emotions as viewed by psychoanalysis and neuroscience: An exercise in consilience. *Neuropsychoanalysis*, 1(1), 15–38.

Panksepp, J. (2004). *Textbook of Biological Psychiatry*. Wiley-Liss.

Panksepp, J., & Trevarthen, C. (2009). The Neuroscience of Emotion in Music. In *Communicative Musicality: Exploring the Basis of Human Companionship* (pp. 105–146). Oxford University Press.

Panksepp, J., & Watt, D. (2011). What is essential about basic emotions? Lasting lessons from affective neuroscience. *Emotion Review*, 3(4), 387–396.

Parisi, G. (2023a). In *a Flight of Starlings: The Wonder of Complex Systems*. Penguin.

Parisi, G. (2023b). Nobel lecture: Multiple equilibria. *Reviews of Modern Physics*, 95(3), 030501.

Park, H.-J., & Friston, K. (2013). Structural and functional brain networks: from connections to cognition. *Science*, 342(6158), 1238411.

Parkinson, K., Minaie, A., & Sanati-Mehrizy, R. (2020). Recognizing fractal behavior in jackson pollock artwork through computer vision. *2020 Intermountain Engineering, Technology and Computing (IETC)*, 1–6.

Paxton, A., & Dale, R. (2013). Multimodal networks of interpersonal interaction and conversational contexts. In *Proceedings of the Annual Meeting of the Cognitive Science Society* (pp. 1121–1126). Cognitive Science Society.

Pearce, E., Wlodarski, R., Machin, A., & Dunbar, R. I. M. (2017). Variation in the β-endorphin, oxytocin, and dopamine receptor genes is associated with different dimensions of human sociality. *Proceedings of the National Academy of Sciences*, 114(20), 5300–5305.

Pecora, L. M., & Carroll, T. L. (1990). Synchronization in chaotic systems. *Physical Review Letters*, 64(8), 821–824.

Peirce, C. S. (1953). *Letters to Lady Welby*. Whitlock's.

Peirce, C. S. (1968). *Chance, Love, and Logic: Philosophical Essays*. Barnes & Noble.

Peirce, C. S., & Fisch, M. H. (1982). *Writings of Charles S. Peirce: A Chronological Edition*. Indiana University Press.

Perrin, B. (1926). *Plutarch's Lives*. Harvard University Press.

Pessoa, F. (2002). *The Book of Disquiet*. Penguin.

Petitmengin, C. (2007). Towards the source of thoughts: The gestural and transmodal dimension of lived experience. *Journal of Consciousness Studies, 14*(3), 54–82.

Pezard, L., Nandrino, J. L., Renault, B., el Massioui, F., Allilaire, J. F., Muller, J., … Martinerie, J. (1996). Depression as a dynamical disease. *Biological Psychiatry, 39*(12), 991–999.

Piaget, J., & Cook, M. (1952). *The Origins of Intelligence in Children*. W. W. Norton & Company.

Pichon, S., & Kell, C. A. (2013). Affective and sensorimotor components of emotional prosody generation. *The Journal of Neuroscience, 33*(4), 1640–1650.

Pichot, P. (1994). The Clinical Approach in Psychiatry. In *Past, Present and Future of Psychiatry* (pp. 910–911). World Scientific.

Pikovsky, A., Rosenblum, M., & Kurths, J. (2001). *Synchronization: A Universal Concept in Nonlinear Sciences*. Cambridge University Press.

Pincus, D. (2009). Coherence, Complexity, and Information Flow: Self-Organizing Processes in Psychotherapy. In *Chaos and Complexity in Psychology: The Theory of Nonlinear Dynamical Systems* (pp. 335–369). Cambridge University Press.

Pincus, D., Cadsky, O., Berardi, V., Asuncion, C. M., & Wann, K. (2019). Fractal self-structure and psychological resilience. *Nonlinear Dynamics, Psychology, and Life Sciences, 23*(1), 57–78.

Pirandello, L. (2021). *One, None and a Hundred-Thousand*. Good Press.

Plato, & Cornford, F. M. (1957). *Plato's Theory of Knowledge: The Theaetetus and the Sophist of Plato* (translated with a running commentary by Francis Macdonald Cornford). Routledge & Kegan Paul Ltd.

Plato, & Griffith, T. (2000). *Symposium and Phaedrus*. Knopf.

Plato, Bloom, A. D., & Benardete, S. (2001). *Plato's Symposium*. University of Chicago Press.

Plato, Gallop, D., & netLibrary, I. (1988). *Phaedo*. Clarendon Press.

Poincare, H. (1929). *The Foundations of Science: Science and Hypothesis, The Value of Science, Science and Method*. The Science Press.

Popper, K. R. (1963). Science as falsification. *Conjectures and Refutations, 1*(1963), 33–39.

Popper, K. R. (1979). *Objective Knowledge: An Evolutionary Approach*. Clarendon Press.

Popple, A. V., & Levi, D. M. (2000). Wundt versus Galton — two approaches to gathering psychophysical measurements. *Perception, 29*(4), 379–381.

Pressman, S. D., Jenkins, B. N., & Moskowitz, J. T. (2019). Positive affect and health: what do we know and where next should we go? *Annual Review of Psychology, 70*(1), 627–650.

Proust, M. (2006). *Remembrance of Things Past* (Vol. 2). Wordsworth Editions.

Przibram, K., Schrödinger, E., Einstein, A., Lorentz, H. A., & Planck, M. (1967). *Letters on Wave Mechanics*. Vision Harrisonburg.

Puchner, M. (2015). Wittgenstein's language plays. *Philosophy and Literature, 39*(1), 107–127.

Pyragas, K. (1996). Weak and robust synchronization of chaos. *Physical Review E: Statistical Physics, Plasmas, Fluids, And Related Interdisciplinary Topics, 54*(5), R4508–R4511.

Pyragas, K. (2001). Control of chaos via an unstable delayed feedback controller. *Physical Review Letters, 86*(11), 2265–2268.

Ramstead, M. J., Friston, K. J., & Hipólito, I. (2020). Is the free-energy principle a formal theory of semantics? From variational density dynamics to neural and phenotypic representations. *Entropy, 22*(8), 889.

Reda, M. A. (1988). *Complex Cognitive Systems of Psychotherapy*. Carocci.

Reda, M. A., & Baskets, L. (2008). Evaluation of Psychophysiological Dyads Patient/Therapist During a Psychotherapy Session: Preliminary Results. In *Studies and Research of the Department of Neurological and Behavioural Sciences*. Siena Ignatius Press Publisher.

Regier, D. A., Narrow, W. E., Clarke, D. E., Kraemer, H. C., Kuramoto, S. J., Kuhl, E. A., & Kupfer, D. J. (2013). DSM-5 field trials in the United States and Canada, Part II: test-retest reliability of selected categorical diagnoses. *American Journal of Psychiatry, 170*(1), 59–70.

Repp, B. H., & Su, Y.-H. (2013). Sensorimotor synchronization: a review of recent research (2006–2012). *Psychonomic Bulletin & Review, 20*(3), 403–452.

Reuderink, B., Mühl, C., & Poel, M. (2013). Valence, arousal and dominance in the EEG during game play. *International Journal of Autonomous and Adaptive Communications Systems, 6*(1), 45.

Reynolds, C. W. (1987). Flocks, herds and schools: A distributed behavioral model. In *Proceedings of the 14th Annual Conference on Computer Graphics and Interactive Techniques* (pp. 25–34). Association for Computing Machinery.

Ricard, M. (2014). A Buddhist view of happiness. *Journal of Law and Religion, 29*(1), 14–29.

Richardson, R. D. (2007). *William James: In the Maelstrom of American Modernism*. HMH.

Richter, J. P. (1970). *The Notebooks of Leonardo da Vinci*. Courier Corporation.

Rietveld, E. (2012). Bodily intentionality and social affordances in context. In *Consciousness in Interaction: The Role of the Natural and Social Context in Shaping Consciousness* (pp. 207–226). John Benjamins.

Rinaldi, S. (1998). Love dynamics: The case of linear couples. *Applied Mathematics and Computation*, 95(2), 181–192.

Rinaldi, S., & Gragnani, A. (1996). Love dynamics between secure individuals: a modeling approach. Working Paper WP-96-69, International Institute for Applied Systems Analysis.

Rinaldi, S., & Gragnani, A. (1998). Minimal Models for Dyadic Processes: A Review. In *The Complex Matters of the Mind* (pp. 87–104). World Scientific.

Rinaldi, S., et al. (2015). *Modeling Love Dynamics*. World Scientific.

Ritchison, G. (2023). Nervous System. In *In a Class of Their Own* (pp. 479–686). Springer.

Rizzolatti, G., & Arbib, M. A. (1998). Language within our grasp. *Trends in Neuroscience*, 21(5), 188–194.

Rizzolatti, G., Fadiga, L., Gallese, V., & Fogassi, L. (1996). Premotor cortex and the recognition of motor actions. *Cognitive Brain Research*, 3(2), 131–141.

Roazen, P. (2013). Freud's Patients First-Person Accounts. In *Freud and the History of Psychoanalysis* (pp. 289–306). Routledge.

Rogers, C. R. (1995). *On Becoming a Person: A Therapist's View of Psychotherapy*. Mariner Books.

Rosenzweig, M. R., Krech, D., Bennett, E. L., & Zolman, J. F. (1962). Variation in environmental complexity and brain measures. *Journal of Comparative and Physiological Psychology*, 55(6), 1092.

Rosenzweig, S. (1936). Some implicit common factors in diverse methods of psychotherapy. *American Journal of Orthopsychiatry*, 6(3), 412.

Rothe, N., Steffen, J., Penz, M., Kirschbaum, C., & Walther, A. (2020). Examination of peripheral basal and reactive cortisol levels in major depressive disorder and the burnout syndrome: A systematic review. *Neuroscience & Biobehavioral Reviews*, 114, 232–270.

Rothstein, A. (2018). *Psychoanalytic Technique and the Creation of Analytic Patients*. Routledge.

Rovelli, C. (2005). Relational Quantum Mechanics. In *Quo Vadis Quantum Mechanics?* (pp. 113–120). Springer.

Russ, S. W. (2009). Pretend Play, Emotional Processes, and Developing Narratives. In *The Psychology of Creative Writing* (pp. 247–263). Cambridge University Press.

Ryan, J. (2005). *How Does Psychotherapy Work?* Karnac Books.

Sadeghi, B., Mashalchi, H., Eghbali, S., Jamshidi, M., Golmohammadi, M., & Mahvar, T. (2020). The relationship between hostility and anger with coronary heart disease in patients. *Journal of Education and Health Promotion, 9*, 223.

Sadegzadeh, F., Sakhaie, N., Isazadehfar, K., & Saadati, H. (2020). Effects of exposure to enriched environment during adolescence on passive avoidance memory, nociception, and prefrontal BDNF level in adult male and female rats. *Neuroscience Letters, 732*, 135133.

Safran, J. D., & Muran, J. C. (2000). Resolving therapeutic alliance ruptures: Diversity and integration. *Journal of Clinical Psychology, 56*(2), 233–243.

Santoso, D. I. I., Yolanda, S., Redjeki, S., Andraini, T., & Ivanali, K. (2020). Continuous environmental enrichment and aerobic exercise improves spatial memory: Focus on rat hippocampal BDNF and NGF. *Comparative Exercise Physiology, 16*(2), 121–128.

Sapir, E. (1956). *Culture, Language, and Personality.* University of California Press.

Sasaki, T., & Biro, D. (2017). Cumulative culture can emerge from collective intelligence in animal groups. *Nature Communications, 8*, 15049.

Saussure, F. de (1986). *Course in General Linguistics.* Open Court.

Sbarra, D. A., & Coan, J. A. (2018). Relationships and health: the critical role of affective science. *Emotion Review, 10*(1), 40–54.

Schachner, D. A., & Shaver, P. R. (2004). Attachment dimensions and sexual motives. *Personal Relationships, 11*(2), 179–195.

Scheffer, M., et al. (2018). Quantifying resilience of humans and other animals. *Proceedings of the National Academy of Sciences USA, 115*, 11883–11890.

Schegloff, E. A., Jefferson, G., & Sacks, H. (1977). The preference for self-correction in the organization of repair in conversation. *Language, 53*(2), 361–382.

Schenk, N., Fürer, L., Zimmermann, R., Steppan, M., & Schmeck, K. (2021). Alliance ruptures and resolutions in personality disorders. *Current Psychiatry Reports, 23*(1), 1.

Schiepek, G. (2003). A dynamic systems approach to clinical case formulation. *European Journal of Psychological Assessment, 19*(3), 175.

Schiepek, G., & Strunk, G. (2010). The identification of critical fluctuations and phase transitions in short term and coarse-grained time series — a method for the real-time monitoring of human change processes. *Biological Cybernetics, 102*(3), 197–207.

Schiepek, G., Aichhorn, W., & Schöller, H. (2017). Monitoring change dynamics — A nonlinear Approach to psychotherapy and feedback. *Chaos and Complexity Letters, 11*(3), 355–375.

Schiepek, G., Eckert, H., Aas, B., Wallot, S., & Wallot, A. (2016). *Integrative Psychotherapy: A Feedback-Driven Dynamic Systems Approach.* Hogrefe Publishing GmbH.

Schöll, E. (2016). Synchronization patterns and chimera states in complex networks: Interplay of topology and dynamics. *The European Physical Journal Special Topics, 225*(6–7), 891–919.

Schöll, E., Zakharova, A., & Andrzejak, R. G. (2019). Chimera states in complex networks. *Frontiers in Applied Mathematics and Statistics, 5*, 62.

Schore, A. N. (2001). Minds in the making: attachment, the self-organizing brain, and developmentally-oriented psychoanalytic psychotherapy. *British Journal of Psychotherapy, 17*(3), 299–328.

Schreiber, T. (1999). Interdisciplinary application of nonlinear time series methods. *Physics Reports, 308*, 1–64.

Schrödinger, E. (1959). *Mind and Matter.* Cambridge University Press.

Schwalbe, M. (1993). Goffman against postmodernism: emotion and the reality of the self. *Symbolic Interaction, 16*(4), 333–350.

Schwalbe, M. (2009). Framing the self. *Symbolic Interaction, 32*(3), 177–183.

Searle, J. R. (1992). *The Rediscovery of the Mind.* MIT Press.

Searles, H. F. (1979). *Countertransference and Related Subjects: Selected Papers.* International Universities Press.

Sebeok, T. A. (1992). *Biosemiotics: The Semiotic Web 1991.* Walter de Gruyter.

Seligman, M. E. (2002). Positive psychology, positive prevention, and positive therapy. *Handbook of Positive Psychology, 2*(2002), 3–12.

Sellars, J. (2021). *The Fourfold Remedy: Epicurus and the Art of Happiness.* Penguin.

Seth, A. K. (2013). Interoceptive inference, emotion, and the embodied self. *Trends in Cognitive Sciences, 17*(11), 565–573.

Shamay-Tsoory, S. G., & Abu-Akel, A. (2016). The social salience hypothesis of oxytocin. *Biological Psychiatry, 79*(3), 194–202.

Shannon, C. E. (1951). Prediction and entropy of printed English. *Bell System Technical Journal, 30*, 50–64.

Shannon, C. E., & Weaver, W. (1949). *The Mathematical Theory of Communication.* University of Illinois Press.

Shannon, C. E., Ashby, W. R., & McCarthy, J. (1956). *Automata Studies.* Princeton University Press.

Shine, J. M., Bell, P. T., Koyejo, O., Gorgolewski, K. J., Moodie, C. A., & Poldrack, R. A. (2015). Dynamic fluctuations in integration and segregation within the human. *Neuron, 88*, 207–219.

Shine, J. M., Aburn, M. J., Breakspear, M., & Poldrack, R. A. (2018). The modulation of neural gain facilitates a transition between functional segregation and integration in the brain. *Elife, 7*, e31130.

Shiota, M. N. (2014). The Evolutionary Perspective in Positive Emotion Research. In *Handbook of Positive Emotions* (pp. 44–59). Guilford Press.

Shiota, M. N., Campos, B., Oveis, C., Hertenstein, M. J., Simon-Thomas, E., & Keltner, D. (2017). Beyond happiness: Building a science of discrete positive emotions. *American Psychologist, 72*(7), 617.

Shockley, K., Richardson, D. C., & Dale, R. (2009). Conversation and coordinative structures. *Topics in Cognitive Science, 1*(2), 305–319.

Shockley, K., Santana, M. V., & Fowler, C. A. (2003). Mutual interpersonal postural constraints are involved in cooperative conversation. *Journal of Experimental Psychology, 29*(2), 326–332.

Short, T. L. (1983). Teleology in nature. *American Philosophical Quarterly, 20*(4), 311–320.

Siegel, D. J. (2020). *The Developing Mind: How Relationships and the Brain Interact to Shape Who We Are* (3rd edition). The Guilford Press.

Simeonidou-Christidou, T. (1998). An analysis of features of meaning by Prieto. *Semiotica, 122*(3–4), 205–215.

Skinner, B. F. (1998). The Experimental Analysis of Operant Behavior: A History. In *Psychology: Theoretical-Historical Perspectives* (2nd ed., pp. 289–299). American Psychological Association.

Sletvold, J. (2011). "The reading of emotional expression": Wilhelm Reich and the history of embodied analysis. *Psychoanalytic Dialogues, 21*(4), 453–467.

Sletvold, J. (2013). The ego and the id revisited: Freud and Damasio on the body ego/self. *The International Journal of Psychoanalysis, 94*(5), 1019–1032.

Smirnov, L., Osipov, G., & Pikovsky, A. (2017). Chimera patterns in the Kuramoto-Battogtokh model. *Journal of Physics A: Mathematical and Theoretical, 50*(8), 08LT01.

Smith, A. (1937). *The Wealth of Nations*. W. Strahan and T. Cadell.

Smith, T. W. (2015). *The Book of Human Emotions: An Encyclopedia of Feeling from Anger to Wanderlust*. Profile Books.

Speranza, C. I., Wiesmann, U., & Rist, S. (2014). An indicator framework for assessing livelihood resilience in the context of social–ecological dynamics. *Global Environmental Change, 28*, 109–119.

Spillius, E., & O'Shaughnessy, E. (2013). *Projective Identification: The Fate of a Concept*. Routledge.

Sprott, J. C. (2004). Dynamical models of love. *Nonlinear Dynamics, Psychology, and Life Sciences, 8*(3), 303–314.

Sprott, J. C. (2008). Predator-prey dynamics for rabbits, trees, and romance. In *Unifying Themes in Complex Systems IV* (pp. 231–238). Springer.

Stacey, R. D. (1995). The science of complexity: An alternative perspective for strategic change processes. *Strategic Management Journal, 16*(6), 477–495.

Stacey, R. D. (1996). *Complexity and Creativity in Organizations*. Berrett-Koehler Publishers.

Stellar, J. E., John-Henderson, N., Anderson, C. L., Gordon, A. M., McNeil, G. D., & Keltner, D. (2015). Positive affect and markers of inflammation: Discrete positive emotions predict lower levels of inflammatory cytokines. *Emotion, 15*(2), 129.

Stengel, E. (1959). Classification of mental disorders. *Bulletin of the World Health Organization, 21*(4–5), 601.

Stern, D. N. (1977). *The First Relationship: Mother and Infant*. Harvard University Press.

Stern, D. N. (1985). *The Interpersonal World of the Infant: A View from Psychoanalysis and Developmental Psychology*. Basic Books.

Stern, D. N. (2004). *The Present Moment in Psychotherapy and Everyday Life*. W. W. Norton & Company.

Stern, D. N. (2010). *Forms of Vitality: Exploring Dynamic Experience in Psychology: The Arts, Psychotherapy, and Development*. Oxford University Press.

Stern, D. N., Brüschweiler-Stern, N., Harrison, A. M., Lyons-Ruth, K., Morgan, A. C., Nahum, J. P., et al. (1998). Involving the process of therapeutic change implicit knowledge: Some implications of developmental observations for adult psychotherapy. *Infant Mental Health Journal, 19*(3), 300–308.

Stockdale, L. A., Morrison, R. G., & Silton, R. L. (2020). The influence of stimulus valence on perceptual processing of facial expressions and subsequent response inhibition. *Psychophysiology, 57*(2), e13467.

Storli, R., & Hansen Sandseter, E. B. (2019). Children's play, well-being and involvement: How children play indoors and outdoors in Norwegian early childhood education and care institutions. *International Journal of Play*, 8(1), 65–78.

Strawson, G. (1997). The self. *Journal of Consciousness Studies, 4*(5-6), 405–428.

Strawson, G. (2022). What I Call Myself. In *Hume on the Self and Personal Identity* (pp. 47–83). Springer.

Strogatz, S. (2004). *Sync: The Emerging Science of Spontaneous Order*. Penguin.

Strogatz, S. H. (1988). Love affairs and differential equations. *Mathematics Magazine, 61*(1), 35.

Strogatz, S. H. (1994). *Nonlinear Dynamics and Chaos: With Applications to Physics, Biology, Chemistry, and Engineering*. Addison-Wesley Pub.

Strogatz, S. H. (2003). *Sync: The Emerging Science of Spontaneous Order*. Hyperion.

Sutherland, J. D., & Winnicott, D. W. (1971). *Psychoanalysis and Contemporary Thought*. Hogarth Press.

Taleb, N. N. (2014). *Antifragile: Things that Gain from Disorder*. Random House.

Talmy, L. (2019). 1. Cognitive Semantics: An Overview. In *Semantics — Theories* (pp. 1–28). De Gruyter Mouton.

Tauber, A. I. (1994). The immune self: Theory or metaphor? *Immunology Today, 15*(3), 134–136.

Tauber, A. I. (2008). The immune system and its ecology. *Philosophy of Science, 75*(2), 224–245.

Taylor, G. J., Bagby, R. M., & Parker, J. D. (1999). *Disorders of Affect Regulation: Alexithymia in Medical and Psychiatric Illness*. Cambridge University Press.

Thom, R. (1975). *Structural Stability and Morphogenesis: An Outline of a General Theory of Models*. W. A. Benjamin.

Thom, R. (1988). *Esquisse d'une semiophysique*. InterEditions.

Thompson, D. W. (1963). *On Growth and Form*. Cambridge University Press.

Thompson, E., & Varela, F. J. (2001). Radical embodiment: neural dynamics and consciousness. *Trends in Cognitive Sciences, 5*(10), 418–425.

Timmons, A. C., Margolin, G., & Saxbe, D. E. (2015). Physiological linkage in couples and its implications for individual and interpersonal functioning: A literature review. *Journal of Family Psychology, 29*(5), 720.

Tracy, J. L., & Randles, D. (2011). Four models of basic emotions: A review of Ekman and Cordaro, Izard, Levenson, and Panksepp and Watt. *Emotion Review, 3*(4), 397–405.

Trevarthen, C. (1993). The Self Born in Intersubjectivity: The Psychology of an Infant Communicating. *The Perceived Self* (pp. 121–173). Cambridge University Press.

Trevarthen, C. (1998). The concept and foundations of infant intersubjectivity. In *Intersubjective Communication and Emotion in Early Ontogeny* (pp. 15–46). Cambridge University Press.

Trevarthen, C. (2009). The intersubjective psychobiology of human meaning: Learning of culture depends on interest for co-operative practical work–and affection for the joyful art of good company. *Psychoanalytic Dialogues, 19*(5), 507–518.

Trevarthen, C. (2012). Embodied human intersubjectivity: Imaginative agency, to share meaning. *Cognitive Semiotics, 4*(1), 6–56.

Trevarthen, C., Delafield-Butt, J., Schögler, B., Gritten, A., & King, E. (2011). Psychobiology of musical gesture: Innate rhythm, harmony, and melody in movements of narration. In *New Perspectives on Music and Gesture* (pp. 11–43). Routledge.

Tronick, E. Z., et al. (1998). Dyadically expanded states of consciousness and the process of therapeutic change. *Infant Mental Health Journal, 19*(3), 290–299.

Tschacher, W., & Bergomi, C. (2015). *The Implications of Embodiment: Cognition and Communication*. Andrews UK Limited.

Tschacher, W., & Haken, H. (2020). Causation and chance: Detection of deterministic and stochastic ingredients in psychotherapy processes. *Psychotherapy Research, 30*(8), 1075–1087.

Tschacher, W., & Haken, H. (2023). A complexity science account of humor. *Entropy, 25*(2), 341.

Tschacher, W., & Meier, D. (2020). Physiological synchrony in psychotherapy sessions. *Psychotherapy Research, 30*(5), 558–573.

Tschacher, W., Greenwood, S., Kirchberg, V., Wintzerith, S., van den Berg, K., & Tröndle, M. (2012). Physiological correlates of aesthetic perception of artworks in a museum. *Psychology of Aesthetics, Creativity, and the Arts, 6*(1), 96.

Tschacher, W., Greenwood, S., Ramakrishnan, S., Tröndle, M., Wald-Fuhrmann, M., Seibert, C., Weining, C., & Meier, D. (2023). Audience synchronies in live concerts illustrate the embodiment of music experience. *Scientific Reports, 13*(1), 14843.

Tschacher, W., Greenwood, S., Weining, C., Wald-Fuhrmann, M., Ramakrishnan, C., Seibert, C., & Tröndle, M. (2024). Physiological audience synchrony in classical concerts linked with listeners' experiences and attitudes. *Scientific Reports, 14*(1), 16412.

Tschacher, W., Haken, H., & Kyselo, M. (2015). Empirical and structural approaches to the temporality of alliance in psychotherapy. *Chaos and Complexity Letters, 9*(2), 177.

Tschacher, W., Scheier, C., & Grawe, K. (1998). Order and pattern formation in psychotherapy. *Nonlinear Dynamics, Psychology, and Life Sciences, 2*(3), 195–215.

Turnbull, O. H., & Salas, C. E. (2021). The neuropsychology of emotion and emotion regulation: The role of laterality and hierarchy. *Brain Sciences, 11*(8), 1075.

Uddin, L. Q., Supekar, K. S., Ryali, S., & Menon, V. (2011). Dynamic reconfiguration of structural and functional connectivity across core neurocognitive brain networks with development. *Journal of Neuroscience, 31*(50), 18578–18589.

Ungvari, G. S. (1993). The Wernicke-Kleist-Leonhard school of psychiatry. *Biological Psychiatry, 34*(11), 749–752.

van Dixhoorn, I. D., Reimert, I., Middelkoop, J., Bolhuis, J. E., Wisselink, H. J., Groot Koerkamp, P. W., Kemp, B., & Stockhofe-Zurwieden, N. (2016). Enriched housing reduces disease susceptibility to co-infection with porcine reproductive and respiratory virus (PRRSV) and *Actinobacillus pleuropneumoniae* (*A. pleuropneumoniae*) in young pigs. *PloS One, 11*(9), e0161832.

van Fraassen, B. C. (2010). Relational quantum mechanics: Rovelli's world. *Discusiones Filosóficas, 11*(17), 13–51.

Van Geert, P., & Van Dijk, M. (2021). Thirty years of focus on individual variability and the dynamics of processes. *Theory & Psychology, 31*(3), 405–410.

Van Orden, G. C., Kloos, H., & Wallot, S. (2011). Living in the Pink: Intentionality, Wellbeing, and Complexity. In *Philosophy of Complex Systems* (pp. 629–672). Elsevier.

Van Praag, H., Kempermann, G., & Gage, F. H. (2000). Neural consequences of environmental enrichment. *Nature Reviews Neuroscience, 1*(3), 191–198.

Varela, F. J. (1997). Patterns of life: Intertwining identity and cognition. *Brain and Cognition, 34*(1), 72–87.

Varela, F. J. (1999). *Ethical Know-How: Action, Wisdom, and Cognition*. Stanford University Press.

Varela, F. J., Thompson, E., & Rosch, E. (1991). *The Embodied Mind: Cognitive Science and Human Experience*. MIT Press.

Vasudevan, K., Cavers, M., & Ware, A. (2015). Earthquake sequencing: Chimera states with Kuramoto model dynamics on directed graphs. *Nonlinear Processes in Geophysics, 22*(5), 499–512.

Verhulst, F. (1998). *The Validation of Metaphors*. In *Validation of Simulation Models* (pp. 30–44). SISWO.

Von Foerster, H. (2013). *The Beginning of Heaven and Earth Has No Name: Seven Days with Second-order Cybernetics*. Oxford University Press.

Waldinger, R. J., & Gunderson, J. G. (1984). Completed psychotherapies with borderline patients. *American Journal of Psychotherapy, 38*(2), 190–202.

Wallot, S., & Kelty-Stephen, D. G. (2018). Interaction-dominant causation in mind and brain, and its implication for questions of generalization and replication. *Minds and Machines, 28*(2), 353–374.

Wang, Z., & Liu, Z. (2020). A brief review of chimera state in empirical brain networks. *Frontiers in Physiology, 11*, 724.

Watanabe, S., & Strogatz, S. H. (1993). Integrability of a globally coupled oscillator array. *Physical Review Letters, 70*(16), 2391.

Watanabe, S., & Strogatz, S. H. (1994). Constants of motion for superconducting Josephson arrays. *Physica D: Nonlinear Phenomena, 74*(3–4), 197–253.

Wauer, J., Schwarzer, D., Cai, G. Q., & Lin, Y. K. (2007). Dynamical models of love with time-varying fluctuations. *Applied Mathematics and Computation, 188*(2), 1535–1548.

Weaver, W. (1952). Translation. *Proceedings of the Conference on Mechanical Translation*. Massachusetts Institute of Technology.

Weaver, W. (1991). Science and complexity. In *Facets of Systems Science* (pp. 449–456). Springer.

Webber, C. L., & Marwan, N. (2015). *Recurrence Quantification Analysis: Theory and Best Practices*. Springer.

Webber, C. L., & Zbilut, J. P. (1994). Dynamical assessment of physiological systems and states using recurrence plot strategies. *Journal of Applied Physiology, 76*(2), 965–973.

Webber, C. L., & Zbilut, J. P. (2005). Recurrence quantification analysis of nonlinear dynamical systems. *Tutorials in Contemporary Nonlinear Methods for the Behavioral Sciences* (pp. 26–94). National Science Foundation.

Webber, C. L., Marwan, N., Facchini, A., & Giuliani, A. (2009). Simpler methods do it better: Success of recurrence quantification analysis as a general-purpose data analysis tool. *Physics Letters A, 373*(41), 3753–3756.

Welch IV, J. L. (2009). *Interdisciplinarity and the History of Ideas*. The University of Texas at Dallas.

West, B. J. (1985). *An Essay on the Importance of being Nonlinear*. Springer.

West, B. J. (1990). *Fractal Physiology and Chaos in Medicine*. World Scientific.

West, B. J. (2006). *Where Medicine Went Wrong: Rediscovering the Path to Complexity*. World Scientific.

West, S. A., Griffin, A. S., & Gardner, A. (2007a). Evolutionary explanations for cooperation. *Current Biology, 17*(16), R661–R672.

West, S. A., Griffin, A. S., & Gardner, A. (2007b). Social semantics: Altruism, cooperation, mutualism, strong reciprocity and group selection. *Journal of Evolutionary Biology, 20*(2), 415–432.

Whitehead, A. N. (1978). *Process and Reality*. The Free Press.

Whorf, B. L. (1956). *Language, Thought, and Reality*. MIT Press.

Wiener, N. (2019). *Cybernetics or Control and Communication in the Animal and the Machine*. MIT Press.

Wijnants, M. L. (2012). *Fractal Coordination in Cognitive Performances* [PhD Thesis, Sl: sn]. https://repository.ubn.ru.nl/bitstream/handle/2066/93590/93590.pdf

Wijnants, M. L., Hasselman, F., Cox, R. F. A., Bosman, A. M. T., & Van Orden, G. (2012). An interaction-dominant perspective on reading fluency and dyslexia. *Annals of Dyslexia, 62*(2), 100–119.

Wiley, N. (1994). *The Semiotic Self*. University of Chicago Press.

Willmore, T. (1988). Riemann extensions and affine differential geometry. *Results in Mathematics, 13*(3–4), 403–408.

Wiltshire, T. J., Philipsen, J. S., Trasmundi, S. B., Jensen, T. W., & Steffensen, S. V. (2020). Interpersonal coordination dynamics in psychotherapy: a systematic review. *Cognitive Therapy and Research, 44*(4), 752–773.

Windelband, W. (1998). History and natural science. *Theory & Psychology, 8*(1), 5–22.

Winfree, A. T. (2001). *The Geometry of Biological Time*. Springer.

Winnicott, D. W. (1954). Mind and its relation to the psyche-soma. *British Journal of Medical Psychology, 27*(4), 201–209.

Winnicott, D. W. (1971). *Playing and Reality*. Tavistock Publications.

Winnicott, D. W. (1988). *Human Nature*. Free Association Books.

Wittgenstein, L. (1961). *Tractatus logico-philosophicus: the German text of Ludwig Wittgenstein's Logisch-philosophische Abhandlung*. Routledge & Kegan Paul.

Wittgenstein, L. (1967). *Philosophical Investigations*. Oxford University Press.

Wittgenstein, L., Anscombe, G. E. M., & Wright, G. H. (1969). *On Certainty*. Blackwell.

Wittgenstein, L., Anscombe, G. E. M., Wright, G. H., & Nyman, H. (1980). *Remarks on the Philosophy of Psychology*. University of Chicago Press.

Worgan, S. F., & Moore, R. K. (2010). Speech as the perception of affordances. *Ecological Psychology, 22*(4), 327–343.

Wu, C. W. (2007). *Synchronization in Complex Networks of Nonlinear Dynamical Systems*. World Scientific.

Xu, L., Zhu, L., Zhu, L., Chen, D., Cai, K., Liu, Z., & Chen, A. (2021). Moderate exercise combined with enriched environment enhances learning and memory through BDNF/TrkB signaling pathway in rats. *International Journal of Environmental Research and Public Health, 18*(16), 8283.

Yao, Z., Hu, B., Xie, Y., Moore, P., & Zheng, J. (2015). A review of structural and functional brain networks: Small world and atlas. *Brain Informatics, 2*(1), 45–52.

Yau, S.-T., & Nadis, S. (2010). *The Shape of Inner Space: String Theory and the Geometry of the Universe's Hidden Dimensions*. Basic Books.

Zachar, P., Regier, D. A., & Kendler, K. S. (2019). The aspirations for a paradigm shift in DSM-5: An oral history. *The Journal of Nervous and Mental Disease, 207*(9), 778–784.

Zenith, R. (1993). Fernando Pessoa and the theatre of his self. *Performing Arts Journal, 15*(2), 47–49.

Zenith, R. (2021). *Pessoa: A Biography*. Liveright Publishing.

Zerubavel, E. (1981). *Hidden Rhythms: Schedules and Calendars in Social Life*. University of Chicago Press.

Index

biosemiotics, 34–36, 63, 76, 165

chimera, 78, 101–103, 106, 109, 110, 138, 145, 162, 167, 168–170
complexity, vii, ix, 2, 3, 7–12, 14, 17, 22, 28, 31, 33, 43, 59, 83, 87, 89, 92, 102, 110, 120, 122, 130, 138, 143, 145, 151, 154, 158, 170
complex system, 7, 8, 16, 32, 67, 68, 83, 99, 121, 135, 154
coordination, 28, 68, 69, 77, 78, 95, 98, 106, 108, 109, 111, 112, 125, 135, 136, 138, 153, 158, 160–162, 166, 169
coupling, 4, 27, 38, 70, 71, 76, 77, 78, 95, 97–102, 109, 112–114, 119, 121, 123–125, 134, 138, 146, 148, 153, 157, 159, 166, 167, 168, 170, 171
criticality, 11, 96, 124–126

determinism, 17, 97, 99, 100, 103, 120, 170
diagnosis, 83, 86–88
disorder, ix, 25, 84, 87, 89, 91, 110, 111, 153
dissonance, ix, 134, 139–145, 147, 148, 160

dynamical system, 2, 16, 28, 65, 67–69, 81, 97, 158, 168

embodiment, 36, 39–41, 43, 63, 66, 67, 100, 109, 112, 124, 151, 154, 161
emergence, 2–5, 7, 9, 11, 12, 14, 17, 28, 30, 51, 53, 68, 70, 72, 76, 78, 96, 97, 102, 155, 156, 159, 160, 165, 167
emotion, 41–45, 48–53, 56, 59, 62, 64, 66, 71, 73, 96, 112, 124, 129, 136

formulation, 16, 17, 20, 61, 73, 88, 91, 92, 122

game, 59, 113, 129, 130, 139

holism, 3
hyper-structures, 3

interdisciplinary, 13–17, 40, 95, 171

language, vii, 2, 3, 13, 14, 18, 19, 24–28, 34, 35, 37, 39, 43, 45, 46, 50, 59, 63, 66, 72, 73, 76, 79, 95, 96, 99, 100, 105, 108, 109, 117, 124, 129,

130, 137, 148, 152, 157–159, 162,
164, 165

model, 17–21, 26, 34, 51, 75, 77, 82,
83, 99, 101, 103, 104, 117, 122, 130,
134, 154, 159, 166–168
morphogenesis, 74, 75, 134, 160, 162

neuroscience, vii, 42, 53, 57, 62, 76,
88, 100, 104, 156, 165, 171

orchestration, 145, 146, 161

pattern, 5, 16–18, 21, 25, 50, 60,
73–76, 78, 82, 83, 89, 90, 97, 109,
152–154, 159, 160, 165, 170, 171
personality, 20, 41, 53, 60, 64, 66, 81,
86–88, 110–111
phase transition, 110, 136, 169
physiology, 36, 47, 51, 65, 69, 71, 95,
98, 100, 104, 110–112
play, 18, 29, 54, 57, 58, 107, 124–126,
128–133, 135–137, 139–141, 144,
146, 156, 160

pragmatism, 15
probability, 9, 10, 100, 103, 163,
164
psychopathology, 82, 83, 85, 86,
89–92, 135, 140, 153, 154, 155

rationalism, 28, 157, 159
repair, 107, 108, 110–112, 114, 135,
138–140
rupture, 107, 108, 110–112, 114, 135,
138, 139, 147, 155, 160

self, 40, 60, 61, 63–74, 78, 81–83,
91, 93, 106, 111, 114, 129, 132,
135, 136, 146, 152–156, 159, 161,
168
self-organization, ix, x, 7, 11, 12, 36,
68–70, 72, 92, 96, 114, 119–121,
123, 125, 132–139, 159, 160
synchronization, vii, 27, 28, 31,
32, 68, 75–78, 95–102, 109–112,
114, 115, 119, 121–126, 134, 138,
145, 147, 148, 153, 157–159, 162,
165–170

9 789811 287367